595

THE
POWER
GAME

EDITED BY

Clay Felker

from the pages of

MAGAZINE

Simon and Schuster / New York

FIRST PRINTING

SBN 671-20375-4
Library of Congress Catalog Card Number 79-92187
Designed by Irving Perkins
Manufactured in the United States of America
By H. Wolff Book Mfg. Co., Inc., New York

Contents

Contents

1. Introducing The Power Game

Clay Felker

"In a complex city like New York, with so many veto-endowed power groups who effectively check each other and prevent actions from being forced down anyone's throat, perhaps the most useful definition—and effective exercise—of power is the negative ability to withhold favors."

Shortly after he stopped being Prime Minister for the final time, Winston Churchill came to New York aboard the private yacht of Stavros Niarchos, which tied up at the 79th Street boat basin. One night there was a small dinner party for Churchill aboard the yacht, and the guest list reported in the morning papers was a short but distinguished roster of world-famous names except for one: Harry Haggerty, identified only as a vice president of the Metropolitan Life Insurance Company. Who was the mysterious Mr. Haggerty, I wondered, and why was he in this exclusive pantheon of the powerful—a mere vice president of an insurance company? I discovered that Mr. Haggerty was no mere vice president but the chairman of the loan committee of the Metropolitan, then a $12-billion company which had financed such real-estate projects in New York as Stuyvesant Town and Peter Cooper Village. The Metropolitan, quite simply, controls the largest pool of private, investable capital in the world. Here was a man with enormous power in the affairs of the city (and, by extension, of the nation), and yet almost totally unknown to the public.

I began to wonder about the men of power in New York, and for years my favorite dinner conversation when I was with knowledgeable New Yorkers was a variation of the old ten-best game:

name the ten men who run New York City. I soon found that The Power Game was not only popular but increasingly complex and confusing. Everyone had (and has) differing lists according to his degree of personal sophistication or point of view from the particular social or economic pyramid he occupies. That is to say, it came down to a question of how power is defined.

Defining power is both a fascinating and elusive enterprise. Professor Edward T. Banfield of Harvard's Department of Government has written a long and carefully reasoned essay on the definition of power running to many thousands of words. But in dealing with a subject as infinitely complex as New York, I felt that we should use as working tools some relatively direct and simple measurements of power—definitions worth keeping in mind as you read *The Power Game,* even though they often raise as many questions as they answer.

The late C. W. Mills, the Columbia University sociologist who wrote *The Power Elite,* said that power, in general, resided at the head of a hierarchic institution. Nelson Polsby, in his study of how power operates in a city, *Community Power and Political Theory,* uses the term "influence" as a synonym of power. The political scientist Robert Dahl defines power as the ability of someone to influence someone else to act in a way he otherwise would not act, and Max Weber said that power was the "chance of a man or of a number of men to realize their own will in a communal action even against the resistance of others who are participating in the action." Two other scholars wrestling with the problem—William D'Antonio and William Form in *Influentials in Two Border Cities* —viewed power as "composed of two subclasses: authority, based on the position a person holds in a formal hierarchical structure; and influence, that more subtle phenomenon manifested in the willingness of people to obey others who lack formal authority." This last kind of power is also known these days as charisma. And in his excellent recent study *The Power Structure,* sociologist Arnold Rose flatly states, after examining these and many other definitions, that "There is an elusiveness about power that endows it with an almost ghostly quality."

In a complex city like New York, with so many veto-endowed power groups who effectively check each other and prevent actions from being forced down anyone's throat, perhaps the most useful definition—and effective exercise—of power is the negative ability to withhold favors. For New Yorkers who want an even handier way to determine who has power in their city, there is another rule of thumb: A person with power is someone who can always get through on the telephone.

Tom Wolfe, whose zoomar perception of crucial nuances in modern society is soundly based academically (he took his Ph.D. in sociology at Yale), creates his own definition of the ends of power in the final chapter, "Seeing 'Em Jump." Whether his definition of the ultimate power is one with which you will totally agree, you will never again look at a powerful person in the same light after reading his essay.

A useful working definition of power in New York City is given in the chapter by Edward Costikyan, the former leader of Tammany Hall (1963–65), who rose to head the New York Democratic organization through the ranks of the Reform Democrats. Costikyan grew up in New York, graduated from Columbia College and Columbia Law School, and is now a prominent trial lawyer and civic affairs leader. He says, "By power I mean the power to control and direct the city's governmental policies, determine its budget, determine the taxes it will impose, allocate its public and private resources, establish its tastes, and determine the quality of New York City life."

As we were considering who runs New York, Costikyan independently came upon the idea of The Power Game—making a list of *his* ten candidates, but from another approach. As he told me, "My hobby is worrying about New York City. I started out by pondering what was wrong with the city, and so, in order to start somewhere, I began to think about who runs it. Everybody is perplexed about how things work here, and they tend to blame everything on the Mayor. It doesn't take much thought to see that this is both simplistic and unfair."

As I played The Power Game over the years, I found the object of the game shifting from the Ten Most Powerful to another focus. Like Costikyan, I wanted to know *how* the city is run, not just *who* runs it. I wanted some answers to questions about the nature and exercise of power in New York.

New York City is particularly well suited to such examination because it is at this moment in history indisputably the greatest city in the world, a fact elaborated on by Gus Tyler in his chapter, "Eight Million Pieces of the Action." Tyler, who is assistant president of the International Ladies Garment Workers Union and director of politics, education and training for that enlightened and powerful union, is not only a man who has been on the inside councils of power for many years, but one who has operated the levers of power in the city and the nation. He refers to the city as Imperial New York. What better place to examine power than in Imperial New York? For if New York is the Imperial City of the modern world, it is a demonstration of how definitions of power change. New York is not a political capital in the way that other imperial cities of the past—such as Athens, Rome, Paris, or London —were. True, the United Nations is located here, but that institution exerts its power primarily on world opinion. The United Nations correspondents are almost as important as the delegates —a fact that reveals one of the important aspects of Imperial New York: it is the communications capital of America and the world. In New York it isn't military might that matters but the power of ideas. Perhaps in no other city can an idea be shaped and transmitted so quickly. An idea, a fact, a piece of gossip, can saturate New York in the space of one working day. And it usually winds up in print in *The New York Times* the next morning, while every influential New Yorker to a man spends an obligatory hour in the morning accepting as gospel those stories he knows nothing about but wondering why they got it wrong in reporting those stories he does know something about; it didn't seem to be that way a few years ago. Two things have happened to create this growing impression of the *Times'* fallibility: one is the death of the *Herald Tribune,* which served as a check on the *Times'* going biases; the other is the rapid increase of interpretive reporting in that paper as new executives have taken over in recent years. Paul Weaver, an assistant professor of government at Harvard, spent more than a year studying the *Times,* and his article on how and why that paper is changing tells why more and more people get angry at the most powerful single communications medium in the world every morning—and why more and more people read it.

Sometimes it seems as if New Yorkers are connected by one mammoth conference call, with everyone on the telephone trading information and talking furiously to everyone else. In his first-hand report on automobile telephones, Ralph Schoenstein, who has participated in New York's information marathon as a columnist for a newspaper and a commentator on television and radio, gives examples of the extremes of New Yorkers' need for constant communication.

This addiction to the telephone is also noticed by Nicholas Pileggi, who spent several months specifically researching his chapter on the rules of The Power Game. A reporter with a background of sixteen years covering the city for the Associated Press before coming to *New York* Magazine, Pileggi notes that "the men who really wield, retain and covet power in New York are the kind of men who answer bedside telephones while making love." Pileggi also told me that in making appointments for the many interviews he had during his research, he noticed that one mark of a man of power is that he makes his appointments by the number, not the name, of the day. That is, he says, "I'll see you on the fourteenth" —not, "I'll see you on Wednesday." This means that for them power must be exercised daily, and not on a convenient five-day week. The powerful work seven days and seven nights a week. And as Peter Maas, a political analyst, demonstrates in his chapter, the "Power Brokers" are part of this tireless group.

The notion that power is New York's sex (even if jealous wives won't believe it) is considered by "Adam Smith" in his chapter on what summer bachelors do when the family is away at the shore. According to "Adam Smith," the competitive lust usually triumphs over the physical and men who don't get to see each other during the rest of the year because they commute to different places or their wives don't like each other, get together for an evening during the summer months and make the deals that keep them busy the rest of the year.

It is true that women do not always understand a man's involvement in the pursuit of power, or are unsympathetic about the endless nature of The Game. Gloria Steinem, a young woman powerful in her own right through her involvement in the vanguard of political action and her writing, discovered that women as a group hold a remarkably small amount of power, despite popular contrary belief. Much to her own surprise, Miss Steinem came to the conclusion, after extensive research, that "the truth is that most women will have to exercise their much denied instincts for power through

men for a while yet, at least until the generation now in college"
takes over. She added that "If society stopped telling girls that men
can and should hand them their total identity on a silver platter,
wives wouldn't be so resentful when it didn't happen. And ambitious women could relax and look for pleasure instead of power
in bed."

Power, of course, is more than a game. The real reason it fasci-
nates (explaining the attempts to understand and codify the rules
and to identify the men who hold power) is that power is the
name we give that mysterious force which shapes our lives in the
city.

The thrust of this book is identical with the force that brought
New York Magazine into being. We live in an urban civilization
and unless we grow to understand it, we will all be overwhelmed
by the scale and complexity of its problems. But if we do begin to
understand the forces that interact in the cities to produce that
culture, we have the opportunity to create a rich and meaningful
existence amid a setting not instantly open to acclaim for its beauty
or even comfort.

The nature of cities is profoundly misunderstood. Often we tend
to label as problems conditions that are more than that. Traffic
congestion, for example, is a problem, but in lamenting it, we tend
to overlook that it is also evidence of the vitality of the city. Density
in general creates problems but it can also bring human dynamism.
People like to be with other people, so long as they are not in each
other's laps. Cities work, despite all prophecies of chaos and doom.

In his recent book, *The Last Landscape,* a persuasively hopeful
analysis of life in the cities, William H. Whyte remarks that "American literature in general has a deep antiurban streak, and the very
reason for the city concentration is viewed as its mortal defect."
In an interview in *New York* Magazine, Mr. Whyte said that "The
essential genius of a city like New York is that it's a center, a place
where large numbers of people *can* come together. That's an exciting thing. The minute you start talking about decentralization,
taking the city's functions and dispersing them, creating a bunch
of little Utopias, you're really talking about destroying something
that may be the most important thing to preserve."

As a magazine setting out to examine the life in the laboratory
city of the world (which is what New York City is, because its very

size and dynamism cause trends that might go unnoticed elsewhere to become full blown here), we find it takes small rationalization on our part to be optimistic about the future of the city: the productive stimulation of daily life is alone reason enough to account for that. Much of that excitement is caused by the swift pace of inexorable change, which has its tragic side. The dying off of our great daily newspapers is an example close to us at *New York* Magazine, since we originated as the Sunday magazine of the *New York Herald Tribune*. But as the patterns of New York life shifted under population and technological pressures, so did the patterns of publishing. The death of the *Herald Tribune* gave us the opportunity to be reborn as an independent magazine, free of the crippling baggage of the past. We shall always mourn the death of the great newspaper that gave us birth, and we shall always be grateful for the vital traditions we inherited—and the opportunity that was created by the vacuum left by the *Trib's* passing.

As a nation we have come to a point in history when the quality of life in the cities will take first priority, and any politician who doesn't realize it risks being swept away in the tide. The challenge of improving urban life needs new voices. It particularly needs a new literature—not a 19th-century, rural-oriented, antiurban literature, but a literature of the city. *New York* Magazine is one of the vehicles helping to create that new literature through what has come to be called the "new journalism." The new journalism requires, among other things, an eagerness to embrace the world today and what Tom Wolfe terms "saturation reporting," combined with the great techniques of English literature: narrative flow, scene-setting, characterization, and dialogue. *New York* Magazine, in its days in the *Herald Tribune* and today, has, at its best, been characterized by an extraordinary group of writers, practitioners of the new journalism, the new literature of the city.

Jimmy Breslin's contribution here, "Life in the City of Gold," is part of the new urban literature, in the form of a series of vignettes on the sources of ghetto unrest and the beginning of recognition of the situation by a few key leaders in New York. The very energy that went into the reporting of this chapter infuses it with a passion and a tension that have made Jimmy Breslin the laureate of New York. When future historians confront life in New York in the 1960s, the vividness of Breslin's reporting and the skill of his writing will prove a valuable source for understanding the period.

Another writer who, like Breslin, essentially draws on basic themes from the "people" of the city—that is, those unglamorous millions who make up the majority of the city and live outside of the spotlight glare of mid-Manhattan—is Pete Hamill. A native of Brooklyn, Hamill returns to the neighborhoods of his youth to bring to the surface the hidden feelings of the lower white middle class in the approximately seventy identifiable "villages" that make up the city—villages that are in revolt. These are the people who, when urged by almost every major political leader and force in the city, including Mayor Lindsay, Senators Robert Kennedy and Jacob Javits, both political parties and *The New York Times,* to endorse the police civilian review board, silently went out and voted it down, two to one. One major political leader asked me afterwards, in talking about this show of power: "Where did they come from?" Hamill tells us where—and why.

On the opposite end of the economic scale from Breslin's report is Jane O'Reilly's series of startling case histories on the economic problems of the moneyed middle class. It has often been said that New York is a place for the very rich or the poor. Miss O'Reilly's detailing of the life styles of those in between, even at what seem luxurious levels, demonstrates why, ludicrous as it may seem, they are as likely as not to be seriously in debt and living on the thin edge economically even if making $80,000 a year.

Although Breslin's use of the phrase "The City of Gold" is ironic, for many ambitious young men, the phrase functions literally, and they cash in big. Such a young man is looked at closely by Chris Welles, a specialist in writing about Wall Street, who tells us about Saul Steinberg, a bright new star on Wall Street who at the age of twenty-nine attempted to take over the Chemical Bank, one of the pillars of the New York banking world, and what happened when he ran into the financial establishment downtown.

The problems of the middle class and the rich who have lost faith in the public school system of the city are painfully revealed in Julie Baumgold's chapter on the world of the private schools. It has been said that the ultimate patronage in New York would be the ability to place a dozen children in New York private schools. A man could land almost any account, make a brilliant deal every hour, if he had the ability to ease the mind of worried parents, afraid to send their child into the violence of New York City's disintegrating public schools. Herself a product of city private schools, Miss Baumgold has written from an unblinking inside view. These, incidentally, are where the young aristocrats learn and practice the "Honk" of power, that distinct tone in New York speech, which is an effective mark of the upper class examined by Tom Wolfe in his survey on New York accents.

The power of exclusiveness and exclusion is examined in two chapters, one on the generally anti-Semitic private clubs (with certain proud exceptions clearly noted) and the archaic restrictive policies still being practiced in some East Side luxury apartments. The blame here lies (if not equally) with both those bigots who perpetuate racial and religious restrictions and those ethnic minorities who refuse to fight for their rights clearly guaranteed by law. If such practices, often thought by many to be buried in the past, still persist, it is because the fight was given up too soon, or because, as in so many things, it is not comfortable or convenient to expose the problems.

Problems have a way of surfacing sooner or later. Alan Rich, who is the arts editor and music critic of *New York* Magazine, has written a well-documented *tour d'horizon* of the state of the arts in terms of who's responsible for what. As the cultural capital of the country, New York has become complacent, and there are severe problems that go far beyond the success or failure of Broadway plays. The quality of city life is accurately reflected by the health of its culture: the environment we live in can be inspiring or depressing.

As the charismatic mayor of the city, John V. Lindsay has often found his job exhilarating, and he has often found it harrowing. In the midst of it all, he occasionally reflects on the peculiarities of New York political life. On one of his rare vacations, as he was trying to repair the ravages to his spirits of a series of nightmare labor clashes and as he was conferring with his family about the forthcoming Mayoral election, he found himself reflecting on the tribal rites of political dinners. He sat down and banged out the essay included in this book, and it showed up on my desk one day unannounced. Soon there was a call from the Mayor, who told me that he hadn't checked it with any of his press aides because he knew they wouldn't like it, and they would try to talk him out of running it. I ran it in the magazine immediately, and sure enough, I began getting angry blasts from some of his personal staff. I still don't know what they were afraid of, but in New York, as John Lindsay told one of the writers who contributed to this book, "The name of the game is not so much power as self-defense."

New York City
May, 1969

2. Power: The Only Game in Town

Nicholas Pileggi

"The most influential of men in New York are at the mercy of deaf waiters, busy retail clerks and pre-occupied elevator starters. Power, in fact, is held by so many people in New York that no one man or visible combination of men can actually control the whole city."

Power in New York is nurtured, fussed over, married, loved, faked and hoarded. New York is as much a city of power as Boston is a city of background, San Francisco a city of style and Los Angeles a city of celebrity. Power is New York's sex and none of the people living here are unconscious of that fact. Watch the face of an off-duty cab driver in the rain, the painfully slow fingers of a token attendant as a subway rumbles into a station, or the deliberate way a patrolman has of writing out a parking ticket. Power in New York is courted like a woman, and even her most ineffectual romancers write of her seduction like erotic monks. One such recollection, despite the implications of the title, *Making It,* actually dealt with a man from Brooklyn becoming the editor of a Manhattan magazine. In New York, power is romanced by everyone from the city's benign Medicis—the Rockefellers—to the Mafia. A magnificent municipal orgy with eight million participants searching for their own particular pleasures. It might be the power to choose the flowers that will be planted down the middle of Park Avenue or the ability to borrow financier Robert Lehman's private museum in midtown Manhattan, hung with over $100 million in paintings, for a charity drive.

Theodore W. Kheel, the labor mediator who earns more than $200,000 a year keeping those possessed from each other's throats, think's the city's passion for power is logical.

"The problem today is how do power groups in conflict get their problems resolved," Kheel said. "And you don't resolve them by saying, 'Isn't it awful that there is Black Power.' What's so awful about it? Or Union Power? Or White Power? Or Consumer Power? This is as natural as can be.

"But the Black Community is going to ask for things that the unions may find objectionable. The problem, the solution, is not to say abolish Black Power, abolish the unions, but to try to resolve these conflicts."

In another city, any one of New York's 442 judges, 487 bank presidents, 19,081 doctors, 40,942 lawyers and 4,310 fully accredited Mafia racketeers would be prestigious neighbors or fearsome citizens. In New York, however, these men are rebuffed by receptionists, wait in line at P. J. Clarke's, get parking tickets outside their homes and have their names forgotten, mispronounced and misspelled. The most influential of men in New York are at the mercy of deaf waiters, busy retail clerks and preoccupied elevators starters. Power, in fact, is held by so many people in New York that no one man or visible combination of men can actually control the whole city. There is no Citizens Council in New York to approximate the one in Dallas where a dozen oilmen and merchants purportedly dictate municipal decisions to elected officials. There is no monolithic political organization in New York to compare with that of Chicago's Mayor Richard J. Daley, despite the fact that New York's mayor is a potential Presidential candidate and its governor, senators and most of its congressmen, national figures. There is no cabal of Pittsburgh Mellons strong enough to control New York, even though Manhattan is the nation's financial capital and the headquarters for, among other economic power blocs, the country's largest banks, insurance companies, industrial combines, utilities, retail firms and transportation companies. In New York control is, at best, short-lived and power is exerted on only a small piece of the city at a time. The acquisition of a valuable building site, the resolution of a labor dispute or even the placing of a boy at the Collegiate School is achieved through clearly defined and delicately balanced accommodations involving sworn enemies, subtle deceits and secret alliances. The men who really wield, retain and covet power in New York are the kind of men who answer bedside telephones while making love. They know that power is kept, whether it was originally inherited or bought, only if it is exercised daily. They know it is the ultimate competitive triumph reserved for those who have risen above their contemporaries, above their elders and above their teachers.

"The name of the game in New York," Mayor John V. Lindsay said a few days after announcing the resolution of the five-week school strike in 1968, "is not so much 'power' as it is self-defense. The name of the game in New York for the average person is to keep his own liberties from being ignored by special-interest groups who are constantly fighting for power among themselves and totally ignoring the average guy's needs."

Lindsay was seated in his corner office, twirling a miniature silver-saber letter opener between his fingers. The morning light came in over his shoulders, and outside in City Hall Park privileged officials and newsmen parked their automobiles on the sidewalks and paths under the guidance of policemen wearing white gloves and friendly smiles.

"There just isn't any one group powerful enough to control New York," Lindsay continued. "Because of the size of this city many of our institutions have become so huge that in their groping for even more power they tend to collide with each other. Take the city's schools, for example. Over the years they have been subjected to two powerful groups—the Superintendent of Schools and Board of Education, to whom the city turned over one billion dollars every year without even a check or double check, and the United Federation of Teachers. These two groups became so totally engaged in their own contest that they bypassed everyone else. Look over their past contracts and you will see a pattern whereby the two groups often merged, often dovetailed. They were inextricable. It became very difficult when parents and children began to demand a place at table because the mountainous bureaucracy began to groan.

"A short while after I was elected," Lindsay continued, "I said there would be no room at City Hall for the power brokers. I also said that I wouldn't identify the power brokers until after I was out of office."

Throwing down the letter opener and leaning back in his chair he smiled. "I will say that while there isn't any one group of power brokers that can control New York, there are many 'pace setters' here who maintain certain *very* high standards."

The waiting room outside the mayor's office that morning was already littered with copies of *The New York Times*. A few of the "pace setters" had already been there waiting to see him. During his conversation, telephone calls were put through, and leaning back in his chair the mayor thanked, encouraged, chided and sympathized with various men. One civil rights leader, addressed by his first name, was thanked for helping to keep tempers relatively calm during the Ocean Hill-Brownsville school dispute. A Republican Party official was sympathized with over the illness of his brother.

To identify the men who can leave their copies of *The New York Times* outside the mayor's office, have their telephone calls put through to Lindsay or leave their cars on the sidewalk and under the trees of City Hall Park is not difficult. They are businessmen, labor leaders, political party bosses and large donors to a variety of causes. They are the administrative officials whom the mayor himself appointed to look over his 300,000-man bureaucracy. They are the men whom Wallace S. Sayre and Herbert Kaufman describe in their *Governing New York City* as members of the four civic activities:

• The race relations and interfaith groups, made up primarily of Catholic and Jewish lawyers and second-level business executives (big businessmen steer clear, too controversial) who watch over the welfare of Negroes, Jews and Catholics.

• The good government groups, made up usually of Protestant lawyers and executives who analyze the records of candidates and elected officials with an eye toward "improving the public morality."

• The culture, museum and university trustee groups, the pinnacle of civic prestige and composed of persons of great inherited wealth and heads of large corporations.

• The business, construction and planning groups, composed of bankers, real estate men and merchants whose future success depends upon the growth and prosperity of the city.

None of these men or groups is ever certain it will get the results it wants from official decisions, because there is always another group demanding almost the exact opposite. As a result, none of these groups and none of the men is ever more than temporarily in a position of enough authority to exercise the dictionary definition of power: "the ability to compel obedience."

David Riesman and the late C. Wright Mills represent two different positions among American sociologists in their definitions of power. Riesman contends that the country has no decisive ruling group and that there is instead an amorphous power structure in which various interest groups struggle and make constant use of the veto to block moves by other groups who might seem to threaten their jurisdictional areas. Mills, on the other hand, described a definite power elite in the United States that is composed of a coalition of top military officials, government executives and the directors of large corporations. Furthermore, he maintained, there is considerable mobility within this "power elite"—an ex-Secretary of Defense will often be found at the head of one of the nation's most powerful corporations. Another sociologist, G. William Domhoff, author of *Who Rules America?* agrees basically with Mills and sets forth the proposition that "the members of the upper class dominate the major corporations, foundations, universities, and the Executive branch of the federal government."

A Wall Street investment banker, a man who might easily be considered part of any "power elite," disagrees with the Mills-Domhoff theory.

"There isn't a real power establishment here," the banker said. "The country is too fluid. Too pluralistic. In the Soviet Union one can pin down a real power structure within the walls of the Kremlin, but not here. The New Left in the United States really show how naïve they are when they talk of seizing the Establishment. They haven't realized yet that there isn't one. Power, when it does exist, is like mercury. It flows subtly. It shifts to where it can be used. It does not reside in marbled halls where it would begin to atrophy."

In New York there *is* a persistent body of special interest groups whose leaders appear to dominate every aspect of the city's life. Certain names and specific groups keep surfacing more often than others, not because of any dramatic or drastic action they might take in any particular situation, but because they are intimately involved in Sunday morning public service television shows, the men who stay up all night at Gracie Mansion and "hammer out" shirtsleeves solutions to labor disputes. They are also the men who endow universities, preserve landmarks, acquire priceless paintings for museums they help to support and endorse political candidates in their newspapers, on their radio and television stations and in their magazines. And, they are those less prominent men whose interests are directed more toward banks, department stores and construction firms, the men who keep a careful eye on urban renewal locations and property assessment rates, expressway routes and parking regulations. All of these men, and the groups they represent, not only have collective entree to the offices of the city's officials, but their advice is often sought and their support on specific issues is often requested. In a sense, these men and their organizations become an intimate part of the city's machinery and of the city's decision-making apparatus in specific spheres. As members of the city's hierarchical institutions (e.g., the New York Stock Exchange), these men have *influence,* rather than *control,* over the city's operation. In *Who Rules America?* Domhoff wrote, "By *control* we mean to imply dominance, the exercise of power (the ability to act) from a position of authority by virtue of some office or legal mandate. *Influence,* for us, is a weaker term, implying that a person can sometimes sway, persuade, or otherwise have an effect upon those who control a position of authority."

At any time, almost any one of these power manipulators can appear to be the most powerful man in New York simply by asserting all of his strength for a brief period of time and then taking the consequences. The consequences usually come in the form of concessions that such men must make to their lukewarm allies in exchange for support. Albert Shanker, the president of the United Federation of Teachers, is a perfect example of a man who for five weeks was the single most powerful man in New York. His stand so enraged the city's citizens that his years and years of active civil rights work and participation in all the important marches in the South were forgotten by the Negro communities; his exemplary liberal voting record was forgotten by the city's liberals; and meetings of his own union were held to see if he could be unseated. In addition, for the support he got from Harry Van Arsdale and the Central Labor Council in the face of grave opposition by the Council's predominantly Negro locals, Shanker will be forever in Van

Arsdale's debt. In the end, the whole power game in New York operates on the barter system. Deals are made and credits and debits scrupulously recorded. Victories are won, enemies defeated and dreams fulfilled only after deftly arranged clusters of single-interest power groups have managed to find agreeable goals.

The accommodations of selfish interest by divergent groups is the key to power in New York, as demonstrated by the influence of professional middlemen like Theodore Kheel and former Supreme Court Justice Arthur J. Goldberg. For if the New York power blocs were left to satisfy their own appetites unmediated, they would very likely gorge themselves to death. New York would be a city of high-rent housing and no people, or low-rent housing and no landlords. Its streets would either be clogged with automobiles or flower-studded promenades. It would be an uninhabitable island of overhead expressways and a paved Central Park, a city where $20,000-a-year patrolmen could hand down sentences upon the "perpetrators" they arrest, or perhaps a rigidly preserved landmark in which no building, tree or window fan could be disturbed. New York's informal single-minded power groups are made up of the nation's most competitive men, who have in common only their shrill denial that they even exist.

Most of the city's powerful and influential men avoid indulging themselves in the superficial trappings of power simply because they see no point in making an unnecessary target of themselves. There is a growing theory, especially among union leaders today, that to show too much power is an invitation to conflict. In fact, in the last five years, more than two thousand union contracts endorsed by the leadership of the nation's unions have been rejected by the unions' rank and file. In New York John J. Cassese of the Patrolmen's Benevolent Association, John J. DeLury of the Uniformed Sanitationmen's Association, and Michael Maye of the Firefighters' Association have all had tentative contracts they endorsed thrown back at them by their own memberships.

The city's most powerful men are usually too experienced in the easy resentments, petty jealousies and competition they would face if they conspicuously displayed the symbols of their power. For instance, New York's most powerful union leader, Harry Van Arsdale, has no limousine, wears inexpensive suits, never drinks, shuns parties, pays himself $225 a week (the average salary of an electrician whose union he runs) and never smokes "big shot" cigars. Van Arsdale, who has a hand in every labor settlement in the city, will purposely withdraw when the announcement of a settlement is being made. He does this not only in order to allow the union official whose membership is directly involved in the settlement to get the Gabe Pressman interview, have pictures taken shaking hands with the mayor and generally be a New York power-for-a-day, but also to help further solidify the official's position with the members of his union.

"Every time a local union president stands up and hears a boo," Jack Mallon, the *Daily News* labor editor said, only half joking, "he knows there's a guy out there after his job. If there are no boos from his membership, then he knows somebody's already got it. The one thing Van Arsdale wants is a group of strong local presidents whom he can depend upon. He'll do anything to make them look good, and sometimes that's hard."

To disavow completely the trappings and presence of power can be just as dangerous of the city's leaders as to flaunt it. In fact, the main trouble with former Mayor Robert F. Wagner during his terms in office was that he never looked as though he possessed the tremendous power that he really did. Wagner, a consummate politician who was groomed by his father, Senator Robert F. Wagner, to exercise power from the day he was born, had cultivated the entire New York Establishment during his rise to the mayoralty. From social workers and labor leaders to big businessmen and philanthropists, Wagner had given time, interest and sympathy to their cases. "Eventually," an aide of the former mayor recalled, "they all felt that they had a stake in keeping him in office." And yet, for all of his real power, Wagner studiously avoided giving the impression that he had any strength at all. Wagner was so defensive about playing the power game in New York that he always sat next to his driver in his official limousine while his detective bodyguard sat in the rear. During traffic jams and when he was behind schedule, Wagner would never request a police department motorcycle escort and would never allow the driver to use the automobile's siren. One day, just before he announced his retirement from City Hall, Wagner stepped into an elevator with his bodyguard after giving a speech at the Waldorf-Astoria. As usual the mayor walked to the rear of the empty elevator and leaned against the wall. On the next floor the doors opened and a tall, well-tanned couple entered. The man stared down at Wagner for a moment and then, in a booming voice directed at his blond companion, asked, "Hey honey! Do you know who that man is?"

The companion gave the mayor a bored, squinty look.

"Why that's the mayor," the man continued, smiling at Wagner. "Ain't that right?"

"You sure that's the mayor?" the woman asked, continuing to peer suspiciously toward the rear of the elevator.

"Go ahead, gowon, tell her you're the mayor," the man said to Wagner.

Wagner smiled weakly as the elevator doors opened and the couple walked into the lobby without waiting for his reply. Wagner was for twelve years the city's most powerful man, but many New Yorkers never really believed it.

For some men, however, it is both psychologically impossible as well as unnecessary to hide the exercise of power. Perhaps the most visible of these men is Chase Manhattan chairman David Rockefeller, the unofficial chairman of the power board, a man whose sense of responsibility and wealth makes all of America's problems Rockefeller problems. As a steward of a family fortune estimated at $6 billion, Rockefeller is just naturally affected by every fluctuation in America's mood, every rustle in the nation's economy, every nuance of the country's life. During his trips abroad (he averages seven a year) Rockefeller pays courtesy calls on the heads of state in the nations he visits. When they visit the United States the calls are reciprocated.

Yet for all of Rockefeller's power and accomplishments, he is still no more than an active participant in the New York power game. His biographical file card system of 20,000 names is not something an office staff maintains for amusement. The breakfasts, luncheons, meetings and dinners Rockefeller attends in the pursuit of business activities are endless. His elaborate file system helps to refresh his memory about whomever it is he is going to meet, cajole or pressure.

"You can imagine the reaction of the average banker or businessman when David Rockefeller walks into his office to pay a call," one breathless Chase executive said. "It's not something he's likely to forget."

In any other city of the world, the Chase executive could be reminded, it would be unnecessary for David Rockefeller ever to go anywhere.

But in New York, even for a Rockefeller, power is achieved through accommodation, not command. Just before Lindsay was elected, a super-citizens council was convened to take Democratic Mayor Robert F. Wagner to task for his inaction and to recommend solutions to some of the city's most desperate problems. The meeting was arranged by John Hay Whitney in the private dining room of the now defunct New York *Herald Tribune*.

"The luncheon was private," a city official recalled, "and it was important. Present were members of the power elite of varying political persuasions. I remember David Rockefeller was there and so were Ken Clark and Ted Kheel and Yunich from Macy's and Levin from the Citizens Budget Commission.

"At the end of the two hours they had reached some disquieting conclusions. Though they agreed to a man that New York was truly a city in crisis, there was little they would do jointly or publicly to halt its decline. Though they did not say as much at the meeting, their reasons were obvious. As part of the business and civic establishment of a one-party city, New York's elite found it more expedient to remain silent. The arrangements and agreements had all been made. Wagner had given up a little bit to each of them to keep them off his back. I remember Rockefeller—he had just reached an accommodation with Wagner on the Downtown development thing—would not join in recommending solutions, even though I know he really felt they were important. He didn't want to get into a brawl. Everyone expected Wagner to be there for another four years and there was no point in jeopardizing other projects that were also important. The power men in New York, rather than moving toward more control, play a holding action. Retain. Hang on. They're constipated. That's really what bugs Lindsay—the fact that it's such a single-interest city. Nobody cares for anyone else and nobody wants to take anyone else on."

The reason for this, of course, is that the city's business leaders and the "power elite" invited to the Whitney luncheon were only a small part of the city's true power structure. New York's core of operational power is simply not limited to society, business, labor and political groups. A committee of "super citizens," for instance, would never include the two men and one woman who literally exercise control over how any of the proposed solutions would be received by the city's people and administration. To invite the media, newspaper and wire-service functionaries to a private meeting with men like Whitney, Rockefeller and Kheel would be unthinkable, yet Arthur Gelb, Adrienne Weil and Thomas Duffy Zumbo are the individuals who prepare the local news schedules for *The New York Times,* the Associated Press and United Press International respectively. As assignment editors it is their news judgment, as well as that of advisory newsmen, assistants and immediate superiors, that determines just what is to be covered, by whom, at what length and when. The assignments made, of course, are based on news value and upon an AP service called "The Daybook," which lists, twice a day, all the possibilities for stories likely to occur in the next twelve hours. While nothing of news value could or would be suppressed by this group, items of minimal news value but of great interest to those involved are covered or not covered at the discretion of these assignment editors. These are the people Kheel will call to announce an expected contract settlement, or the mayor's press secretary will call to announce one of Lindsay's "impromptu" walks through the city's streets. These are the men to whom Governor Nelson A. Rockefeller announced his divorce and to whom district attorneys, senators, congressmen and ambitious policemen announce their victories and their enemies' defeats. The men who must mold and sometimes manipulate favorable news coverage for their clients or causes know these editors well, know their days off, the hours they work and who relieves them. Again, of course, accommodation prevails. Kheel might call the AP's Tom Crane and arrange a midnight to 8 A.M. news blackout on a negotiating session, thereby allowing Crane to go home to bed guaranteed that no progress reports will be released until he returns.

Robert Moses, a consummate artist of New York power politics, was one of the earliest and most successful practitioners of the manipulation of the functionaries of the "working press" as well as their publishers.

"He knew instinctively that the man who hands out the news gets the advantage in the handling of it," Warren Moscow, a former executive assistant to Mayor Wagner, wrote in a book of memoirs, *What Have You Done for Me Lately?* "He [Moses] had a fine sense of public relations, keeping reporters, editors, editorial writers and publishers in his corner through his willingness to keep them informed. There was a period when it could be said without documented challenge that he 'owned' the editorial pages of the city's principal newspapers. He was too smart ever to brag about it, either."

Moses, as well as the city, had to pay a price. Moscow quotes a Moses biography by Cleveland Rogers published in 1952 which recalls Moses' part in the building of the Triborough Bridge. "The Manhattan side of the structure had been planned to land at 125th Street, at least a mile north of the logical location. The Manhattan arm of the bridge should have gone across Ward's Island instead of Randall's, but powerful real estate and business interests had brought about the acquisition of land at 125th Street, and Moses had to leave this part of the old plan unchanged to avoid a controversy that might have jeopardized the whole undertaking."

Moscow adds, "What Rogers was saying politely was that the approaches at 125th Street had been bought up, on the basis of advance information, by William Randolph Hearst, and that Moses preferred to build the bridge in the wrong place rather than fight the Hearst newspapers."

Apart from the city's business, in the world of culture there is another power elite, and its influence is absolute. Here, the names of men like John Hay Whitney and William S. Paley, chairman of the Columbia Broadcasting System, and David Rockefeller appear in support of a dazzling variety and number of cultural and philanthropic projects. Recently *The New York Times Magazine* reported that a cache of thirty-eight paintings that had belonged to Gertrude Stein was in the process of being sold. "The buyer has not yet been announced," the article read, "but it is believed that a trustee—or a syndicate of trustees—of the Museum of Modern Art in New York, has actively engaged in the secret negotiations. Although spokesmen for the museum have refused to comment, the names most often mentioned in connection with the sale are William S. Paley, president of the museum; David and Nelson Rockefeller, chairman and member of the board, respectively; and John Hay Whitney, the board's vice chairman."

Women like Mrs. William S. Paley and her sisters, Mrs. John

Hay Whitney and Mrs. James Fosburgh (formerly Mrs. Vincent Astor), exercise social power in New York, not only because of their great wealth, family ties and powerful husbands, but because of their personal drive and the fact that they operate within a rigidly insular social unit. The influence of these ladies would not be half so impressive as it is were the boards, trustees and corporations of the city's museums, universities and cultural centers not already made up of so many people from their immediate circle. One of the principal routes to social power in New York today is via the propagation of culture, and there is hardly a museum, cultural center or university upon the board of which one of the three Cushing sisters or their husbands do not sit. There is another, largely informal, bloc in New York—the donors. It is made up of extremely wealthy men and women who have chosen to champion specific power-game combatants. These donors, who are sought after, catered to and indulged, are women like Mary Lasker, long a supporter of the Stevensonian wing of the Democratic Party. There is Arthur Krim, president of United Artists Corporation, another Democratic Party supporter. There is Mrs. Edwin Hilson, a Republican Party contributor, a close friend of Mamie Eisenhower and a financial backer of Mayor Lindsay. The donors also include, among others, Mrs. Marshall Field, Mrs. Brooke Astor, Rebekah Harkness, John H. Schiff, John L. Loeb, the imperial Robert Lehman, Andre Meyers and the Rockefeller brothers. These donors are usually herded together for various causes by a select circle of fund raisers, men like Gustave Levy, the multimillionaire partner in Goldman Sachs. Levy recently raised $4 million in four months for the Urban Coalition. Financier John Coleman, an official of the New York Stock Exchange, has long been the major fund raiser for the Roman Catholic Church in New York. Fund raising in the tradition of these men, as well as others like them, is accomplished the way Jacob Schiff once raised $5 million in a single day. Schiff simply telephoned twenty friends who donated $250,000 each. The power to give away money, after all, is the power to withhold favors. In some cases it is foundation money that is being given away, and in these cases the strings attached are clearly discernible. Shortly after McGeorge Bundy took over as the president of the Ford Foundation, that organization began to demonstrate more muscle. Bundy, who believed that heavily endowed universities were much too conservative with their investment portfolios, let it be known that schools refusing to be more adventurous with their capital would be cut off from Ford Foundation funds.

Donations, of course, need not always be in the form of money. There is in New York a list of social mandarins whose names and reputations alone can lend such prestige to a cause that often they are courted and show deference far out of proportion to their real power. For instance, until her marriage to Aristotle Onassis, the social empress of New York was, without question, Jacqueline Kennedy. Restaurants, designers, museum openings, Broadway shows could be made by her presence and destroyed by her scorn.

"Jackie's influence won't diminish a bit," *The New York Times'* perceptive women's news editor Charlotte Curtis said. "She has always had enormous influence on New York society and fashion and will, I'm sure, continue to have. She's been leading a gypsy sort of life for the past couple of years anyway, so actually she won't really be in New York that much less now. The only really close rivals Jackie has had are people like the Duchess of Windsor and Princess Margaret. These are the people who can really stop New York, but she'll be here a lot more than any of them. In fact, it would be fascinating to see what would happen if all those people arrived in New York at the same time."

An excellent example of the omnipresence of the monied and social leaders in New York is the Board of Trustees of Columbia University. The thirty-five trustees are drawn almost exclusively from the business and banking worlds. Early this year, when students and faculty members demonstrated against the school's building-expansion policies and its relationship with the military-oriented Institute of Defense Analyses, there was almost no aspect of the dispute in which one of the trustees was not personally involved. For example, Columbia trustee Percy Uris, chairman of the Uris Corporation and one of the nation's largest builders, had been scheduled to oversee the university's controversial expansion program. Another trustee, financier William A. M. Burden, was the board chairman of the same Institute of Defense Analyses against which the students were protesting. The story of their demonstrations and arrests was covered by *The New York Times* and CBS, whose chief executives, Arthur O. Sulzberger and William S. Paley, respectively, are both Columbia trustees. And, after more than 600 students were arrested, another Columbia trustee, District Attorney Frank S. Hogan, was their prosecutor.

In a borough of as much undiscovered larceny as Manhattan, Frank S. Hogan, the dour, tight-lipped district attorney, is a man who is feared. His reputation for stubborn determination when he's out to "get somebody" chills the bones of even the honest. His bitter jurisdictional feuds with other prosecutors—most recently with Assistant U.S. Attorney Robert Morgenthau—are well known. He differs from the rest of the city's district attorneys in that his cases invariably stand up in court and are almost never leaked in advance to the press.

Occasional individuals are able to create power for themselves from the dynamism of their personalities and drive. Metropolitan Museum Director Thomas P. F. Hoving, as the city's commissioner of parks, was an excellent example of an infectiously enthusiastic man who through deft manipulation of media, balloons, be-ins, cycle fetes and parades managed to reawaken a jaded city to the pleasures of its parks and recreational facilities. Before Hoving, Joseph Papp, the founder of the city's Shakespeare Festival, was another case of a one-track aggressive keeping an idea alive over the objections of police officials, former recreational czar Robert Moses and parks-are-only-for-the-trees enthusiasts.

The city's political party bosses exert their influence in myriad other ways. Stanley Steingut, the Brooklyn Democratic leader, an affable heir to the city's strongest party machine, has not only his own lifetime of friendship, favors and debts to rely upon, but those of his father, who was the leader before him. Steingut, an old-fashioned, benevolent Daley, controls the Democratic Party in Brooklyn through a web of patronage that involves the anointing of judges, the distribution of insurance premiums on government property, the judicious placement of state bank deposits and the awarding of urban renewal contracts worth millions to politically connected sponsors.

Vincent Albano, the New York County Republican Party chairman, exerts considerable local power today by virtue of the fact that the city, state and nation are now in the hands of Republicans and that some of the patronage honey pot, long under the control of the city's overwhelming Democratic majority, is now available to him. In addition, Albano, like all other political bosses across the country, acts as a conduit to power simply by being able to introduce individuals interested in doing business with the city to the officials they must reach. He was recently admonished for the practice in a special report ordered by Mayor Lindsay, but even the report acknowledged, "We realize that the practice is apparently widespread in both major parties and that there may be nothing inherently improper in the mere introduction. However, we believe that such communication can carry an implication of possible benefit to the government official flowing from a powerful political party." The practice, proper or not, is one way to compensate the party's most ardent supporters and largest contributors for their efforts and cash.

Alex Rose, the Liberal Party boss in New York, has neither the base of patronage available to the Democrats nor the national importance of the Republicans. Nevertheless, he has managed to construct a third party by using a voting coalition of union-oriented garment workers, liberals and old-world socialists as leverage against the candidates of the other two parties. The Liberals have supported, at one time or another, both Democrats and Republicans, depending upon who at the given time presents Rose and his party with the best opportunity to strengthen their own position. The arrangements are made away from the eyes of the press and the party rank and file, but the fruits of these accommodations are evident in every voting machine when judgeships are dealt like cards by the city's political partisans. Rose developed a unique ability to offset his weightier Republican and Democratic opponents. Early in his career of political masterminding he learned that there were political reporters of sound judgment and wooden tongues who could be trusted. For well-connected political writers like Clayton Knowles and Peter Kihss of the *Times* and Tom Poster of the *Daily News,* Rose was always a first-class source. When the negotiations in smoke-filled rooms became so clouded that even these reporters could no longer understand all of the ramifications, they always knew they could "call Alex" and get an objective and authoritative interpretation, regardless of whether the subject was the Democrats or the Republicans. No one, however, would ever call Alex Rose for an objective report on his own party.

Kieran O'Doherty, the Conservative Party's state chairman, has nurtured his power by almost single-handedly pushing his party toward the position of prominence it now holds. O'Doherty has worked in the conservative cause twelve months a year for the last ten years, and he was a familiar figure in the city's newsrooms long before he managed to persuade William F. Buckley, Jr., to run for mayor against Lindsay. Until then, the Conservative Party was largely made up of sincere, dull candidates, and its membership was predominantly middle-aged. O'Doherty plugged away, calling reporters at three in the morning to refute "unfounded charges" or "challenge" opposing candidates to debate. He was tireless, and his work has begun to pay off.

There are two other backstage political powers in New York, and neither of them holds any official post whatever. They are Steven Smith, who is trying to pick up the pieces of the city's Democratic Party, which shattered with the assassination of his brother-in-law, the late Senator Robert F. Kennedy; and Herbert Brownell, the Republican attorney general under President Eisenhower and the closest of political advisers to Mayor Lindsay. "It's difficult to discuss the 'power' of Steven Smith," one long-time Kennedy ally said. "So much of his power is potential rather than actual, or at least definable. He manages the Kennedy family finances, and he was essentially Bobby's campaign manager. Humphrey asked him to become his chief fund raiser after Bobby's death, but he refused. He said at the time, 'I've never had a title in my life.' "

When Robert Kennedy decided to run for his party's presidential nomination, many of the state's Democrats complained at the pressure Steve Smith was able to exert. "It's just a matter of whether you're with them or against them," one local pro-Humphrey Democrat recalled. "If you didn't support them, by God they'd go out and support somebody against you in a primary. It happened all over the state. A lot of guys, you know, would rather switch than fight."

Herbert Brownell, meanwhile, would exert just as much pressure and just as much persuasion to promote his political protégé, John Lindsay, as Smith would to help a Kennedy. At the Miami Republican convention, after sleepless negotiating, unfaltering encouragement and repeated reminders of the possibility that Lindsay's rival, Governor Nelson Rockefeller, might remain for the next six years, Brownell was able to press the Republican vice presidential spot for Lindsay. "Herb ran in and out of more campaign wagons, while juggling Lindsay's vicissitudes and Nixon's coolness, than any hooker in the place," said one reporter who paid particular attention to Brownell.

Not all of the city's political power is generated or exercised in the five boroughs. In fact, many people believe that the four most powerful men in New York maintain offices in Albany. The governor, the Senate majority leader, the Assembly speaker and the chairman of the Committee of the Affairs of New York City have the power to determine the fare charged on the city's mass transit system, what kind of educational system the city runs and how and when the city can tax its own residents. The Albany legislature, in fact, has such control over the administration of the city's government that any mayor who wishes to institute just a modest number of his proposals must reach some accommodation with those four men. They are perfect examples of the difference between "real" power inherent in the individual, a property he can take with him from place to place, and "mandated" power which remains an inherent part of a job rather than an individual. The distinction is one that many elected officials tend to forget the longer they occupy their posts.

There are other men in the city whose posts hold no inherent power whatever, but who, by their own ambition, talent and power-playing expertise have risen from the ranks of flacks, negotiators and hatchetmen to become the power behind some of the city's most powerful men. The real power behind the paper throne of the PBA's John Cassese, for instance, is the organization's slick, dapper and gray-haired public relations spokesman, Norman Frank. Frank is not a policeman—he's too short—and has no organizational mandate from the 20,000 patrolmen who are members of the PBA. He did, however, mount a successful, if somewhat groin-level, campaign against Lindsay's Civilian Review Board. Public-relations man Frank appears with PBA chief Cassese wherever and whenever he makes a public appearance or gives an interview.

Another behind-the-scenes player in the city's power game works very closely with the high-strung and verbally explosive Sanitationmen's Association president, John J. DeLury. Jack Bigel, an officer in the union, is a calm, ponderously reflective man, a master tactician of the collective bargaining process and a theoretical economist of a caliber rarely found at a bargaining table. Bigel, like Norman Frank, always appears with his boss during interviews.

Harry O'Donnell, who was the press secretary to Mayor Lindsay until May, 1969, is another man who has been credited with giving advice that has, more often than not, been sound. O'Donnell, many of the newsmen who cover city affairs regularly claim, has been largely responsible for the remarkable national image the city's mayor enjoys. It was O'Donnell, newsmen insist, who convinced Lindsay to reject on principle Governor Rockefeller's plan for solving the 1968 garbage strike. "It was beautiful," one City Hall regular said with reverence. "Poor Rockefeller came out looking bad, even though his position was basically sound, and Lindsay came out looking nobler than ever by standing up to union pressure. It was pure O'Donnell, and it may have cost Rockefeller a presidential nomination."

"One of the most intriguing realities about New York," A. M. Rosenthal, the associate managing editor of *The New York Times* wrote after prize-winning years of plumbing power depths in Europe and the Orient, ". . . [is that] no one group, clique or power center can count on being able to 'get things done' all the time—or even, no one combination of forces. New York is run by a coalition of powers and pressures that change constantly."

Among those powers are the endless number of organizations, committees, citizens commissions, and trusteeships who can whip out charters dating back a hundred years or reappear as ad hoc committees within minutes of a Board of Estimate hearing. And there are the wholly independent men who speak out indignantly for a flying wedge of sentiment behind them. They have, to a great extent, replaced the city's clerics as the moral power base in New York, though their subjects and interests are largely temporal. This group includes men like columnist Murray Kempton, tweedy, witty and committed to an individual brand of lucid liberalism that is on occasion befogged by his own prose. A lot like Kempton in both passion and sincerity of style is Reuben Maury, the editorial writer for the New York *Daily News*. An irascible and outraged, cane-waving stylist, Maury can still bring many blue-collar, low-income, debt-ridden Americans to their feet against social security, do-gooders, jaywalking and crime in the streets. William F. Buckley,

Jr., columnist, editor of the *National Review,* TV personality and power in the Conservative Party, would have to be included in this group, as well as James Wechsler of the New York *Post.*

"Run a test balloon through Wechsler and you'll know how every middle-aged, middle-income, pro-union, small merchant, Roosevelt Democrat will react," one Democratic city official explained. "And the same goes for Buckley, except in his case it's all the sons of those guys who read the *Daily News* editorials but have done two to four years at Fordham or St. John's. These writers cannot really change anything, but by the nature of their presence and the followers you know they have, they all have entree to city government, business and labor circles. You don't want them stirring up their flocks against you if it's not necessary. In fact, that's just what they're like. They're like old-fashioned priests."

Two other men, James Reston, executive editor of *The New York Times,* and John B. Oakes, its editorial page editor, generate considerable power too. Oakes, who is a grandnephew of the paper's founder, is read every day by the nation's most powerful men, and whereas they can ignore most newspaper criticism, it is impossible for them to ignore a critical editorial in the *Times.* It is, or has assumed or has been given the role of recorder of our time, and no one, from Vice President Spiro Agnew to Fidel Castro, is unaffected by John B. Oakes. Reston, on the other hand, because of his recent promotion to the very apex of the *Times'* editorial pyramid, has editorial control over the country's most influential newspaper. Through a hierarchy of underlings, Reston can assign dozens of the nation's most serious, industrious and relentless reporters to probe and clarify the actions of anyone, from the President of the United States to Mafia hoodlums. In fact, the *Times'* exhaustive coverage of the Mafia earned it a reputation among policemen as *The Wall Street Journal* of the mob.

Newspapers are just as much single-interest power brokers as any other group in New York. Newspapers have interests both economic and editorial. They have, because of their constitutionally guaranteed access to government, tremendous editorial muscle. Some of it rubs off on the newspaper's other departments. Newspaper delivery trucks, for instance, are immune from parking tickets and are only rarely ticketed for speeding, passing red lights and using the West Side Highway and East River Drive, where commercial vehicles are prohibited. Several years ago a proposed tax on services, which included plumbing, auto repairs *and* those services rendered by newspapers and their advertising media, was so blasted by newspaper editorials that the measure was withdrawn. Just before leaving office Mayor Wagner again pushed for a similar tax on the same services, this time however excluding those rendered by newspapers and other advertising media. The bill was enacted without any editorial clamor or even any reference to the change.

The owners of newspapers, whether they have a monopoly on a given market as does the New York *Post*'s publisher Dorothy Schiff, or the nation's largest circulation as does the *Daily News,* influence their publications without ever having to say or do anything. Newsmen have long contended that no publisher or functionary of a publisher on a reputable newspaper ever tells a reporter what to write.

"But it's obvious, for heaven's sake," one nightside rewrite man explained. "I mean, if I'm writing for the *Daily News* I'm not going to turn in seven or eight takes on a poverty program story unless I've found someone's hand in the till. You just know what your newspaper prints. It has an image. You either buy it and work there or quit and go into public relations."

Not all of the city's powerful men are as visible to the public eye as the interviewers and the interviewed. There are men—approximately 4,000—who live and operate and breathe in a subculture of New York City life and nevertheless exercise tremendous control over whole areas of the local economy. In one sense, it is as important a part of that economy as any other. It supplies the city's gamblers with an off-track agency for their bets, supplies cash to businessmen involved in enterprises too risky for banks, and has kept the city's night life and tabloids humming for years. It has helped arrange sweetheart contracts between crooked unions and avaricious bosses and has helped cool at least one racial dispute.

The power of some of the city's racketeers can surprise even their lawyers. A few years ago Edward Bennett Williams was defending gambler Frank Costello during deportation proceedings and, while the two men chatted at the Federal House of Detention where Costello was being held, Costello noticed that the attorney seemed momentarily distressed.

"What's bothering you, Mr. Williams?" Costello asked.

Williams explained that he and his wife were taking her parents out that night to celebrate their thirty-fifth wedding anniversary and that he had promised them tickets to a sellout Broadway musical, but the agent who had promised Williams the tickets—reliable in the past—had failed him for the first time.

"You should have told me," Costello said. "Maybe I could have done something."

Shortly after Williams got back to his hotel room that day, there was a knock on the door. A broad-shouldered man handed him an envelope, grunted and disappeared. It contained four tickets to the musical that Williams' agent could not supply. Williams later recalled that it had never occurred to him that a man in jail could help get four tickets at the last minute to a Broadway sellout. Today the old flair may be gone, but the city's Mafiosi—according to local law enforcement agencies—still control most of what New York listens to on jukeboxes, drinks in after-hours bars and gambles away with bookmakers. There are notoriously greedy and cautious men whose $8-billion-a-year profits from illicit activities (estimated by the McClellan Committee hearings on organized crime) are being invested in selected legitimate ventures in which the odds on staying out of jail are slightly better. The day of Mafia-backed congressmen and judges seems to have passed, but the syndicate's huge cash reservoirs, its ties with elements in some unions and their "management consulting firms" still make them a force in New York.

Within the last five years, one of the city's largest ethnic groups has left the casual fraternity of melting-pot insolubles and become an extremely active, if directionless, force. The city's Negro community today lacks not only a single leader, but a single group of leaders. As a result, almost any articulate member of the Negro community can attract the attention of the city's institutions, government and press. Ex-gang leaders, old Harlem Democratic Party bosses, helmeted and ax-carrying militants as well as back-to-Africa Garveyites have all marched with the governor and the mayor in public and talked with them in private. New York's Negro community is so fractured that it is sometimes impossible to locate the right combinations of individuals in agreement on any one point, even one advantageous to the entire Negro community.

There are men in the city's administration whose importance depends not so much on their effectiveness with the city's black community, as on their ability to identify specific Negro leaders. Meanwhile, of course, the city's Negro leaders are not sitting back waiting to be categorized and contacted. They are involved in a dazzling variety of enterprises, from Jesse Grey's rent strikes to studies by sociologist Kenneth B. Clark's Metropolitan Applied Research Center. Ex-CORE leader Roy Innis was the architect for President Nixon's position papers on black business power and helped start a West Side newspaper aimed at liberal white, Puerto Rican and Negro leaders. Men like Urban League President Whitney Young, Jr., Manhattan Borough President Percy Sutton, City Councilman J. Raymond Jones, Harlem antipoverty dispenser Andrew Tyler, Sonny Carson of Brooklyn CORE, Board of Education member Milton Galamison and recently re-elected Representative Adam Clayton Powell are all involved in multitudinous projects and are all constantly jockeying with one another and the city to fill the Negro community's leadership vacuum.

A. H. Raskin, the labor editor of *The New York Times,* thinks the lust for power in New York City is destroying the city.

"We are just working ourselves into a ditch of hatred that is utterly meaningless," he said on a television debate with Theodore Kheel.

"It seems to me," he continued, "that our big problem in this city is that we have been carried away by the worship of power."

3. Life in the City of Gold

Jimmy Breslin

". . . The job is not to shoot or throw bombs, but to get people out of these falling-down ghettos and put them in life . . ."

They drank with their hats on and folded *Wall Street Journals* under their elbows. They stood with faces that showed nothing and they stared at the bottles behind the bar. There were almost no sounds. A man choked on cigarette smoke. Ice clicked against the side of a mixing glass. A cigarette lighter snapped. Once, drinking was fun. Now it is some kind of morose duty. It was 5 P.M., and the market had closed higher and NBC radio's rate card had been raised 10 per cent and Xerox shifted its account and Manufacturers named three new senior vice-presidents. And now the people who conducted this business stood in the dimness of the Oyster Bar at Grand Central Station and they waited for trains, and for the whiskey in their hands to do something good to them.

Outside the bar, the footsteps sounded on the stairs and passageways and the people poured into the station from the streets, from Fifth and Madison and Park, and from the subways coming up from Wall and Beaver and Pine. They came into the station, walking under this block-long Kodak color photo which dominates the main waiting room. It is a pretty ad, with reds and whites and violets, and it has a boy in a plaid shirt and a blonde in blue holding a camera. The lettering on the ad says, "Springtime Calls for Color Snapshots." The ad talks for a world of things to own, and of pretty flowers and pretty people. And the ones who live in this world were walking under the big Kodak picture and their footsteps filled the station as they came down the stairs and past the Oyster Bar and went onto the commuter trains.

The New Haven's 5:51 Stamford Local-Express was at Gate 100. The sign said the first stop was Larchmont. After that, Mamaroneck, Harrison, Rye, Port Chester, Greenwich, Cos Cob, Riverside, Old Greenwich, Stamford; towns people like to say they are from. The billboards in the railroad platform dusk advertised Avis, the Dreyfus Fund, Durene Yarn, *Time, Newsweek*. The train was filling quickly, but the smoking car was almost empty. The smoking car always is the last to get crowded. People who ride the New Haven read and believe the U.S. Surgeon General's reports on smoking. The rise in cigarette sales comes from the people in the streets, who are behind in everything. In the car, a poster noted that 72 per cent of New York's bank officers commute. Another poster carried the only ad for Finnair I've ever seen. "In Finland, one will get you four—one U.S. dollar equals 4.18 Finnish Marks. Fly Finnair!" A bald guy in horn-rimmed glasses, smoking a pipe, came in and sat down in front of me. He pulled the green shade down so he couldn't look out the window.

The smoking car began to fill up. A man with a mustache took off his topcoat and stood in a military-cut twill jacket. The shirts coming through the door were splashed with pinks and yellow stripes. Bank accounts make people bold. Four men, their faces pink from hot showers, came on with blue plastic cases which look like overly long airline bags. These were their squash cases. They had just played a round of squash at the Yale Club, right across Vanderbilt Avenue from the station. The last man to come into the car was carrying a Peal's attaché case, $125 at Brooks Brothers. The train shook and moved and the platform lights ran past the window. The 5:51 to Stamford started up the tunnel under Park Avenue.

The train comes out of the ground and becomes elevated at 96th Street, which is the street everybody in Harlem calls "The Frontier." Raul's Barber Shop is the first thing you see when the train comes up. It stands there with garbage cans lining the curb and fluorescent lights coming through smeared windows. The train moves very quickly. It comes past tenements with fire escapes where people put mattresses down and sleep in the heat of a summer night. It comes past sooty windows with cheap material tacked to the window frames to form curtains. You can see the dirt of East Harlem and Harlem better from the train than you can from the street. On the street, you can't see the alleys behind the tenements. You can from the train. It goes past alley after alley, all of them long mounds of garbage running for the entire block behind the houses. The rats live inside the mounds of garbage. The rats breed litters of eight and nine at a time. The baby rats reach sexual maturity at three months and breed litters of their own. The rats share in the life of everybody in New York who lives above The Frontier.

The blocks go by quickly. Only two people in the smoking car of the 5:51 to Stamford are looking out the window. One of them is a young guy who looks like Jack Lemmon. He has a paperback book in one hand. He holds up his chin with the other hand. He looks down at the black kids standing on the street corners. The other person looking down is back in the rear of the car. Everybody else reads, or stares ahead. The blocks they never see go by quickly: 105th, 108th, 111th.

Cathy and Ebro Marrero live at 220 East 111th. At eight o'clock at night, the rats come up from the spaces around the sewer pipes under the boiler room. They have slept all day and now they cling to the rusted pipes with these strong toenails they have and they start up the pipes which are inside the walls of the old five-story tenement. Cathy and Ebro Marrero live in Apartment 3, on the third floor, and one night Cathy Marrero shrieked and Ebro was standing with a big smile. Two rats had come up the pipes and they came out under the kitchen sink and walked across Cathy's feet while she stood at the sink and washed the dishes. Ebro had chased the two rats and the rats had run into the bathroom. Ebro slammed the door on them. He smiled. Now he had them. Rats always stayed in the bathroom, licking water from the tub. Ebro leaned against the bathroom door and took off his right shoe. Cathy came and handed him a flatiron. He said he didn't want it. He held the shoe in his right hand and opened the bathroom door slowly and slid through. He slammed the door behind him. He began shouting, "Ho! Ha! Ho!" while he beat the rats to death with his shoe. The shoe sounded hollow against the sides of the bathtub. When the door opened, Ebro was beaming. He pointed to the rats in the bathtub. They were small rats for East Harlem. Once, they put two big tomcats into the basement of Ebro's tenement. The next day there was only cat fur and blood in the basement. Cathy came into the bathroom with a handbrush and a paper bag. She swept the two rats into the paper bag. She emptied the paper bag into the toilet and flushed it. She dropped the paper bag into the tub. Ebro lit a match and set the paper bag on fire. Cathy took a bottle of strong disinfectant from a shelf in the bathroom. After the paper bag had burned down, she poured the strong disinfectant all over the bathtub.

Now 111th is gone and the train goes past 115th and 118th and the White Rose Bar at 125th and it continues on through all of Harlem and then it crosses the river and comes into the Bronx. They still don't look out the windows. The train goes right to Larchmont this way. Larchmont is another kind of Frontier. From Larchmont and on up, there is not a house which can be bought for under $25,000. The average house costs closer to $40,000. The train slows to a stop at Larchmont with men standing in the aisle waiting to get off. Men whose income, if averaged out, would be close to $35,000 a year.

When you get off the train, there is this young girl with long hair who is in a navy-blue college sweatshirt, sitting on the rear fender of a LeMans convertible. The dog inside the car puts his nose out the window and starts barking furiously. The woman at the wheel pushes the dog's nose back inside the car. She calls out to her husband, who is coming off the train with an attaché case in his hand.

"Hey," the man calls out. The nose comes out of the window and the dog begins barking. *"Okay,* guy," the man calls to the dog. "Hey," he says to his daughter, ruffling her hair. He walks in the headlights of the Karmann Ghia parked behind his wife's LeMans convertible.

The rest of them spilled out of the train after him and the posters on the station told them to read *Forbes* and *Business Week* and their wives waited in station wagons and convertibles and it is a world of pretty things and pretty people you can take pictures of and they all ride the train that goes through Harlem with only a couple of people looking out the window.

None of them knows Charles Patterson. He stands on 115th Street and looks up at the trains going by. He looks at them so much that he sat down and wrote a poem about these trains which go through Harlem and take people to Larchmont and Mamaroneck and Harrison and Rye and all the way to Stamford. This is what Charles Patterson wrote about the 5:51 Stamford Local-Express:

> You stand there amid
> The city of gold
> 115th Street
> Children laugh, fight, play and kill
> But you killed them first
> 115th Street
> You murdered their fathers
> And filled their mothers' wombs with pain
> The whites pass by seeing only their newspapers
> Return home to laugh at misery
>   up on the tracks, commuters commute
> You are down in Hell, on your dirty street
> And still the whites laugh, saying these niggers
> Are having a ball
> If we are then come play with us you bastards ©

Nobody who is white knows about the poem. It was published in a magazine called *The Liberator,* which says it is the voice of African-Americans. In June of 1967, *The Liberator* carried an ad for the Second Annual Black Arts Convention in Detroit. It was to be held in Detroit because one of the major Black Nationalist leaders in the nation, the Reverend Albert Cleage, Jr., was involved. Cleage is pastor of the Central United Church of Christ in Detroit. Glanton Dowdell, an artist, had painted a chancel mural of a Black Madonna in the church. The mural is nine feet wide and eighteen feet high. The mural was admired at the Black Arts Conference. Dan Watts, the *Liberator* editor, LeRoi Jones and Rap Brown spoke at the conference. Then the Reverend Cleage spoke. He promised that

Detroit would burn. The brothers and sisters were clapping and swaying and saying, yes, Detroit will burn and the Reverend Cleage kept saying burn and the swaying and clapping was louder and nobody who was white in all of Detroit knew who he was. Two weeks later, Detroit blew.

On Sunday night, the night it was at its worst, Federal troops were moving toward the city and there was rifle fire everywhere. At 4 A.M., Jerry Cavanagh, the mayor of the city, came home for a few minutes. He sat in the garden behind his house with his heart broken and the drink shaking in his hand.

"I had a council for human rights," he was saying. "We set up offices, we held meetings, we planned and asked and talked and I did whatever they thought we should do and then I prayed and now look at what we have. And what do I find out now? I find out all these, quote, Negro leaders were the last ones to know what the people in the street were going to do and when the trouble began my people were the first ones to go under the bed."

"Have you ever had anything to do with this Reverend Cleage?" Cavanagh was asked.

"I never heard his name before this," he said. "I don't know how to start finding him now. We just don't know. We're white. We grew up with white people. We don't know. None of us knows."

There was a movie called *The Battle of Algiers*. The reviews, written by white people, mentioned the parallels between Algeria and our own troubles in Vietnam. On a Sunday night, when it was 10 degrees and a cold wind ran along Third Avenue, there was a long line in front of the Cinema I movie house, where the picture was showing. Almost half the line was black. I remember thinking that it was strange, all these people down from Harlem, and on a cold Sunday night, to pay $2.50 for a movie that didn't star Sidney Poitier.

The movie was very good and it had two big scenes which told you the story. The story of the audience. In the first scene, the Algerian rebels had three of their women hide bombs under their skirts and go out and plant the bombs in an airlines office and a restaurant. One of the women took her five-year-old with her so nobody would suspect what she was doing.

"Cool," a black guy sitting directly in front of me said.

"Those sisters are cool," somebody else said.

"The sisters got the whole game," another voice said.

"The sisters, they stay mad all the time so they don't have to get mad."

And at the end of the picture, all the Algerians spilled onto the streets, making this noise by putting their tongues against the roofs of their mouths. They fell on the French and killed them. And as the Algerians killed the French in the movie, the black guy in front of me was snapping his fingers. "Kill the mothers, baby."

The newspaper stories written by white people told you to compare the picture with what we were going through in Vietnam. Nobody knows.

A few days later, Dan Watts, the editor of *The Liberator,* was at the United Nations, sitting over coffee in a little vault of a lunchroom on the third floor.

"Have you seen the movie about Algeria?" he was asked.

"Do you mean our black Academy Award winner?" he said.

"Is that what you call it?"

"The brothers and sisters turned out to see this one like it was the story of their lives. I don't know a brother in the whole country who hasn't gone to see it."

"Why are they so strong for it?" he was asked.

"It gives them ideas," he said.

This is, of course, not sane. The job is not to shoot or throw bombs, but to get people out of these falling-down ghettos and put them in life with the rest of us. Programs used to tumble out of legislatures and executive offices. The idea was to save the inside of a nation. There was one night when Lyndon B. Johnson hung over the lectern and told a joint session of Congress, "We shall overcome." Then the inspiration became lost in battle reports from Chu Lai and Khe Sanh. And all over the country there were these little scenes. Two military policemen getting out of a car in front of a two-story frame house on 64th Place in Glendale, Queens. It is ten o'clock on a Saturday night in March. The MP's stand nervously on the brick stoop and ring the bell. There are two doors, a storm door and the regular door. A woman opens the regular door. It is dark and she can't see well. She looks through the storm door while she begins opening it. She sees the two MP's and she knows. Her eyes roll up into her head and she faints. Her son, Gregory Ambrose, twenty, a private in the 1st Division, is dead in the jungle outside Saigon. Gregory Ambrose had nine days left before he was to leave Vietnam and come home. In the cellar of the house his mother has a big sign. It says, "Welcome Home Gregory."

With this going on, the Report of the President's Commission on Civil Disorders, a report which stands as a major American document, came to Lyndon Johnson's desk. He made no comment on it. The President of the United States became another man sitting in the train and not looking out the window. And if the President does not look any more, then the country does not look.

"I thought something would happen," Jack Rosenthal was saying one day. "I thought he would react to it in some way." When Jack Rosenthal was with the Justice Department he was one of the main people responsible for the march from Selma to Montgomery. He has taken a year out to study urban affairs at Harvard and M.I.T. He spent six weeks doing some of the raw writing for the introduction to the summary of the report. But there has been no answer.

Bobby Kennedy came out of the bedroom in his fourteenth-floor apartment at the United Nations Towers and he walked into the living room and stood by the windows and lit a cigar. It was eleven o'clock and he had changed for dinner. It was one of the nights before he declared for the Presidency.

"How is everything?" he said to the people waiting for him.

"I think it's bad," one of them said.

"What do you mean by bad?" Kennedy said.

"I think the white people and the black people are pulling away from each other. They're beginning to get polarized."

"Not beginning, they *are* polarized," Kennedy said.

"Well then what do we do?" another man said.

"I don't know. What would you do?" Kennedy said.

"Well somebody has to put some direction into the thing. It's got to come from the top."

"I agree," Kennedy said. "How would you do that?"

"Isn't that something for you, not me?" he was told.

He put the cigar in his mouth and his eyes half closed against the smoke. He stood by the windows and said nothing. He knew what he was going to do.

The trouble begins at the top. The government relied heavily on sociologists who have big names and are at big universities. But the sociologists live in frame houses on college streets and they have leaves on the lawn in the fall and greeting card snow in the winter and grass and birds in the summer and they do not know what it is like to lead a life where little things determine so much. They advocated busing. The black people do not like it. They have to give the children lunch money in many cases, and they do not have the money. And the children come home from school too late to work at delivery jobs or, one of the most important occupations of all in the ghetto, baby sitting.

Joe Hilgreen is a tall, graying, soft-spoken man who works for the New York City Department of Welfare. Every once in a while, Joe Hilgreen gets so depressed by what he has to see all day that on the way home he says to hell with it, let me go someplace nice even if it empties me. One night Joe Hilgreen was standing in Toots Shor's when he should have been going against neighborhood prices, and he had a Bloody Mary and he talked about his job.

"We had this regulation," he was saying, "which told us we were supposed to go into the apartment, if it was a woman on relief, and open the closets to see if there was a man's clothes hanging up. People who were experts in social work put that rule in. The dignity of a human being, hell, they never thought of that."

"And you actually had to open a woman's closet and look inside?" a newspaperman at the bar named Richard Wald asked him.

"Me?" Joe Hilgreen said. "I don't know how to do a thing like that."

Mayor Hugh Addonizio stood in his office in Newark City Hall at eleven o'clock on a night when Springfield Avenue was seething and the first fires were starting. Hugh Addonizio, mayor of Newark, was saying, "I have decided to promote six police lieutenants to the rank of captain." Somebody around him began saying, There, now that should do it. One of the police lieutenants was black. This would give Newark its first black captain of police. The white politicians of Newark thought a black police captain would make the people of Springfield Avenue so happy they would not riot.

At one o'clock in the morning, Hugh Addonizio moved from City Hall to an office in an armory. Governor Richard Hughes was with him. The National Guard was turning out for a riot which nearly took the life of a city.

White religious institutions, which are run so much like political parties, generally have displayed the same mentality as the ward politicians. The churches and temples offer love, but only in sermons. The priests and ministers and rabbis are adept at issuing statements.

The worst section of the City of New York is Brownsville, in Brooklyn. Once, it was crowded and vibrant and famous for its Jewish lore and its comedians and prize fighters, and for gangs like the Amboy Dukes and Murder, Inc. Brownsville now is black and Puerto Rican and it is empty. The car driving down Sutter Avenue passed block after block in which four and five and six stores were broken-windowed and empty. Meyers Ice Cream Parlor at 527 Sutter is gone. There used to be a big, tough Jewish shylock who came into Meyers on Saturday night to collect. Either you were sitting there with the money for him or you were in trouble. At the corner of Sutter and Hinsdale, Club 521 is gone. Once it was a bar run by a guy they called Pacy. Now it is empty and the windows are dark with dirt. At the corner of Hopkinson and Sutter, a four-story building has all the windows broken. The candy store on the ground floor is gone. Next to it, the Famosa Grocery is gone, too. On the opposite corner is a yellow stone building with a sign saying "Catholic Mission Good Shepherd Center." When you come through the school-building double doors into a shabby hallway the first thing you see is stained glass with the Star of David on it. When Brownsville was white, the place was a synagogue.

A young nun sat in an office off the hallway. She was a Sister of St. Joseph. In the Diocese of Brooklyn, the Sisters of St. Joseph do most of the teaching in Catholic grammar schools. It was surprising to see a nun in a place like the Good Shepherd Center, and she was asked about it.

"Five of us are here," she said. "We live in an apartment right down the street. We're only here a short time. I used to teach in Maspeth and Flatbush. But I think this is so much more important. We're not up on a pedestal. We're with the people, working for them, trying to help even a little. Two of us are nurses. The other three of us teach these people how to deal with landlords and welfare. And their own lives."

A Puerto Rican woman wearing sneakers came in. She had a drained face which made her seem ancient. She stood silently, with the aimless stare of people who have been defeated so often.

"The housing is the worst thing here," the nun said. "I was in a place the other day. The landlord was renting it for ninety dollars. He listed it as four rooms. Four rooms! I told the landlord, 'You must be charging for the walls.' And the rats. They just come through in hordes. Here, Isabelle, how long have you looked for a place to live?"

"A year," the Puerto Rican woman said.

"Where have you looked?" the nun said.

"All the place. Bushwick, Nostrand, Bronx."

"She has ten children," the nun said. "The welfare will go as high as $175 a month for her. But there is no place in this city at that price for a family of her size. So she lives here." The nun shrugged. "Lives. That's only a word."

"What does her husband do?"

Isabelle held out a wrinkled hand. "He chop the fingers off. Four fingers off. He work chop the vegetables in a restaurant. One day chop the fingers off. The Welfare tells him stay home and help mind babies. He no can work."

"How does the rest of it around here look, Sister?"

"If you mean the summer, very bad. The feeling is so bad. They're so alienated. I just don't know. When it gets warm and all these people come out of the houses. They are so beautiful, these people. But so alienated."

"What about yourself down here?"

"I don't know," she said. "I told my father when I came here that, no, I couldn't guarantee him that I'd be safe here. I had to tell him the truth. There is no guarantee that I'm safe. But then I made my father come down here and see just how these people have to live. He couldn't believe what he was seeing. On Saturdays, he's been driving back here with his friends and they go all around so they can see for themselves. It's so hard for them to believe. White people out in the neighborhoods, they just don't know."

"How old are you, Sister?"

"Twenty-eight."

"And your name?" she was asked.

She sat up and looked over the desk and saw that notes were being taken on scraps of paper balanced on a knee.

"What are you doing?" she said.

"Taking down notes."

"Notes? What kind of notes?"

"For a story."

"A *story?*" She was up from her chair and grabbing the notes.

"You'll get me in trouble," she said.

"What trouble?"

"With the community." The "community" is the word for the directors of the order of nuns to which she belongs.

"There's a great deal of controversy over us being here," she said, her hand over the notes. "Some people don't think we should be living in an apartment and doing this sort of work."

"What do they think you should be doing?"

"Never mind what anybody thinks. I want to stay here and you can get me in trouble. I was nearly removed from here already. I went through an apartment on Herzl Street where a child died from pneumonia. The child had gotten a cold and there was no heat in the house and he died. The landlord was telling somebody, 'I give heat twenty-four hours a day.' And I said, 'Yeah, twenty-four hours once every three months.' That got back to the community and I was in trouble. I was nearly removed."

"In other words, the people in your order don't like the whole idea of you being here?" she was asked.

The phone rang and she answered it, and waved goodbye to us while she talked.

It was April now. The winter was long and the streets were empty in the cold. But now it was April and we began to play a game with time again.

"When do you start?" John Lindsay was asked one night. "In June?"

"No. In May," he said.

There was a story out of Washington about Federal troops being trained specifically for riot duty. Lindsay was asked whether he knew anything about it.

"There'll be no troops with me," John Lindsay said. "When I walk, I go alone."

The envelope was mailed from New York. It contained a ten-page booklet of instructions for a riot. The material on page two was under the heading "In a Revolution You Either Win or Die." The booklet was written by somebody who uses English well. It was printed on an offset press. It was not the crude mimeographed sheets they used to hand out in 1964 in Harlem, when riots were young.

Individuals should make phone calls to the police department during an uprising (telling of emergencies such as being robbed, shot at or someone's being killed, a store or bank being broken into, etc.). The address that you give to the police department should be outside the area of revolt but in the same borough. Also report snipers that do not exist in areas outside the revolt. Women are good for this type of job.

These pamphlets don't produce action. So far, nothing planned or threatened ever really came off. Money from Cuba was coming into New York, maybe $70,000, all totaled, to help people in the Revolutionary Action Movement make trouble. Happily, the RAM members are as inept at their end of the civil rights proposition as the white people are on their end. Most of the money went into new cars and blond girls.

"All right, move it on now," the cop called over to the two men who were standing on the corner and pushing each other in an argument.

One of them, a brown hat low over his eyes, turned on the cop. "Move where?" he said.

"Just break it up and move it on," the cop said.

"You better do the movin'. You goin' be in for a nice long hot summer," the guy said.

"If it's a long summer, it may be your last summer," the cop said.

While they talked, you could look straight down the street, down 114th Street, and make out the railroad tracks in the darkness. No train was passing. The commuter rush hour was over. The people on the trains had gone through without seeing. They were home now. Home, knowing nothing about what the cop and the guy in the hat were talking to each other about.

4. The Big Ten, or: Who Runs New York?

Edward N. Costikyan

"The power to run New York is so ephemeral, and the structure rests upon such unsure foundations . . . that the ten men who run New York . . . change, month to month, year to year."

About a year ago Frances Low, the wife of City Councilman Robert A. Low, mentioned the problem a friend was having in trying to make a list of the ten men who run the city. I pooh-poohed the alleged difficulties in compiling such a list, and, to prove my point, within four weeks I had completed a draft of an article which explained who the ten were (there were really only nine when I got finished), and why.

But, between the time my first draft was finished and the time it took to publish a completed—and revised—version, the list didn't look so solid to me. So I started making some changes, and by the time the revision was finished some of those whom, two months earlier, I had left on the list looked out of place.

Another revision, and, as the course of events continued to reflect changes in the allocation of power, I despaired of compiling a sufficiently permanent list.

More important, however, the exercise demonstrated that the power to run New York is so ephemeral, and the power structure rests upon such unsure foundations, that month-to-month fluctuations thrust one or another New Yorker to the front ranks. For the ten men who run New York City do not combine their power and exercise it collectively. Nor do they exercise it to repress new faces, which are constantly appearing. The group of ten is thus not a permanent one. New York City's governing establishment changes from month to month and year to year.

Nevertheless, at any given time there is a small group of people who have the power to run New York City. By "power," I mean they have the power to control and direct the city's governmental policies, determine its budget, determine the taxes it will impose, allocate its public and private resources, establish its tastes, and determine the quality of New York City life. This definition excludes many powerful people in New York like David Sarnoff of RCA and William Paley of CBS, and Robert Lehman and Gustave Levy of Wall Street. They have power, but not over New York City, in part because such power as they have is only intermittently directed against New York City's problems.

The volatility of membership in the group is the result of the intermittent crises which thrust one or another person into the position where he seems to be and is running New York City. Mike Quill was running New York City for the first two or three weeks of Mayor Lindsay's administration in 1965. Albert Shanker ran the school system of New York City during the fall of 1968.

I believe, however, that the list of ten I suggested a year ago and the list of ten I suggest this year would have the power to run the city in any area—if all of them joined together and put all their power into the effort.

My first nominees to the list of ten were three men in the labor field, John DeLury, Harry Van Arsdale and Theodore Kheel.

John DeLury is the head of the city's Sanitationmen's Association. (I put him on the list before the recent sanitation strike.) DeLury is a gruff, feisty, tough labor leader. He is, as we five-foot-fivers like to say, of average stature—i.e., about five foot six—and is usually found with a Sherlock Holmes curved pipe in his mouth.

His union is the best political machine left in town. He doesn't believe in strikes by public employees (his union has really had only one major strike in its history—in 1968), but rather that their legitimate objectives should be achieved through political activity.

My reasons for putting DeLury among the top ten were that John DeLury for some years has been the man who did the most to establish New York City's expense budget. DeLury's union has only 10,000 members, all city employees. They clean the streets.

But DeLury's unique power is derived from the strategic position occupied by his union and by his brilliant exploitation of the union's political power and importance in the day-to-day life of the city.

The union's strategic position flows from the fact that garbage collection in New York City is essential, but not dangerous like police or fire work (he disputes this assertion). Exploiting the necessity of the service, DeLury has step by step forced, coerced, conned, and persuaded the city to extend to sanitationmen benefits accorded to the police and fire departments because of the hazardous nature of the duties the policemen and firemen perform— such as one-half pensions after twenty years of service.

More than any other labor leader, he has conceived of new negotiating objectives, such as having the city pay first part, and ultimately all, of various fringe benefits. He has forced pay increases, more vacations, more sick leave, more of everything for his men.

Each concession to the sanitationmen has inevitably been followed by similar concessions to the remaining 300,000-or-so city employees, whose unions have patiently awaited the word as to the latest concession DeLury has extracted. The result has been that DeLury has played a major role in determining the city's expense budget. The small concession obtained by DeLury, at a cost to the city of say $5 million, becomes a budget item of $125 million or more in a year or two as soon as other unions demand and obtain what DeLury's men have.

The city budget reacts accordingly. For the past five years expenditures have increased at a rate of 13 to 14 per cent per year (without any additional services) while tax revenue from existing sources expands by 3.9 to 5 per cent. Hence every year New York City has a bigger budget gap. John DeLury was for a long time— until the welfare budget started leaping upward—the man most responsible for creating that gap.

I would no longer put John DeLury on the list of ten. Last winter's sanitation strike resulted in a change in the sanitationmen's contract year. Now the contracts of sanitation, police and fire end at the same time. Their contracts are dealt with together. Gone is the tactical advantage which DeLury once had of negotiating his contract separately, after the fire department and the police department contracts had been negotiated. As a result of the 1968 strike, he and his union have been promoted to the level of the police and fire. No longer does DeLury have the chance to pioneer the fight for new concessions from the city which other unions pick up in turn. Now he is one of the big boys, but in being thus promoted he plays a far less significant role in determining New York's labor relations and the size of the city's budgets. His role as innovator is buried in his promotion.

The next man on the list of ten a year ago was Harry Van Arsdale, and Van Arsdale is still on anyone's list. Van Arsdale is (1) financial secretary and international treasurer of the electricians' union, (2) head of the taxi union, and (3) the head of the Central Labor and Trades Council, a committee of New York City's major unions. But Van Arsdale is more than that. He is labor's man in government—its trader, negotiator, wheeler-dealer, spokesman and broker.

When a strike threatens to paralyze the city its mayor—whoever he is—usually calls on Van Arsdale to help straighten it out. When voting machines couldn't get delivered to the schools because of the teachers' strike, the Board of Elections called on Van Arsdale. When the economy slows down because of a cutback in construction projects, the unions are likely to call on Van Arsdale to persuade the mayor or governor to approve a new housing or highway project. When public officials need votes to be re-elected, they seek out Van Arsdale to ascertain what special legislation is needed to attract support from a given union. Thus, when Robert F. Wagner broke with the Democratic Party in 1961, he turned to Van Arsdale for help, and Van Arsdale formed a new party—the Brotherhood Party—just in case the Democratic "bosses" beat Wagner in the primary and he needed a line to run on.

When Nelson Rockefeller was at the bottom of the pile in January 1966 and looked as if he were politically dead, he turned to Van Arsdale. The governor delivered the legislation—such as minimum wage—and some new major construction projects which Van Arsdale said the union wanted, and, that November, Van Arsdale was in the successful Rockefeller's corner.

In the 1968 Presidential election, when the Democratic Party was shattered by the McCarthy phenomenon, the death of Senator Kennedy, and the Daley convention, Van Arsdale kicked off the Humphrey campaign in New York by marching down Fifth Avenue with him on Labor Day. Thereafter it was labor as much as the party organization which produced a 370,548-vote margin for Humphrey in New York State on Election Day.

Van Arsdale resuscitated the Lower Manhattan Expressway, which everyone thought was dead, in order to make work for union members, and he may yet succeed in putting it through. Van Arsdale organized the taxi drivers—a feat which proved too much for John L. Lewis—and, in order to get his men more pay, he engineered the first taxi fare increase in New York in many years. Van Arsdale's support for the Port Authority's grotesque World Trade Center was a major factor in its approval—it meant work for the Building Trades Union.

Because of his strong voice in determining the nature and location of construction projects built with public funds, his important role in determining the labor legislation of this state, his power in delivering support to candidates for public office, and his participation in the negotiation and settlement of every major labor dispute in New York City, Van Arsdale must be placed in the top ten.

The next man on my 1967 list was Theodore W. Kheel.

Because of his key role in formulating the resolution of earlier controversies which shape the new controversies, and because of the necessity for his services to prevent strikes which will paralyze the city, Theodore W. Kheel must be placed in the top ten. Kheel is New York's strike settler. Whether it's a strike or a threatened strike by government employees, such as transit workers, or teachers, or a dispute involving private employers such as the newspapers, Kheel is involved. Beyond the labor disputes of public attention, Kheel acts in dozens of unpublicized disputes. As a mediator, arbitrator, fact finder or referee, Kheel has had more of a voice than any other man in determining the quality of labor-management relations in New York. More than that, his intellect and judgment have left their impact in literally hundreds of resolutions of disputes—and given both the disputes and their resolution a direction and momentum which tend to shape the nature of future disputes and in turn the resolution of those disputes.

The result of Kheel's activities has been to create a kind of framework of precedents—not entirely dissimilar from the early years of the English common law—which help to shape the decisions of today's and tomorrow's labor disputes. The way in which last year's disputes were settled (often by Kheel) is a factor in deciding what "demands" should be advanced this year. The tentative small steps won three years ago suggest the areas where further progress should be sought by the union this year. What has been done in one dispute becomes the pattern for settling a half-dozen others. Kheel's cumulative activities over the years have been a major factor in shaping and formulating this body of precedent.

Kheel is still on my list of the top ten, although his position is somewhat shakier. In the last year the city has turned less and less to him. He was not involved in the sanitation settlement in the spring of 1968 or the police, fire and sanitation settlement in the fall, when Justice Arthur Goldberg was introduced to New York City government the hard way. Kheel was briefly involved in the teachers' strike, but the union rebuffed his efforts.

Nevertheless, no new Kheel has emerged, and the accumulation of activities in the labor field over the years leaves him among New York's top ten. The mere fact, however, that any question arises as to his renewed listing reflects the volatility and evanescence of power in New York.

A year ago, I placed on the list of the top ten the name of Austin W. Tobin, executive director of the New York Port Authority.

The Port Authority is a bi-state agency created by New York and New Jersey. New York and New Jersey each appoint half of its commissioners. The agency runs the Holland Tunnel, the Lincoln Tunnel, the George Washington Bridge, the three major airports and smaller ones as well, the marine terminals, bus terminals and Hudson Tubes, and is presently building the World Trade Center, a massive complex including office space on Manhattan's Lower West Side.

Last year I said that Tobin was on the list because of the tremendous power of the Authority which Tobin heads. Tobin, at $70,000 a year, is one of the nation's best-paid government officials. The Port Authority, under his direction, has had the power to do pretty much as it pleases and to require the city to do pretty much what the Authority wants it to do. For example, thirty-six years ago it started to collect fifty cents a car for the use of the George Washington Bridge on the promise that the toll would go when the bonds were paid off. Drivers have given up complaining about the toll, although the costs of the bridge have been repaid five times over.

The Port Authority and Tobin occupy a position of pre-eminent power similar to that Robert Moses once held. Like Moses, the Authority and Tobin can do no wrong. When the Authority decided it wanted to build a World Trade Center which no one particularly wanted (except the unions, but they would have accepted some other project) and which would uproot hundreds of businesses, play havoc with television reception, and provide publicly financed competition for private real estate interests such as those which owned the Empire State Building, the Tobin-Port Authority juggernaut was not to be stopped.

The Authority is an independent corporation. Its books are closed to the public and the legislature. Its finances are its *own* business, although it is concededly engaged in public business.

Tobin is no longer among the top ten, only because the Port Authority has been exceeded in power by the newly created Metropolitan Transportation Agency, and he by the MTA's chairman, William J. Ronan, whom I will discuss below.

Of the next three on the 1967 list, two are casualties of one year's changes. The three were Nelson Rockefeller, Anthony Travia, and Earl Brydges. I said of them then:

> These three men control New York State's legislature and what it does or does not do. When all three agree on anything, it is done. When one of the three dissents, it is not done.
>
> Brydges, a Republican, controls the State Senate; Travia, a Democrat, controls the Assembly; and, Rockefeller has a veto on both. Neither house has a party with a large enough majority to override a Rockefeller veto.
>
> The three together therefore determine, directly or indirectly:
> the fares charged in New York City's public transportation;
> what taxes the city can impose to meet its budget gaps;
> how much of the gap must be closed by new taxes;
> how much must be closed by increasing existing taxes.
>
> In short, they have the power to determine the structure of New York City's government. They have the power to fix its taxes. They have the power to require the city to spend money, which the city must raise. And they have the power to forbid the city to impose taxes to raise the money it must spend.
>
> Because these three men hold the power of the purse strings and the residual political power over the city, they must be in-

cluded in the city's ten most powerful men—even though Earl
Brydges lives in Wilson, New York, near Niagara Falls, and
Rockefeller in Tarrytown.

Of the three, only Brydges—the man from Niagara Falls—remains as one of the top ten. He remains in control of the State
Senate. Anthony Travia, after years of the rough and tumble of
New York politics as assemblyman, minority leader, Wagner's
Brooklyn county leader, and speaker of the Assembly, was appointed to the Federal bench in Brooklyn, where he is now one of
eight Federal judges. His Assembly seat was filled in 1968 by Vito
Battista, the flamboyant and conservative head of the Taxpayers
Party. His successor as speaker is a Republican, Perry Duryea, a
Montauk assemblyman. However, Duryea in the speakership will
not command the power which his predecessor wielded for some
time, for a number of reasons. He is new and yet to be tested as a
speaker; he commands a thin majority of Republicans, some of
whom will likely vote with their fellow representatives of the cities,
even though they are Democrats, on issues affecting New York
City; and John Lindsay's power is likely to rise because of the decline in Governor Rockefeller's position. An increase in Lindsay's
power means a decline in the power of a Republican speaker vis-à-
vis New York City.

As for Nelson Rockefeller, the garbage strike of 1968 started a
chain of events which knocked him out of New York City's top ten.
By proposing a settlement of the garbage strike which avoided calling out the National Guard and put the garbage men under state
jurisdiction, Rockefeller made a hero out of Lindsay, and made
himself look as if he had surrendered to unreasonable demands of
labor.

Though most impartial observers believe and privately say that
Rockefeller, not Lindsay, was right, the public reacted otherwise.
Rockefeller's stock plummeted.

The strike and Rockefeller's role in it probably cost Rockefeller
a good chance at the Presidency, opened Nixon's path to the nomination and election, made Lindsay a popular national figure, and
for the first time propelled Lindsay into a role among New
York City's top ten.

Rockefeller has not yet restored his power over New York City.

He could not persuade the legislature to support his program for solving New York City's garbage strike. He has not tried to exercise similar power over New York City since.

Number eight on my list a year ago was David Rockefeller. I said then that the governor's brother is president of the Chase Manhattan Bank, which has over $18 billion in resources—one of New York's two largest banks. As such, he plays a pre-eminent role in the commercial life of New York City. For money is New York's biggest business. New York City is still the banking and financial and corporate headquarters of the country.

David Rockefeller is more than a banker. Through and with his brothers, he plays a leading role in the city's cultural life. With them he played a major role in the creation of Lincoln Center, which houses or will house the New York Philharmonic, the Metropolitan Opera, the New York City Opera Company and Ballet, the Lincoln Center Repertory Company, the Juilliard School of Music, and others. He epitomizes and to a great extent represents the banking-cultural-commercial life of the city. His presence on a committee for civic virtue makes the committee significant and indicates it is well directed, well financed, and peopled with ladies and gentlemen who can be counted upon to behave as such. A partial list of the committees and projects with which he has been identified—Rockefeller University, Rockefeller Center, Inc., Council for Latin America, Center for Inter-American Relations, International Executive Service Corporation, General Advisory Committee on Foreign Assistance Program (AID), Downtown Lower Manhattan Association, Inc. (chairman), Morningside Heights, Inc., Council on Foreign Relations, Inc., Museum of Modern Art (chairman)—reflects the breadth of his interests.

Despite all his activity, David Rockefeller does not seek publicity. Like his father, John D. Rockefeller, Jr., David Rockefeller at times seems more interested in keeping his name out of the papers than in them. Even securing the foregoing list required some delicate negotiation.

David Rockefeller's position in New York City does not seem to have changed in one year and he remains among the top ten.

Number nine a year ago was John B. Oakes, editorial page editor of *The New York Times*. He remains on the list. A year ago I said that Oakes is principally responsible for the content of the *Times* editorials and for its overall editorial policy. The editorial board also has a major voice in the news which the *Times* will elect to find fit to print. Oakes wields tremendous power over government, over labor, over business, over urban development, over politics, not to mention national and international affairs. Oakes's *New York Times,* for example, in large part deserves the credit for Lindsay's stand in the transit strike with which Lindsay launched his administration. Day after day Oakes publicly instructed Lindsay, whose election was in part the result of the *Times'* daily editorial support, on how to deal with the threatened strike. Some say that Abe Raskin, another *Times* editorial writer (who has been called the unofficial secretary of labor of the Lindsay government), is the author of the *Times'* labor views. But whoever is author, Oakes has adopted and declared them.

It was Oakes's *Times* which invented the notion that the transit workers had been repeatedly rewarded by earlier Democratic administrations for transit union political support for the Democrats by being given excessive wage increases. This time, thundered Oakes through the *Times,* the strike threat should be met and settled "on the merits," not by "power brokers" (like Van Arsdale and, presumably, Kheel).

Mayor Lindsay did as he was told by Oakes, only to learn that "on the merits" the transport workers were entitled to almost twice what they were originally willing to settle for. But, irked by Oakes and Lindsay, the TWU's Mike Quill got mad enough to make Lindsay accept his own myth. Quill insisted on settling "on the merits." He got twice as much as ever before.

An Oakes endorsement for a candidate to the Assembly, State Senate, or Congress or a lower court judgeship in a close district means victory instead of defeat. An endorsement for a higher office means victory if the race would otherwise be close. Oakes can deliver more votes—about 10 per cent more votes in the Silk Stocking District, for example—than can any party leader. Indeed, once upon a time voters marched into the polls clutching a piece of campaign literature emanating from one of the political parties with instructions as to how to vote. Today, well-dressed New York East Siders line up at the polls waiting to vote their educated independent judgment, one out of two clutching his copy of the morning *New York Times* editorial-endorsement check list. This same power enables Oakes to kill or revive almost any government program by blessing or damning it. In short, an Oakes editorial establishes for most New Yorkers who think they think for themselves what is right and good, what is wrong and bad.

In the last year, nothing much has changed, and Oakes's power remains. His candidates still get elected (Humphrey carried New York State with the *Times* endorsement while the Democrats lost the Assembly), his voice in labor policy is still heard (in the garbage strike some say the *Times* editorial caused Mayor Lindsay to reject a settlement which the governor had understood he was willing to accept), and his political judgments on candidates for lower political office remain persuasive (e.g., Peter A. A. Berle, endorsed by the *Times,* the first Democrat elected to the 64th Assembly District in the history of the district).

A year ago I could not find a tenth man. I said:

> The position of the Tenth Man is temporarily vacant. It has been held in the past by such men as Rabbi Stephen Wise [Rabbi of the Free Synagogue, who was always ready to lend his voice to the support of every good fight], John Haynes Holmes [Minister of the Community Church, who was usually alongside Rabbi Wise], Charles C. Burlingham [distinguished lawyer who played a key role in the fight for political reform in the first half of this century], Samuel Seabury [another political reformer, who drove New York City's Mayor Walker out of office], Bernard Baruch, Eleanor Roosevelt [although she was really a world, rather than a city, power], and Herbert H. Lehman. These were the repositories of wisdom and spokesmen for morality, justice, and other virtues. Their voices could create a movement or stop an injustice. Their counsel could change a policy. Their support could elect a mayor over what were then, but are not now, powerful political machines.
>
> No one seems to qualify for the tenth-man role today. There is no spokesman in the pulpit who carries with him the power of a Rabbi Wise or a John Haynes Holmes. We have no park bench font of wisdom like Baruch.
>
> I do not know whether the absence of a likely candidate for the tenth man role is a temporary accident or whether it is symptomatic of something basically wrong with our city's life. Perhaps it is a little of both.

I think what I wrote a year ago about the missing tenth man is still true today.

A year ago I did not include Mayor Lindsay on my list. I said then that Mayor Lindsay was not on the list as yet, and that perhaps someday he would be, as his predecessor, Robert F. Wagner, would have been five years ago.

Of the ten people who run the city, the people of the city can vote for or against only one of them—the mayor. Small wonder the mayor has become the man who is always held responsible whenever anything goes wrong. For he is the only one over whom the citizens of the city have any apparent control.

Six months ago, after the garbage strike, I put Lindsay on the list, because it seemed to me he was, at last, in some degree of control of the city. After the garbage strike, the mayor's stock went up. Aso, when Martin Luther King, Jr., was assassinated, the mayor did exercise control, by his example as well as by the orders he gave. As New York remained peaceful over the summer, it seemed more and more that the mayor was clearly among the ten who ran the city and high among them.

Despite subsequent doubts, today Lindsay must be included among the ten who run New York City, because in some areas, on some occasions—such as the end of the garbage strike and when he was dealing with the threat of a racial explosion—the mayor has been in control, even though in many other areas, he is not.

Van Arsdale, Kheel, Brydges, David Rockefeller and John Oakes survived from last year's list, and the "tenth man" role has not yet been filled, although for a time it seemed as if McGeorge Bundy of the Ford Foundation had arrived. More and more his prestige was sought to develop and launch new programs, such as school decentralization. But the lack of foresight with which that experiment was launched, and the attendant collision with the teachers' union, accompanied by Bundy's belated statements concerning the Vietnam war policy, of which he had been a principal architect, sapped public confidence in his, until then, growing reputation.

Other new arrivals from Federal service are candidates for the "tenth man" role. Justice Arthur Goldberg, retired U.S. Supreme Court Justice and U.N. Ambassador, is one whose counsel is increasingly sought. Presiding Justice Bernard Botein, who is retiring from the bench, is another likely candidate for that position. So is Cardinal Cooke, Cardinal Spellman's successor as Archbishop of New York. But again, his tenure has been too short to say that he has restored the somewhat eroded status of the hierarchy which he inherited.

In addition to the five men who have remained on last year's list of nine, plus Lindsay, who makes the list this year, there are three new arrivals—one who promises to be permanent and two whose permanence is questionable, but for the time at least, they are there.

The permanent one is William J. Ronan, former academician, former counsel to Governor Rockefeller, and now the head of the new Metropolitan Transportation Authority.

The MTA has replaced the Port Authority as the most powerful government agency operating in New York. It is building subways and bridges, spending hundreds of millions of dollars per year, operating commuter railroads and planning massive construction in New York City. Within ten years ingress and egress to New York City and movement within it will be the product of Mr. Ronan's decisions.

Recently he was the subject of some public criticism because his salary had been raised to $70,000 a year without much if any publicity. The lack of publicity concerning internal affairs is a hallmark of any large public authority. But if Mr. Ronan isn't worth $70,000 a year, he shouldn't be head of the MTA in the first place.

The other two additions—possibly temporary but obviously there now—are Albert Shanker, head of the teachers' union which represents New York's 55,000 teachers, and Rhody McCoy, administrator of the Ocean Hill-Brownsville decentralized school district.

Shanker lives in Putnam County and McCoy in Nassau. But the clash between the two men and the forces they represent closed New York City's schools. Their clash has probably cost our school children one year of education, their parents one extra year of child support, and the city thousands upon thousands of tax-paying citizens as the flight to the suburbs turned into a stampede by parents seeking education for their children *now*.

The struggle over decentralization, teachers' rights versus students' rights, stability versus change, will continue. For underlying the Shanker-McCoy battle is a rejection by a substantial part of the population of the present educational administration. And Shanker's union finds itself on the side of the status quo.

I do not believe McCoy's position among the top ten is a very permanent one. He will probably be supplanted by a less parochial spokesman—or perhaps more than one spokesman—of minority groups. Three people are likely substitutes—Manhattan Borough President Percy Sutton, Bronx Borough President Herman Badillo, and first-term Brooklyn Congresswoman and Democratic National Committeewoman Shirley Chisholm.

At present none of the three is pre-eminent. As time passes, however, it is likely that the power will gravitate to one of the three as it earlier gravitated to Adam Clayton Powell. If the Negro and Puerto Rican populations were to come to look to one of the new three for leadership, that one would certainly become one of the top ten in New York City.

The police commissioner is not on the list. There just does not seem to be any reason why he should be. His power is diffused by the police bureaucracy through which he must operate. Nor is there a leader of the underworld. The years when a Frank Costello could select judges seem to have passed, and while there are powerful criminals in the city, none seems to qualify for the list of the top ten.

In part for the same reasons, neither Frank Hogan, District Attorney of New York County, nor Robert Morgenthau, the United States Attorney for the Southern District of New York, is on the list, although some of their predecessors would have been. One reason is that the position of organized crime in the city is not as powerful as it was twenty or thirty years ago, when the underworld involved itself in all areas of governmental life. The adversaries being weaker, the law enforcement officials find fewer occasions to exercise their power in a way which can be characterized as "running the city." A second reason is probably routinization of law enforcement. While crime rates have increased substantially, the major part of the increase is in non-organized petty crime such as narcotics, robberies and the like. Dealing with this kind of crime is something different from the case where a Thomas E. Dewey is dealing with a Lucky Luciano.

Finally, the bureaucratization and routinization of the district attorneys' offices have hindered efforts to deal with the area where the underworld is moving into the city's life—the commercial area.

In any event, neither Hogan nor Morgenthau qualified for membership in the elite top ten.

There are undoubtedly other candidates for membership among the top ten whose names have been omitted. Some are national or world figures, not New York City ones. Others have reputations but no real power.

But, if this list fails to convince you—or if you want to have some fun—consider what the impact would be if

Harry Van Arsdale
Theodore Kheel
William J. Ronan
John V. Lindsay
Earl W. Brydges
David Rockefeller
John Oakes
Rhody McCoy
Albert Shanker

—*all* using their full powers and resources—and the tenth man—all joined to support or oppose a particular candidate or policy or program, public or private.

You pick a team to take the other side, and I will see you when they count the votes.

5. The Rites of Power

John V. Lindsay

". . . part of the initiation . . . includes a demonstration of skill in the art of making hand contact with each of the celebrants without . . . making eye contact."

There is a special form of torture in New York called "the affair."

Cool down. This is not the kind of affair you undoubtedly have in mind, assuming you take a relatively normal and sane view of life. No, it's not remotely as interesting, nor as worthwhile, nor even in its own way as exasperating. It's far too dull to be any of these.

The "affair" I regrettably have in mind is, inevitably, a four-course, five-hour, six-dais, seven-speaker ordeal for politicians and their power brokers which takes place in a midtown hotel and is ritualistically attended by the political flagellants of our town. Attendance at these primitive rites is thought to be mandatory, because the penalties of avoidance are generally understood to be worse.

I once knew a politician called Al, a tribal member in good standing, whose fall out of grace became noticeable when pejorative comment about him was being voiced at one of the "affairs" by other members of the tribe. "I haven't seen Al at any of the affairs recently," I overheard one saying. I knew right then that the curse was being put on Al; it was only a matter of time until it would be generally accepted that Al would be left naked and alone beyond the compound to be devoured by outside powers. Al's violation of the tribal laws was, of course, in the private language of the elders and members, his absence at lunch three hours earlier, or the night before, or last week, or whenever it was, at Joe's or Jimmy's or Charlie's "affair."

The "affair" rotates from hotel to hotel, ballroom to ballroom, under different names, party labels or other insignia, but generally it's the same old crowd. The erstwhile member of the tribe who, like poor Al, ignores the tribal tradition of attendance is, of course, quickly discovered because by "affair" custom a certain percentage of the faithful, many of them respected elders, travel from dais to dais, table to table, shaking the hand of each person they pass. Although the established member in this role never looks in the eye of the person with whom he is making hand contact, he is nevertheless very watchful because he is looking past that person to see who the next person is. Hence, despite the impression that one is never looked at while the hand contact process takes place, and perhaps therefore unnoticed, one is still accounted for, and discovery of absence is inevitable. "We don't see Al at the affairs any more" is the first blackball.

Like all tribal customs, over generations certain variations or embellishments may appear, some explainable according to the needs of tribal development or survival, and some not.

There is, for example, in the more elaborate rituals, a "filing-in" ceremony, which begins in another room (called "Dignitaries") with a kind of primitive game developed in childhood called "Musical Chairs." By some still-unexplained process, certain of the membership is chosen for this ceremony, and having arranged themselves in rows of chairs, looking not at each other or anyone else, but at a wall, they then rise all at once, face left, or right, at a given command, and file from that room to the other room, where they again sit down in the same fashion. They apparently have full confidence that they are not being blindly marched into a gas chamber or over a precipice. All this is accompanied by music from an organ and hand-clapping by all of the other members in the ballroom, as it is called, who now face the ceremonial dais-sitters, as they are called.

Those not chosen for this "dais" ceremony don't seem to object, for submission to the process of choosing is one of the unwritten rules of the "affair." It is also understood that part of the initiation rite for the members, particularly the younger ones reaching manhood, who look forward one day to participation in the dais ceremony, includes a demonstration of skill in the art of making hand contact with each of the celebrants without, of course, simultane-ously making eye contact.

Students of the "affair" have noticed markings on certain mem-bers that set them a bit apart from the rest as seasoned elders. The latter will be noticed wearing ruffled shirts, white with black edg-ing, or possibly powder blue, and occasionally pink. The older, slightly stouter ones, who have been rewarded for their fidelity, will have a shining clear polish on their fingernails and gold cuff links the size of half dollars. Many will have even, white teeth which they show to the other members by clenching them together and holding the face and lips fixed into a wide grin. For these members especially, status in the tribe calls for the holding of the tribal em-blem, a cigar in the left hand, leaving the right free for clutching some portion of another member's upper body.

The "affair" then goes according to established custom. Ritual calls for invocations, salutes and tributes to the ceremonial dais-sitters, all of whom are then called "distinguished" as well as "dig-nitaries," and occasionally one is called "our very own" or "our very good friend," or, simply, "swell fella."

One of the distinguished dais-sitters who is called "M.C." then addresses the throng for quite a while, standing behind a large square block of wood with metal arms coming out of it and a large round emblem on the front, which is not the identifying symbol of the "affair" or of the dais dignitary behind the block, but is rather the name of the hotel. Students tell us that the reason for this is that unless it is known the "affair" is conducted in a midtown hotel ball-room, it is not a proper "affair" and will lose face in the eyes of the other "affairs."

The ceremonial dais-sitter who is known as "M.C." then calls upon many other distinguished dignitaries on the dais, usually with some liturgical words having special meaning, as follows: "At this time I want to . . ." or sometimes, "Now it is my special privi-lege . . ."

Each of the chief dignitaries will then address the members for about a half-hour or more, each in the same fashion, as deviation from the customary words is not orthodox. Most of the members during this process will sit very still, their chins resting on their chests out of respect for the ceremonial dais-sitter who is speaking.

It is, however, permitted by the tribal code that some members move about in the back of the room in small clusters, where occasionally they are seen tapping each other on the chests—even on the ruffles—and speaking through the teeth and the cigar. Some are permitted still to continue making hand contact without eye contact from table to table.

Hours later the members and celebrants, dignitaries and distinguished dais-sitters are spent and it is apparent that the rites are concluded. There are final appeals to the deities and to tribal regularity, some last hand contacts, although eye contact is now permitted because exhaustion makes it difficult to keep moving, and the members disappear in the darkness to their places of rest. And rest will be needed, because, depending on the season and the tribal harvest, there will be a whole series of similar affairs in the nights ahead. Few will fail to participate, for, after all, who really knows what became of Al?

P.S. Any resemblance to any person in this article, living or dead, is strictly coincidental.

6. Eight Million Pieces of the Action

Gus Tyler

"Each of these entities—economic, ethnic, geographic, sometimes ideologic—is a political power, with the result that there are so many power centers in New York that the formal center, City Hall, is almost powerless."

New York City's number one problem is its greatness. It's too much. Behold the Imperial City.

It is the center of world finance: Wall Street. It is the greatest manufacturing city in the country, dominated by an industry that sets the fashions for the Western world: Seventh Avenue. It is the atelier of the image makers: Madison Avenue. It is the greatest sea and airport in the nation: waterfront, JFK, LaG, Newark. It is the greatest theatrical center in the world: Broadway, off Broadway, and off-off. It is the cultural center of America: fifty-five public libraries, added private libraries, more than twenty-six million volumes, thirty-six museums, thirty-eight colleges, six hundred thirty-four art galleries. It is the commercial hub of the New World, handling a volume of trade equal to one-tenth of America's gross national product. It is the headquarters of corporate headquarters immortalized in buildings named after companies: ATT, Chrysler, Colgate-Palmolive, Con Ed, Con Can, Esso, Gen Dyn, Gen Elec, Gen Mot, Lever, Lorillard, Nat Biscuit, and Union Carbide—for instances. It is the headquarters of great national unions, including those in women's apparel, men's clothing, millinery, stage handlers, sailors, musicians, legit actors, transport, wholesale and retail, photoengravers and lithographers, textiles, toys, furniture, jewelry, leather goods, longshoremen, office and professional, porters, utilities. It is the largest publishing and printing center in the U.S., with ninety-three firms each with a net worth of at least a million in the city. It is a convention city entertaining more then eight hundred conferences per annum with more than a million conferees. It is the greatest medical, artistic, philatelic, numismatic, gastronomic, ideologic, criminal and theologic city of the Western world.

New York City is the home of the rich: Park Avenue below 96th Street. It is the home of the poor: Park Avenue above 96th Street. It has more Italians than Milan, more Jews than Tel Aviv, more Irish than Dublin, more Germans than Bonn, more Puerto Ricans than San Juan, more blacks than Nairobi plus Lagos, more Catholics than Rome, and nearly as many voters as Texas. Finally Greater New York contains within its legal boundaries more than a hundred historically defined communities whose cultures are as much tribal as metropolitan, inhabited by the small towners of the big nation of eight million.

Each of these entities—economic, ethnic, geographic, sometimes ideologic—is a political power, with the result that there are so many power centers in New York that the formal center, City Hall, is almost powerless. At best, City Hall is a skillful power broker; at worst, it is a broken power whose bits and pieces are manipulated by the real powers. When Mayor Lindsay denounced the "power brokers" early in his administration he was discarding the glue that traditionally held the city together, offering *Hochpolitik* for *Realpolitik*.

The symbol of *Realpolitik* in New York is the Democratic machine (Tammany) that, according to popular legend, can generally count on the electorate to give thumping majorities to the party's nominees in the city. But is that so? In the twenty-one mayoralty elections since 1897, the Democratic Party line showed a *majority* count on only six occasions: less than one-third the time. Seven elections were lost by Democrats to Fusion candidates (Low and Mitchell) or to Republicans with leftish backing (La Guardia and Lindsay) or to an independent like Impellitteri. Eight other Democratic victories were won *without a party majority* because of a broken field (three to five real candidates) or because Democrats had minor-party backing (O'Dwyer with the American Labor Party in 1945; Wagner with the Liberal and Brotherhood Parties in 1961).

The Democratic Party has not done much better *on its party line* for other top candidates whose names appeared on the city ballot. Since 1944, there have been thirty-one contests, covering—in addition to mayor—governor, senator and President. The Dems polled a majority in only seven.

The point? New York is no one-party or even two-party town. It's a multi-party city in which minority parties (Jeffersonian, Fusion, Socialist, American Labor, Conservative, Liberal) more often than not have held the balance of power. New York's political pluralism is a reflex of its power pluralism.

The illusion that New York is a Democratic Party (machine) town is based on the fact that in neighborhood elections for the old alderman or the new councilman, for the Assembly or State Senate, or for borough president, the "machine" generally does well. The foundations of this "machine"—and of the Republican machine outside the silk-stocking district—are the many urban villages that compose the geographic (and political) jigsaw of New York. These "villages" are fairly homogeneous communities, many of whose denizens may spend a lifetime within the political boundaries of the metropolis without ever having visited Times Square. The villages are cities within the city, with known political leaders (even non-constitutional mayors), with marked ethnic traits that become apparent in restaurants, diverse delis, places of worship, accents, in-jokes, groceries; with local shopping centers and even local manufacture that is just a half-step removed from the old homework system. These communities, like the clichéd iceberg, are hardly visible to the tourist or even to the inhabitants of other urban villages like Greenwich Village, Village East, or Brooklyn Heights, but their submerged might has often sunk the titanics of reform in the city. (In 1966, a proposal to establish a Civilian Police Review Board, backed by Lindsay, Javits, Kennedy and O'Connor, was beaten badly to the dismay of many lifelong New Yorkers who had never explored the bush country of the urban villages.)

In these villages are located the one- and two-family houses that constitute 80 per cent of the residential construction in the city. Here lives the white middle class with a median income of $7,600 a year (1966 statistic). Here also live many of the poor whites who in the last census (1960) made up 63 per cent of New York families with incomes under $3,000. (By 1969, whites are still more than half the poor of the city.)

There are, of course, other villages of the "other" people: There is Harlem where population density is so thick that if all America were to live that way the whole country could be crammed into three boroughs of New York. And in contrast, there are the rich preserves of Riverdale in the Bronx, Shore Road in Brooklyn, and Grymes Hill in Richmond, where the Cunards and Vanderbilts erected their mansions.

To service neighborhood needs there are sixty-nine local publications. To cater to ethnic needs there are sixty-nine more foreign language papers in twenty-four tongues, including six in Chinese, seven in Lithuanian, three in Arabic, three in Armenian, and two in Japanese.

While some of these communities are purely synthetic, the invention of real estate developers, as in the case of Elmhurst, Corona, and Forest Hills, most of these villages have real historic roots. There are the old Dutch settlements of Haarlem, Breuckelen, Bushwick, Gravesend, Flushing (Vlissingen), and New Utrecht; there are the very British names of Chelsea, Yorkville, New Brighton, St. George, Murray Hill; the Indian names like Maspeth (the Mespat Indians); the French names like Huguenot and La Tourette Park. In most cases the current ethnic stamp is clear: Bath Beach and Northeast Bronx are Italian; Ridgewood is more German than Yorkville; Sea Gate and Brighton Beach are Jewish; Sunset Park is Scandinavian with its Leiv Eiriksson Square; Eighth Avenue in its teens and low twenties is Greek; East Harlem is Puerto Rican; and Chinatown is what it is expected to be, except that it is now several times its original size as it has—like the Bohemians further north—spread eastward, bringing cleanliness and quiet to the original camping grounds of the city's early gangs.

New York City is less a melting pot than a casserole, crammed with distinct chunks stewing in one another's juices. That's why party tickets are always balanced and why power is always unbalanced.

A counter power to that of the communities is that of the "corporations," the mighty economic fiefdoms whose lords may live outside the city limits but whose institutions are pillars of public policy. These economic baronies are commerce, finance, manufacturing, shipping, publishing, culture, tourism, public authorities, public employees, and the underworld. They live a life of symbiotic sovereignty: free and fettered.

Commerce and shipping came first to New York, hand in hand. The discovery of New Amsterdam by Henry Hudson was the by-product of a commercial venture by the Dutch West Indies Company. Around the port city gathered the merchants (buying and selling), the financiers (accumulating and lending), the manufacturers (gathering rare skills and cheap labor in a creative combo), the talents (creating designs, informing the worldly, keeping the books, titillating the taste), the builders (creating the vertical city of crowded homes, high hotels, crammed lofts and skyscraping office buildings), and the underworld (preying on all these riches and dispensing the services that the law and an alien Puritan ethic forbade).

As of 1969, shipping remains a major power in the city. Along the 650 miles of New York waterfront are 1,630 piers, bulkheads and wharves. Total ocean and airborne trade ran to more than $15 billion in 1966. The airports handled about twenty-five million passengers, a hundred thousand tons of mail, and a half-billion tons of cargo. Most of that cargo is not made in New York City: steel products, grain, vehicles, fruits and vegetables, copper, ore, petroleum. New York is the port of the nation, carrying on its work through sixteen railroads, a hundred and seventy steamship lines, thirty-nine airlines, and ten thousand registered trucks. To discover the romance and reality of New York as a seafaring town, spend a few hours with the photos of Steiglitz and a few more with the police blotters along the waterfront.

With shipping came commerce (the original reason for the voyage) and the underworld, the flotsam and jetsam of mankind that drifts into every port city in the world and that, in New York, found special reason to grab hold and to grow. The extent of commerce in New York today (wholesaling and retailing) is measurable: wholesale trade of about $53 billion carried on by 27,000 establishments (1963) plus a retail trade of another $10 billion. The extent of organized crime is not quite so measurable for obvious reasons, but there is little doubt that New York has been the financial, intellectual and organizational center of the American underworld for more than a century. New York provides a congenial atmosphere for honest and dishonest commerce.

For the merchant prince, New York is a proper manor from which to build a commercial empire. At hand are ships, trains, planes, trucks and at one time, the Erie Canal. If the seller needs a hawker, there is Madison Avenue and a horde of pushy peddlers to burn up the country to make a buck so that they may return to the hot city to burn up their money. There are film companies (932 of them in the city) to make and distribute commercials. There are artists with a taste for human foible to design packages worth more than the product. There are lures for the buyers—belly and ballet dancers, live plays and live participation in TV shows, a bunching of front offices to allow the purchaser to walk from one empire to another in twenty paces. There are accountants, lawyers and handy founts of credit: legitimate lending institutions or underworld factors. There are insurance companies and rumors to hedge bad judgments. There are *The New York Times* and *The Wall Street Journal* (powers in themselves) to tell about the world of men and money. There is a home far away (forty-five minutes on the Long Island, New Haven, or Penn Central Railroad) that is close enough to the dashboard and the steering wheel of the company to see to it *in person* that nothing goes too wrong. And for the "better half," there are the theaters, concerts halls, art galleries, stylists, antiques, and anonymity.

All these supporting services and environmental goodies are also on hand for the retailers of New York—the little ones in the "villages" and side streets and the big ones on 34th Street and on Fifth Avenue. There are also plenty of customers: eight million residents, an added seven and a half million who come for business, plus a million for conventions, and another seven and a half million who come to rubberneck and shop. Indeed, some come only to buy, flying in from New Orleans or Nome for a style—in hemlines or hair. To meet this omniverous demand, the retail trade offers 75,000 outlets, including 4,661 bars, 2,053 liquor stores, 101 emporiums of religiosa, 107 pet shops and 1,056 antiqueries.

The supporting services on which New York trade leans so heavily are a vital part of the "external economies" that cause many businesses to locate in a city that might, otherwise, be an uneconomic area. This applies particularly to manufacturing, New York's largest employer. The rationale for running a production plant in a city where space is tight and costly, wages high, taxes onerous, and loading, unloading and movement awkward, is to be found in the "external economies."

These "externals" create an environment for manufacturers who have to be creative. Are you in *haute couture?* Then you need designers who, in turn, need designers to stay hot in mutual friction. The fashion makers also need culture: the cross pollination of the crossroads. Are you in popular-priced lines? Then you need the high-style people to create so you can "knock off" the creation to sell ersatz class to budgeted housewives. You want to know what's doing in the market? *Women's Wear* helps, even if it is more interested in undress than dress, but it comes out only once a day. If you want instant info, go *schmoose* on the corner, or slap backs at The 500 Club (Seventh Avenue's Harmonie), or, if you're orthodox, break bread at Lou Siegel's. You need advice on how to run the business? There are 2,477 business management consulting agencies. You need a special something for your product? There are specialists in pleating, tucking, bonnaz, embroidery, nailheads, buttons, bangles, and spangles. You need credit? The banks are waiting with $21 billion in deposits (1965 figure) and the money factors with all kinds of money—clean and dirty.

What is true for apparel is true for other New York manufacture. The city has irresistible attractions for those sectors of production that require an ecology congenial for creativity. Hence the types of producers in garments, printing, and electronics (the three big makers) who seek out New York are those under tension, living on invention, copying, credit, craft and craftiness. Several years ago, a voluminous Harvard study (*Made in New York*) offered the city as psychotherapist for the industrially nervous. "Establishments for which uncertainty is a normal way of life," it intoned in scholarly manner, "cannot generally achieve a high degree of self-sufficiency. Rubbing elbows with others of their kind and with ancillary firms that exist to serve them, they can satisfy their variable wants by drawing upon common pools of space, labor, materials and services."

Not all New York production, however, is high strung; much of it is quite pedestrian, depending heavily on a reservoir of cheap labor, engaged to perform simple repetitive chores in manufacture. Much of this manpower (more often womanpower) is found in the urban villages where plants locate for workers who walk to work. The reservoir is replenished by immigration from other countries and by in-migration from the South and Puerto Rico.

Manufacture, consequently, is New York's largest single employer: about one-fourth the labor force. This figure actually understates the importance of manufacture in the city. For cost reasons, many plants needing larger space locate outside the city but inside the metropolitan area (within the radius of a one-hour truck run), taking advantage of space in the outskirts and savvy in the city. New York has also increasingly become the front office for manufacturing establishments that may not have any production plants in the area. Of the 178,000 white-collar people employed in central administrative offices in the city, 117,000 are attached to manufacturing firms (1966). A recent *Fortune* count showed 153 of the 500 largest industrial corporations in the U.S. headquartered in New York.

Why is New York the headquarters of headquarters? Because of all the "external economies" mentioned above plus—plus the prestige of a New York address. The trend to New York has been hastened as onetime family firms with a traditional base in a fixed community go public. Business judgment, once liberated from the *lares and penates* of the founding father, favors moving from Main Street to the main city.

Housing headquarters (four of the top ten utilities, six of the seven largest banks, the four biggest insurance companies) has given New York a new profile, a changing skyline. The city is more vertical than ever. Manufacture likes long lofts; executive offices like high aeries where prestige rises with the altitude. Result? There was more office space built in Manhattan alone from 1947 to 1955 (66.5 million square feet) than in the rest of the nation. The amount built in Manhattan since World War II is as great as the total available office space in the whole city before Pearl Harbor. As the skyline goes up, it carries construction, finance, real estate, and insurance to new heights. The last three are old powers in New York. (The New York Stock Exchange was organized in 1792 at 68 Wall Street; the first real estate firm in America was established in 1748 and is now run by descendants of the founder, as Cruikshank Company on Wall Street; the Mutual Life Insurance Company—the pioneer of life insurance—was founded in 1843 at 56 Wall Street, the residence of Captain Kidd, an acknowledged pirate.) In the century or two that finance, realty and insurance have flourished in New York, they have added to their power—politically as well as economically.

One of the great New York mysteries is property ownership. The big building at 999 Blank Street, for a mythical for-instance, is owned by the 999 Blank Street Corporation, a legal entity concealing identity. (The city's difficulties in pinning down slumlords are cases in point.) Finding the biggest owners is a guessing game with the best-informed guesses suggesting the Astors, the Rockefellers, the Catholic Church, Columbia University, the Mafia and the British Crown. Who knows? The art of property holding in New York is the *ars celare artem.*

The incongruous mix of big realtors in New York suggests that history does repeat itself in the city—constantly creating new powers. When a British frigate in 1664 took over New Amsterdam from an enraged Peter Stuyvesant at gunpoint, the city set a pattern of accumulation by aggression. (Since the Dutch had taken Manhattan from the Indians for twenty-four dollars in beads, the British hold-up was only petty larceny.) As colonial wealth was real estate and the earliest aristocracy was landed, the descendants of these first families represent a sizable body of anonymous wealth in the city, hidden behind estates, corporate veils, dummies and institutions. The notion that the Crown should be a big holder after all these years hints that wealth (and power) in New York is as much part of an *ancien regime* as of a *nouveau riche* that includes upstarts like Astor and Vanderbilt. (Institutional holdings are so large in the city that 30 per cent of the property is tax-exempt, held by non-profit entities.)

The real upstarts of the century, of course, are the Mafia whose original New York ancestors were as British as the Queen of England. The first gangsters came into the port as indentured servants, as societal dropouts, as escaped and paroled convicts, or as just plain poor. The waterfront was a good place to survive, since this port, like any port, is a crossroads where commerce is booty. For the modern highwayman, the gangster, the transfer point of the world's goods is a natural habitat. A century ago, the Daybreak Boys—a juvenile gang whose leaders were hanged in their teens—looted the docks. A century later, a well-oiled syndicate looted the airports. At the turn of this century, the gangs developed the racket of delayed delivery: use of force to hold up shipment for a ransom—a diabolically effective stratagem when dealing with perishables like fruits and fashions.

The ethnic succession of the underworld in New York followed the waves of immigration. After the first settlers came the Irish, then the Jews (Arnold Rothstein was the model for *The Great Gatsby*), then the Italians—each enlarging and refining the operations of corporate crime.

What made the underworld in New York both tolerated and respected was the fact that, although admittedly malignant, it was also benign—in its own bloody fashion. The neighborhood gangs democratized wealth and power. At gunpoint they redistributed wealth. Through the neighborhood political clubs they redistributed influence. In due time they washed unclean money in the cleansing waters of the accepted economy, factoring manufacture, bankrolling construction, moving into the market, endowing churches and colleges.

One of the most recent additions to New York's power complex —more recent than La Cosa Nostra—is the quasi-public authority, the private monopoly with a public mien. The two greats are the Triborough Bridge and Tunnel Authority and the Port of New York Authority. Their bonds are tax-exempt—as if they were municipalities. Their properties are not taxed—except as they agree to pay a sum in lieu of taxes. Their monopoly is built-in: they own bridges, tunnels, airfields. In the days when Robert Moses was the symbol of the public authority in New York, it was charged that his control of billions of dollars enabled the authority to "tear down homes and businesses . . . to condemn and demolish entire neighborhoods . . . to establish parks, playgrounds, and public beaches, works of great good, but works in which private contracts and concessions mean veritable fortunes; to control vast networks of bridges and tunnels, collecting millions of dollars in fees that are never reduced, that serve as a tax on the traveling public over which that public has lost all control, that pile up surpluses used to bankroll other and more private enterprises."* The big brouhaha

* Fred J. Cook in *Dissent* (Summer 1961).

over the World Trade Center, won by the Authority, proves that—for better or worse—it is a power.

Although New York is the richest city in the land, it is poor in many ways. Its biggest outlay is not for health or education but for relief: $1,800,000,000 in 1969 to 1,200,000 recipients, about one-seventh the total population. The poor are now a power, organizing, demanding, demonstrating, voting, rioting.

The pressure of the poor puts a new squeeze on a City Hall that has long been living in poverty itself. For many years the Tammany mob treated the public trust as a private trough: steal from the city to give to the poor to get votes from the poor to protect the rich in their right to steal from the poor. Result? A bankrupt city, living in riches it could not touch and poverty it could not end.

When "good government" took over, it was burdened by the past—politically as well as economically. The State of New York was in the hands of Republicans, heavily Waspish, who looked upon the namesake city as the den of those dirty Democratic foreigners, as a rich colony whose wealth was to be tapped and whose right to self-government was to be severely limited. When the city needed funds it had to beg: for financial aid, for authority to tax or borrow. It had to *beg* because although the city had, at times, more than half the state population within its boundaries, the state legislature was so apportioned as to keep power "upstate," a euphemism for non-New York City Republicans.

When the city finally did get the right to borrow, it found itself—as it still does—at the mercy of the lending institutions. Although the law calls for competitive bidding, recent history records the lone bid put in by a syndicate of lenders, who, under these circumstances, can set their own high interest rate, adding new burdens to old. The financiers can always justify the high rate by pointing to the city's low credit rating, an incubus brought on by Democrats in New York City and Republicans in New York State.

If the city did not have enough pressures on it, there have arisen new "pressures" of the public employees, now organizing in militant unions. New York is a union town. These unions have long been much more than bargaining agents: they have erected housing and health centers, they run banks and insurance operations, they register and vote. Their traditional base has been in manufacture, construction, shipping, transport. Unions now have reached into the ranks of the 350,000 employees of government and public authorities. The "new" unions of public employees are interested in more than wages and hours: teachers are concerned about the character and content of education; the police about the degree of law enforcement; the firemen about their safety in riot areas; the transit workers about the condition of trains and the size of the fare. Any one of these "powers" could discomfort the town and, collectively, they could disintegrate New York.

If in moments of tribulation New York appears to be the city that God forgot, it is only necessary to walk down any avenue or byway to discover that the Lord is very much with his wayward children in the modern Babel. There are 3,492 churches and synagogues, half of which are Protestant (most blacks are non-WAS Protestants). Synagogues run to 1,240, of which more than a thousand are Orthodox. (The urban villages of the Hasidim are a transplant of the Old World *shtettl.*) Although Roman Catholics have only 442 churches they are about half the city population.

Once it was smart to stereotype: "Columbia prepares Protestants for Wall Street; Fordham prepares Catholics for Tammany; CCNY prepares Jews for isms." The Archdiocese was "the power house," Morningside Heights was the seat of the upcoming Establishment, City College was "the revolution" maker.

Today Columbia is the stamping ground of the disestablishmentarians, Fordham can't find Tammany's address, and the job-minded kids at the many city colleges are among America's most reluctant rebels.

Old stereos dissolve in the heat of New York's ethnic, economic, geographic, political, ideologic and now generational frictions. New forces arise to compete in the good old game of Gotham:

"Power, Power—Who's Got the Power."

7. The Power Brokers

Peter Maas

"Lindsay never did single . . . [them] out . . . by name. At the time, however, there was no doubt that the list included the old-line labor leaders who had been negotiating union contracts here for years."

One of the mayor's most famous pronouncements was occasioned —if you can remember that far back, past the city nurses, the welfare workers, the police and the firemen, the sanitationmen and, of course, the teachers, whom perhaps we shall never be able to forget —by the great transit strike in January 1966. "The government of this city," said the mayor a few days after he took office, "will not capitulate before the lawless demands of a single power group. It will not allow the power brokers in our city, or any special interest, to dictate to this city the terms under which it will exist in New York."

Lindsay never did single out these power brokers by name. At the time, however, there was no doubt that the list included the old-line labor leaders who had been negotiating union contracts here for years—the late Mike Quill, for one, and, most especially, Harry Van Arsdale, head of the city's Central Labor Council. But despite his brave words, the battle rages on, and the outcome is still in doubt.

Now the mayor's own chances for re-election are in real jeopardy, his apparently unassailable power base throughout the Jewish community gravely damaged because of the school strike and all the racial hatred it triggered.

The situation is as unstable as it has ever been. Indeed, we are rapidly approaching the point of no return, which in the end may provide the only way out. The other day I was talking to Vic Gotbaum, executive director of District Council 37 of the American Federation of State, County and Municipal Employees, AFL-CIO. It is the biggest public service union in the city, bigger than the policemen, firemen, sanitationmen, transit workers and teachers combined. Gotbaum is a pretty levelheaded fellow. He came out of Chicago to run the local here not long before Lindsay took office, and he can speak with a certain dispassion. But when I remarked that at least we won't have to go through another subway crisis this New Year's Eve, he said, "What makes you so sure?"

"Well," I said, "didn't they sign a two-year contract last January?"

"That may not mean much," Gotbaum said. "I wouldn't guarantee anything these days."

The city strikes have had a particular impact because we never had them to any degree, and certainly not in such numbers, before Lindsay's election. Some of the blame is his, but far from all of it. Pre-Lindsay City Hall was occupied by Bill O'Dwyer and Robert Wagner with Impy Impellitteri, who captured the public fancy for one brief, dubious moment, sandwiched in between. Each was a Democrat and each quite at home with the trade union establishment. Of the canny O'Dwyer, Theodore Kheel, the most experienced and successful labor mediator around town, says, "No one had more alertness, quickness and sensitivity to the problems of labor leadership than he had." This translated means, to a large extent, that O'Dwyer never did anything to make union chieftains look bad to their membership or did anything to indicate that they were not fighting for the last buck in the municipal treasury.

Wagner faithfully copied O'Dwyer's tactics. A rough scenario, as gathered from several of those present at various times, ran as follows. A union leader would wrangle hot and heavy with Wagner's budget and personnel directors in secret sessions over a period of months after which union delegates would report to the rank and file that so-and-so was "really fighting for us." Finally the day would arrive when the mayor's men said they could go no higher. Enter Wagner, who might raise the ante somewhat, and who would declare in effect, "That's it. We can't go for a penny more. Now I know you fellows have a problem, so you ask for ten per cent more and we'll offer ten per cent less." Then, after a couple of weeks, the contract would be negotiated at the agreed-upon price, and everyone was happy.

Implicit in these negotiations was camaraderie of long standing, mutual interest and basic mutual trust. This was the kind of thing that *The New York Times* editorialized as "shoddy deals" and "politically contrived settlements." But as Kheel has often pointed out, "The fact that it was a deal was portrayed as being corrupt in itself. The fact that it solved a problem seems to be irrelevant."

It, at any rate, was not Lindsay's style. And even if he wanted to, it was doubtful that he could have carried on in the grand old tradition. He was, however liberal, aloof and often imperious. He was not "one of the boys." He made union leaders nervous with his clipped tones, and he wound up with a hell of a credibility gap. They just didn't trust him. Searching for the right disparaging words, one unionist was reduced to describing Lindsay as "that Yalie." No labor man ever sneered at Wagner, himself a Yale graduate, as "that Yalie."

What turned everything around was the 1966 transit strike. It had gotten so that New Year's Eve was not New Year's Eve in New York without the threat of no subways or buses, but it never happened. A fairytale quality grew up around the last-minute negotiations with Wagner at Gracie Mansion. The last time, even Wagner was a bit unnerved by the angry growls of Quill accompanied by his top lieutenants. Then as he was leaving, with the matter still unresolved, it is said that the mayor's wife, the late Susan Wagner, gently touched Quill's hand and asked, "Oh, Mr. Quill, are all those poor people going to have no way to get home on New Year's Eve?"

"Do not concern yourself, my dear," Quill replied. "There will be no strike."

But with Lindsay the strike happened. At the time he was roundly knocked for not getting swiftly, and personally, in the negotiations. The mayor told me recently, however, that he had in fact met secretly with Quill at least four times as the strike deadline neared. It is Lindsay's contention that the transit workers would have gone out no matter who was mayor. Some of Wagner's former aides agree. The transit workers, once predominantly Irish, were now about half black and Puerto Rican, and the tension between these groups regarding wage differentials was practically out of control.

The transit strike did not start all the subsequent labor trouble the city has had. It was simply the first example to pop of a growing unrest and militancy among municipal workers of all sorts. As Paul Screvane, the former president of the City Council who rose through sanitation ranks himself, says, "Take the sanitationmen. There was a time these fellows were right off the boat and all they did was want to work. They got their pay check and they didn't ask any questions. Now they see what is being achieved by demonstrations and other forms of militancy. They also have motivation now. They are much better educated, they often live in areas where they have more affluent neighbors and they want all the things they see these other people enjoying."

What the transit strike did demonstrate to other city unions was that municipal workers could walk out despite a state law expressly forbidding it, and in getting away with breaking the law they not only did pretty well for their pocketbooks but for their collective ego. The spillover is clear. As a Consolidated Edison official told me last September, "We're going to have a strike no matter what we offer. It's just the thing to do these days."

While none of this was John Lindsay's making, there are a couple of things he could have done which might have eased the almost continual crisis the city has found itself in. "He should have shared some of his power with the Van Arsdales," a labor leader was saying the other day. "People want to be called on by the mayor. They like to be part of the big picture. He should have put them on some kind of an advisory board. Instead he alienated a lot of them, and the truth is that now they would love nothing more than to help throw him out of City Hall." Another thing is the mayor's predilection for open battles in labor disputes. "The question," says one negotiator, "is whether you bargain through the *Times* or in a quiet room. When you make public statements during the middle of negotiations, you're simply not negotiating."

Lindsay himself professes to see a brighter future in the city's labor picture. He is pinning a great deal of his hopes on his Office of Collective Bargaining, which he set up earlier this year. "I think we've got through an apparatus where there is a third party available whenever there is an impasse."

A labor leader in the city like Vic Gotbaum is also optimistic. "Municipal unions," he says, "are new, and it's going to take a little time for everything to settle down."

Maybe so, but you have to wonder how much time is available.

8. The Power of the Working Class

Pete Hamill

"It is very difficult to explain to these people that
. . . one reason the black family is in trouble is
that outfits like the Iron Workers Union have practically excluded blacks through most of their history."

They call my people the White Lower Middle Class these days.
It is an ugly, ice-cold phrase, the result, I suppose, of the missionary
zeal of those sociologists who still think you can place human beings
on charts. It most certainly does not sound like a description of people on the edge of open, sustained and possibly violent revolt. And
yet, that is the case. All over New York City tonight, in places like
Inwood, South Brooklyn, Corona, East Flatbush and Bay Ridge,
men are standing around saloons talking darkly about their griev-
ances, and even more darkly about possible remedies. Their griev-
ances are real and deep; their remedies could blow this city apart.

The White Lower Middle Class? Say that magic phrase at a
cocktail party on the Upper East Side of Manhattan and monstrous
images arise from the American demonology. Here comes the
murderous rabble: fat, well-fed, bigoted, ignorant, an army of
beer-soaked Irishmen, violence-loving Italians, hate-filled Poles,
Lithuanians and Hungarians (they are never referred to as Americans). They are the people who assault peace marchers, who start
groups like the Society for the Prevention of Negroes Getting
Everything (s.p.o.n.g.e), the people who hate John Lindsay and
vote for George Wallace, presumably because they believe that
Wallace will eventually march every black man in America to the
gas chambers, sending Lindsay and the rest of the Liberal Estab-

lishment along with them. Sometimes these brutes are referred to as "the ethnics" or "the blue-collar types." But the bureaucratic, sociological phrase is White Lower Middle Class. Nobody calls it the Working Class anymore.

But basically, the people I'm speaking about *are* the working class. That is, they stand somewhere in the economy between the poor—most of whom are the aged, the sick and those unemployable women and children who live on welfare—and the semi-professionals and professionals who earn their way with talents or skills acquired through education. The working class earns its living with its hands or its backs; its members do not exist on welfare payments; they do not live in abject, swinish poverty, nor in safe, remote suburban comfort. They earn between $5,000 and $10,000 a year. And they can no longer make it in New York.

"I'm going out of my mind," an ironworker friend named Eddie Cush told me a few weeks ago. "I average about $8,500 a year, pretty good money. I work my ass off. But I can't make it. I come home at the end of the week, I start paying the bills, I give my wife some money for food. And there's nothing left. Maybe, if I work overtime, I get $15 or $20 to spend on myself. But most of the time, there's nothin'. They take $65 a week out of my pay. I have to come up with $90 a month rent. But every time I turn around, one of the kids needs shoes or a dress or something for school. And then I pick up a paper and read about a million people on welfare in New York or spades rioting in some college or some fat welfare bitch demanding—you know, not askin', *demanding*— a credit card at Korvette's . . . I *work* for a living and *I* can't get a credit card at Korvette's . . . You know, you see that, and you want to go out and strangle someone."

Cush was not drunk, and he was not talking loudly, or viciously, or with any bombast; but the tone was similar to the tone you can hear in conversations in bars like Farrell's all over this town; the tone was quiet bitterness.

"Look around," another guy told me, in a place called Mister Kelly's on Eighth Avenue and 13th Street in Brooklyn. "Look in the papers. Look on TV. What the hell does Lindsay care about me? He don't care whether my kid has shoes, whether my boy gets a new suit at Easter, whether I got any money in the bank. None of them politicians gives a good goddam. All they worry about is the niggers. And everything is for the niggers. The niggers get the schools. The niggers go to summer camp. The niggers get the new playgrounds. The niggers get nursery schools. And they get it all without workin'. I'm an ironworker, a connector; when I go to work in the mornin', I don't even know if I'm gonna make it back. My wife is scared to death, every mornin', all day. Up on the iron, if the wind blows hard or the steel gets icy or I make a wrong step, bango, forget it, I'm dead. Who feeds my wife and kid if I'm dead? Lindsay? The poverty program? You know the answer: nobody. But the niggers, they don't worry about it. They take the welfare and sit out on the stoop drinkin' cheap wine and throwin' the bottles on the street. They never gotta walk outta the house. They take the money outta my paycheck and they just turn it over to some lazy son of a bitch who won't work. I gotta carry him on *my* back. You know what I am? I'm a sucker. I really am. You shouldn't have to put up with this. And I'll tell ya somethin'. There's a lotta people who just ain't gonna put up with it much longer."

It is very difficult to explain to these people that more than 600,000 of those on welfare are women and children; that one reason the black family is in trouble is that outfits like the Iron Workers Union have practically excluded blacks through most of their history; that a hell of a lot more of their tax dollars go to Vietnam or the planning for future wars than to Harlem or Bed-Stuy; that the effort of the past four or five years was an effort forced by bloody events, and that they are paying taxes to relieve some forms of poverty because of more than 100 years of neglect on top of 300 years of slavery. The working-class white man has no more patience for explanations.

"If I hear that 400-years-of-slavery bit one more time," a man said to me in Farrell's one night, "I'll go outta my mind!"

One night in Farrell's, I showed the following passage by Eldridge Cleaver to some people. It is from the recently published collection of Cleaver's journalism: "The very least of your responsibility now is to compensate me, however inadequately, for centuries of degradation and disenfranchisement by granting peacefully—before I take them forcefully—the same rights and opportunities for a decent life that you've taken for granted as an American birthright. This isn't a request but a *demand* . . ."

The response was peculiarly mixed. Some people said that the black man had already been given too much, and if he still couldn't make it, to hell with him. Some said they agreed with Cleaver, that the black man "got the shaft" for a long time, and whether we like it or not, we have to do something. But most of them reacted ferociously.

"Compensate him?" one man said. "Compensate him? Look, the English ruled Ireland for 700 years, that's hundreds of years longer than Negroes have been slaves. Why don't the British government compensate me? In Boston, they had signs like 'No Irish Need Apply' on the jobs, so why don't the American government compensate *me?*"

In any conversation with working-class whites, you are struck by how the information explosion has hit them. Television has made an enormous impact on them, and because of the nature of that medium—its preference for the politics of theater, its seeming inability to ever explain what is happening behind the photographed image—much of their understanding of what happens is superficial. Most of them have only a passing acquaintance with blacks, and very few have any black friends. So they see blacks in terms of militants with Afros and shades, or crushed people on welfare. Television never bothers reporting about the black man who gets up in the morning, eats a fast breakfast, says goodbye to his wife and children, and rushes out to work. That is not news. So the people who live in working-class white ghettos seldom meet blacks who are not threatening to burn down America or asking for help or receiving welfare or committing crime. And in the past five or six years, with urban rioting on everyone's minds, they have provided themselves (or been provided with) a confused, threatening stereotype of blacks that has made it almost impossible to suggest any sort of black-white working-class coalition.

"Why the hell should I work with spades," he says, "when they are threatening to burn down my house?"

The Puerto Ricans, by the way, seem well on the way to assimilation with the larger community. It has been a long time since anyone has written about "the Puerto Rican problem" (though Puerto Rican poverty remains worse than black poverty), and in white working-class areas you don't hear many people muttering about "spics" anymore.

"At least the Puerto Ricans are working," a carpenter named Jimmy Dolan told me one night, in a place called the Green Oak in Bay Ridge. "They open a grocery store, they work from six in the mornin' till midnight. The P.R.'s are willin' to work for their money. The colored guys just don't wanna work. They want the big Buicks and the fancy suits, but they jus' don't wanna do the work they have ta do ta pay for them."

The working-class white man sees injustice and politicking everywhere in this town now, with himself in the role of victim. He does not like John Lindsay, because he feels Lindsay is only concerned about the needs of blacks; he sees Lindsay walking the streets of the ghettos or opening a privately financed housing project in East Harlem or delivering lectures about tolerance and brotherhood, and he wonders what it all means to *him*. Usually, the working-class white man is a veteran; he remembers coming back from the Korean War to discover that the GI Bill gave him only $110 a month out of which he had to pay his own tuition; so he did not go to college because he could not afford it. Then he reads about protesting blacks in the SEEK program at Queens College, learns that they are being paid up to $200 a month to go to school, with tuition free, and he starts going a little wild.

The working-class white man spends much of his time complaining almost desperately about the way he has become a victim. Taxes and the rising cost of living keep him broke, and he sees nothing in return for the taxes he pays. The Department of Sanitation comes to his street at three in the morning, and a day late, and slams garbage cans around like an invading regiment. His streets were the last to be cleaned in the big snowstorm, and they are now sliced up with trenches that could only be called potholes by the mypoic. His neighborhood is a dumping ground for abandoned automobiles, which rust and rot for as long as six weeks before someone from the city finally takes them away. He works very hard, frequently on a dangerous job, and then discovers that he still can't pay his way; his wife takes a Thursday night job in a department store and he gets a weekend job, pumping gas or pushing a hack. For him, life in New York is not much of a life.

"The average working stiff is not asking for very much," says Congressman Hugh Carey, the Brooklyn Democrat whose district includes large numbers of working-class whites. "He wants a decent apartment, he wants a few beers on the weekend, he wants his kids to have decent clothes, he wants to go to a ballgame once in a while, and he would like to put a little money away so that his kids can have the education that he never could afford. That's not asking a hell of a lot. But he's not getting that. He thinks society has failed him and, in a way, if he is white, he is often more alienated than the black man. At least the black man has his own organizations, and can submerge himself in the struggle for justice and equality, or elevate himself, whatever the case might be. The black man has hope, because no matter what some of the militants say, his life is slowly getting better in a number of ways. The white man who makes $7,000 a year, who is 40, knows that he is never going to earn much more than that for the rest of his life, and he sees things getting worse, more hopeless. John Lindsay has made a number of bad moves as mayor of this town, but the alienation of the white lower middle class might have been the worst."

Carey is probably right. The middle class, that cadre of professionals, semi-professionals and businessmen who are the backbone of any living city, are the children of the white working class. If they are brought up believing that the city government does not care whether they live or die (or how they live or die), they will not stay here very long as adults. They will go to college, graduate, marry, get jobs and depart. Right now, thousands of them are leaving New York, because New York doesn't *work* for them. The public schools, when they are open, are desperate; the private schools cost too much (and if they can afford private school, they realize that their taxes are paying for the public schools whose poor quality prevents them from using them). The streets are filthy, the air is polluted, the parks are dangerous, prices are too high. They end up in California, or Rahway, or Islip.

Patriotism is very important to the working-class white man. Most of the time he is the son of an immigrant, and most immigrants sincerely believe that the Pledge of Allegiance, "The Star-Spangled Banner," the American flag are symbols of what it means to be Americans. They might not have become rich in America, but most of the time they were much better off than they were in the old country. On "I Am an American" Day they march in parades with a kind of religious fervor that can look absurd to the outsider (imagine marching through Copenhagen on "I Am a Dane" Day), but that can also be oddly touching. Walk through any working-class white neighborhood and you will see dozens of veterans' clubs, named after neighborhood men who were killed in World War Two or Korea. There are not really orgies of jingoism going on inside; most of the time the veterans' clubs serve as places in which to drink on Sunday morning before the bars open at 1 P.M., or as places in which to hold baptisms and wedding receptions. But they are places where an odd sort of know-nothingism is fostered. The war in Vietnam was almost never questioned until last year. It was an American war, with Americans dying in action, and it could not be questioned.

The reasons for this simplistic view of the world are complicated. But one reason is that the working-class white man fights in every American war. Large numbers of poorly educated blacks are rejected by the draft because they can't pass the mental examinations; the high numbers of black casualties are due to the disproportionate number of black career NCOS and the large number of blacks who go into airborne units because of higher pay. The working-class white man (and his brothers, sons and cousins) get deferments only if they are crippled; their educations, usually in parochial schools, are good enough to pass Army requirements, but not good enough to get them into the city college system (which, being free, is the only kind of college they could afford). It is the children of the rich and the middle class who get all those college deferments.

While he is in the service, the working-class white hates it; he bitches about the food, the brass, the living conditions; he tries to come back to New York at every opportunity, even if it means two 14-hour car rides on a weekend. But after he is out, and especially if he has seen combat, a romantic glaze covers the experience. He is a veteran, he is a man, he can drink with the men at the corner saloon. And as he goes into his 30s and 40s, he resents those who don't serve, or bitch about the service the way he used to bitch. He becomes quarrelsome. When he gets drunk, he tells you about Saipan. And he sees any form of antiwar protest as a denial of his own young manhood, and a form of spitting on the graves of the people he served with who died in his war.

The past lives on. When I visit my old neighborhood, we still talk about things we did when we were 18, fights we had, and who was "good with his hands" in the main events at the Caton Inn, and how great it was eating sandwiches from Mary's down near Oceantide in Coney Island. Or we talk about the Zale-Graziano fights, or what a great team the Dodgers were when Duke Snider played centerfield and Roy Campanella was the catcher, and what a shame it was that Rex Barney never learned how to control the fast ball. Nostalgia was always a curse; I remember one night when I was 17, drinking beer from cardboard containers on a bench at the side of Prospect Park, and one of my friends said that it was a shame we were getting old, that there would never be another summer like the one we had the year before, when we were 16. It was absurd, of course, and yet it was true; the summer we were 17, guys we knew were already dying on the frozen ridges of Korea.

A large reason for the growing alienation of members of the white working class is their belief that they are not respected. It is an important thing for the son of an immigrant to be respected. When he is young, physical prowess is usually the most important thing: the guy who can fight or hit a ball or run with a football has more initial respect than the guy who gets good marks in school. But later, the man wants to be respected as a good provider, a reasonably good husband, a good drinker, a good credit risk (the worst thing you can do in a working-class saloon is borrow $20 and forget about it, or stiff the guy you borrowed it from).

It is no accident that the two New York City politicians who most represent the discontent of the white working class are Brooklyn Assemblyman Vito Battista and Councilman Matty Troy of Queens. Both are usually covered in the press as if they were refugees from a freak show (I've been guilty of this sneering, patronizing attitude toward Battista and Troy myself at times). Battista claims to be the spokesman for the small home owner and many small home owners believe in him; but a lot of people who are listening to him now see him as the spokesman for the small home owner they would like to be. "I like that Battista," a guy told me a couple of weeks ago. "He talks our language. That Lindsay sounds like a college professor." Troy speaks for the man who can't get his streets cleaned, who has to take a train and a bus to get to his home, who is being taxed into suburban exile; he is also very big on patriotism, but he shocked his old auditors at the

Democratic convention in Chicago last year when he supported the minority peace plank on Vietnam.

There is one further problem involved here. That is the failure of the literary/intellectual world to fully recognize the existence of the white working class, except to abhor them. With the exception of James T. Farrell, no major American novelist has dealt with the working-class white man, except in war novels. Our novelists write about bullfighters, migrant workers, screenwriters, psychiatrists, failing novelists, homosexuals, advertising men, gangsters, actors, politicians, drifters, hippies, spies and millionaires; I have yet to see a work of the imagination deal with the life of a wire-lather, a carpenter, a subway conductor, an ironworker or a derrick operator. There hasn't even been much inquiry by the sociologists; *Beyond the Melting Pot,* by Nathan Glazer and Daniel P. Moynihan, is the most useful book, but we have yet to see an Oscar Lewis-style book called, say, *The Children of Flaherty.* I suppose there are reasons for this neglect, caused by a century of intellectual sneering at bourgeois values, etc. But the result has been the inability of many intellectuals to imagine themselves in the plight of the American white working man. They don't understand his virtues (loyalty, endurance, courage, among others) and see him only through his faults (narrowness, bigotry, the worship of machismo, among others). The result is the stereotype. Black writers have finally begun to reveal what it means to be black in this country; I suppose it will take a working-class novelist to do the same for his people. It is certainly a rich, complex and unworked mine.

But for the moment it is imperative for New York politicians to begin to deal with the growing alienation and paranoia of the working-class white man. I really don't think they can wait much longer, because the present situation is working its way to the point of no return. The working-class white man feels trapped and, even worse, in a society that purports to be democratic, ignored. The tax burden is crushing him, and the quality of his life does not seem to justify his exertions. He cannot leave New York City because he can't afford it, and he is beginning to look for someone to blame. That someone is almost certainly going to be the black man.

This does not have to be the situation, of course. If the government were more responsive to the working-class white man, if the distribution of benefits were spread more widely, if the government's presence were felt more strongly in ways that benefit white communities, there would be a chance to turn this situation around. The working-class white man does not care if a black man gets a job in his union, as long as it does not mean the loss of his own job, or the small privileges and sense of self-respect that go with it. I mean it; I know these people, and know that they largely would not care what happens in the city, if what happens at least has the virtue of fairness. For now they see a terrible unfairness in their lives, and an increasing lack of personal control over what happens to them. And the result is growing talk of revolt.

The revolt involves the use of guns. In East Flatbush, and Corona, and all those other places where the white working class lives, people are forming gun clubs and self-defense leagues and talking about what they will do if real race rioting breaks out. It is a tragic situation, because the poor blacks and the working-class whites should be natural allies. Instead, the black man has become the symbol of all the working-class white man's resentments.

"I never had a gun in my life before," a 34-year-old Queens bartender named James Giuliano told me a couple of weeks ago. "But I got me a shotgun, license and all. I hate to have the thing in the house, because of the kids. But the way things are goin', I might have to use it on someone. I really might. It's comin' to that. Believe me, it's comin' to that."

The working-class white man is actually in revolt against taxes, joyless work, the double standards and short memories of professional politicians, hypocrisy and what he considers the debasement of the American dream. But George Wallace received 10 million votes last year, not all of them from rednecked racists. That should have been a warning, strong and clear. If the stereotyped black man is becoming the working-class white man's enemy, the eventual enemy might be the democratic process itself. Any politician who leaves that white man out of the political equation, does so at very large risk. The next round of race riots might not be between people and property, but between people and people. And that could be the end of us.

9. Culture Power

Alan Rich

"The playwright in London or San Francisco creates for his own locality only secondarily, thoroughly aware that Broadway audiences will react stupidly to his work but will pay a $9.90 top for the privilege."

Joe and Sally went to the theater one night. It was Sally's birthday and, therefore, an Occasion. They weren't able to get a sitter before 7:30, so they decided to eat in and save dining out for some other time. Finding a Broadway play worthy of the night hadn't been easy, because neither Joe (Swarthmore '63) nor Sally (Bard '65) is the sort that likes to leave its brains at home when going out for entertainment. Tickets to the English import they finally agreed upon cost Joe close to thirty dollars through an agency.

They came downstairs at their West Side brownstone at 7:45, and Joe walked over to Central Park West to try to get a cab. As soon as he had gone, two kids came out of the house next door, knocked Sally against a wall and made off with her purse which, by luck, didn't have much of value in it. After a few moments she got over her anger, and Joe and Sally made it to Times Square by 8:20. The cab driver refused to go down the side street the theater was on, so they had to push their way for half a block through the thick and disorganized crowd that is one of New York's trademarks. They had, therefore, a rotten time at the show, an even worse time getting home on the bus, and Joe resolved that for Sally's next birthday he'd give her a color television set which they would then stay at home and watch.

The talk this year is about crisis in the arts. Actually, the word should be *crises,* because they are numerous, diverse, complementary at times and self-contradictory at other times. There is a self-

contradiction in the fact, for example, that the APA-Phoenix repertory company has had to curtail its New York program this year
for lack of box-office support, while people like Joe and Sally complain that you can't get tickets to anything worth seeing on Broadway. The producers of New York's live entertainment complain
against the public, whenever they're not complaining against the
labor unions that force expenses up, and the public complains right
back against the producers.

Up avenue and down canyon, the cries resound. Before the
leaves had turned last autumn, Broadway had already witnessed its
first major casualty: despite good notices, the Edward Albee-Rich-
ard Barr repertory company, Theatre '69, had been dumped after
losing $130,000 in its first two weeks. The APA-Phoenix repertory
dropped its fourth scheduled production for lack of funds. Shortly
before Christmas the *Times* ran a concerted lament from the music
industry, to the effect that attendance at concerts and recitals was
off this year for a tangled counterpoint of reasons. Brooklyn Museum cut back its visiting hours from six days to five, and just last
month the city announced that lack of funds may cause further
cutbacks in museum and library hours. Despite Ford Foundation
support, the excellent Festival Orchestra didn't even begin its pro-
jected 1968–69 season. And so it has gone.

It has gone this way while social and cultural observers talk on
endlessly about the cultural explosion, and how contemporary society can no longer regard culture as a luxury but a necessity
against the troubled times, etc. They are right about the latter, beyond any argument. About the former they are both right and
wrong. The explosion in the arts is not merely a matter of statistical
growth in the number of entertainments available. It is also a matter of statistical growth in the number of headaches.

The crises are not confined only to New York, of course, but
they are intensified here. They are intensified, first of all, because
New York is still the cultural capital of the country, the place
where more things happen in culture than anywhere else, the place
where styles are set for the rest of the country and the world. They
are also intensified by the peculiar nature of the city itself; the fact
that you can't drive a car in New York, that public transportation
—transit and taxis—offers its own web of imponderables and im-
possibilities during those hours when it is most in demand, that the

mere experience of being on the streets of New York at any time of day or night presents more threats to personal safety than astronauts face in outer space,* and that the cost of entertainment and cultural uplift excludes from the city's arts life the very people who could benefit from it the most.

Discomfort and danger, costs and chaos, these are the specters that haunt the cultural world these days. If there are villains to be identified—a cut-and-dried process that answers some questions but not all—we can ascribe the first two to the realities of New York itself. So can the the third, in part: theater and concert-hall rentals have risen scandalously, *and* taxes *and* labor costs. Old theaters are torn down to make room for more profitable real estate; when new ones are built a new and inflated price structure is installed along with the new and improved facilities. For the added comfort (and, to some, prestige) of giving a recital at Lincoln Center's Philharmonic Hall, a musician pays 150 per cent over what he would at Carnegie, a differential passed along, of course, to the ticket buyer.

The fourth of these specters, chaos, is more difficult to pin down, perhaps, but it plays a major role. There is a sense of alienation, of non-communication in today's cultural life. It is not a bad thing in itself that Broadway has relatively little to offer today's younger and intellectually sophisticated audience, because there are alternatives off and off-off Broadway. It isn't fatal that at the moment Lincoln Center's Establishment-oriented programing (as well as its prices) bars all but the conservative and well-heeled, because there are plenty of good concerts and even operas to be found elsewhere. But what is going to happen when today's tired businessman becomes even older and more tired? Who from the next generation is going to buy the tickets to the Broadway musicals and underwrite the Metropolitan Opera's deficits? The most impressive tragedy in today's culture industry (for such it is) is that it is digging its own grave by its failure to make any real accommodation with its own times. It can, when left to its own devices, even betray the spirit of its times, as anyone who cares to contrast the original off-

---

* Note, by the way, that New York's area of highest crime density, Times Square and vicinity—where the rate, by the way, rose 92 per cent from January 1968 to 1969—is also the area of highest density of entertainment facilities.

Broadway *Hair* with its fancied-up Broadway counterpart can attest.

New York's cultural scene is largely supported on a basis that can at best be considered democratic. There are no, or very few, cultural czars or Maecenases as there were a century ago; the Joes and Sallies make themselves felt in the overall structure, because if they don't buy the tickets nobody else will pick up the tab. The role of governmental subsidy in the arts is still hazy and chancy; certainly nobody expects very much from Washington in the next four years, although Governor Rockefeller's Arts Council has been a model for state-level programs throughout the country and the city's participation is above average. (Even so, there is something New York City could learn from, for example, San Francisco, which has firmly committed its tax revenue from a specific area, hotel rooms, to the support of culture.) Business support of the arts consists for the most part of gestures and statements both pious and ludicrous, while the foundations have frequently erred in heeding the advice of conservative (not to say interested) parties. In seeking individual support the arts these days are thrown into competition with Vietnamese war orphans, Biafra, the ghetto—you name it. The squabbling that goes on for the little remaining available money is in itself destructive to the arts. Witness the present mess at Lincoln Center, brought about by, as much as anything, the fact that the Center itself is actively raising funds to support its own educational programs while its constituent members are also raising funds to pay their stagehands.

Small wonder, then, that an aura of chaos hangs over New York's cultural life, rich and distinguished and pace-setting though it may be. Small wonder that, faced with this cloud of confusion through which gleam the beady eyes of the street mugger and the "off duty" signs of the taxicabs, Joe and Sally will stay home on her birthday next year and watch television.

Back in the 1890s one of the Vanderbilt dowagers wrote a letter one day to the management of the Metropolitan Opera House. She had heard, the letter ran, that Mr. de Reszke, the Met's leading basso, had a nice aria to sing early in the first act of *Aïda,* but she wondered if it *had* to come where it did. The problem was, she and her party weren't accustomed to arriving at the Met quite that early. Jean de Reszke himself later confessed to a colleague that in the nineteen performances of *Aïda* he had sung at the Met, he had only sung the aria "Celeste Aïda" four times. Obviously, if he couldn't sing it for Mrs. Vanderbilt and her friends, there was no point in singing it at all.

All this has a somewhat quaint ring today. There is no one dowager or small, discernible power group that tells the Metropolitan or New York City Opera, the Philharmonic or any of the other major performing groups which operas, plays or symphonies it may or may not perform, or where the arias should come. This is not to say, of course, that the managements of those organizations can experiment daringly with their programs. They have tickets to sell, and the vast majority of ticket buyers prefer to wallow in the familiar, checking their brains in the cloakroom along with their furs. This is the genuine power group behind the performing arts in New York City, but it numbers tens of thousands, and is therefore as diffuse and diverse in the way it exerts power as the city's cultural resources are numerous. Los Angeles has Dorothy Chandler, whose power to make basic cultural decisions as to what may or may not come to her city is thrice renowned. Chicago had, until recently, Claudia Cassidy, a critic no less, but one who as spokesman for the McCormick family's Chicago *Tribune* could whisk conductors on and off the podium of the Chicago Symphony and plays in and out of town as easily with her pen as Mrs. Chandler can with her checkbook.

To some extent, that kind of direct power structure is still with New York in the visual arts, where a small group of collectors, patrons and gallery owners function directly as taste makers to the masses. It has long since vanished from the performing-arts scene, however. As long ago as, say, 1907.

That was the year the Metropolitan Opera appointed Otto Kahn as chairman of its board of directors. The Vanderbilts had built the Met at 39th and Broadway in 1883, largely as a means of perpetuating their own species. They were well aware of the long-standing European tradition, whereby monarchs and noblemen vied among themselves for the privilege of supporting the arts to their own greater glory, and they actively hoped for a little of the same glory for themselves. They were disturbed particularly by the rise in the city of the new money being made in barrelfuls by immigrants, especially the German-Jewish merchants and that upstart Andrew Carnegie, and looked with horror on the way that crowd was also beginning to buy its way into the box seats at the old Academy of Music on 14th Street. And so they packed up and moved uptown, where they remained secure in their fortress until 1907 when, in dire financial straits and public disrepute—Enrico Caruso having been jailed for molesting a woman in Central Park and Strauss's *Salome* having brought down the wrath of press and clergy—the company was finally forced to make its peace with the new money. (Attempts to brand the Met an anti-Semitic bastion, as was done by one of the more bizarre groups that was trying to save the house from the wreckers in 1966, produced a drastic oversimplification, of course. The point between the Vanderbilts, etc., and the others was not a question of religious bias, merely of who happened to own New York first.)

Nevertheless, culture power is a force that produces both light and heat, variously definable and everywhere discernible. The seat of that power is New York, and its emanations, both positive and negative, penetrate the local gloom anywhere in the world. The inevitabilities are all here, made all the more inevitable because of their money potential. The playwright in London or San Francisco creates for his own locality only secondarily, thoroughly aware that Broadway audiences will react stupidly to his work but will pay a $9.90 top for the privilege. The painter in Warsaw (Poland or Indiana) knows all about 57th Street, and the singer in Paris can locate Lincoln Center on the map as readily as the Conservatoire.

The emanations work in both directions. If Lincoln Center is the glamour magnet, its power to pull in is balanced by its power to send out. The existence of Lincoln Center has not only profoundly affected the real estate developments in the West Side blocks that surround it, but the Lincoln Center idea, the concept of the cultural supermarket, has also spread to Los Angeles and hundreds of points in between, and has thereby affected real estate developments in each of *these* points. Los Angeles' new cultural center is surrounded by new apartment buildings every bit as ugly as Lincoln Towers.

Thus, culture power is felt today even by those uncountable millions who couldn't care less about the source of that power. A strike in Broadway theaters affects not only audiences and actors, but hotel and restaurant owners, as well as newspaper dealers and managers of clothing and souvenir shops in the Times Square area. New Yorkers often encounter the raised eyebrows of those from civilizations where a cultural centrality has been a fact of life for centuries; they are often informed in words heavy with Teutonic accentuation that they cannot apprehend the import of true culture. But nobody can ever accuse them of not knowing how to live off culture. Anyone who witnessed the brisk sale of *Mona Lisa* ashtrays while that famous painting was "visiting" the Metropolitan Museum can very well speak to that point.

The extent and diversity of New York's cultural resources preclude the possibility of their being dominated, or even greatly affected, by any specific power group; in that respect, at least, there has been some forward movement from the Vanderbilts' palmy days. Carnegie Hall, rescued from the wreckers thanks to a citizens' movement headed by Isaac Stern, has enjoyed its most prosperous booking seasons in its history in the years since the opening of Lincoln Center, thus allaying at least partially the fears that the new halls would monopolize the city's symphonic life. The fact that George Balanchine does set his heavy hand on decisions concerning dance at Lincoln Center has not precluded a nearly explosive proliferation of dance events in recent seasons almost everywhere else in town. New York may have only one public school system, reduceable to ruins in the crossfire between a Shanker and a Mc-Coy; it may possess only a single transit system, wreckable at the wave of a picket sign. But its cultural life threads its way through a forest of viable alternatives.

Thus, the question "Who needs Lincoln Center?" which has been voiced in one quarter or another almost continually since the project was first announced in 1958, has considerable justification. If anything, the revelation by William Schuman, upon his resignation as president of the center late in 1968, that the organization was in just about every conceivable kind of mess, has brought that question to a gigantic crescendo.

The failure of Lincoln Center—if such it be—arises from a complex interweaving of elements, some of them so incompatible that it is only a wonder that anybody could have ever believed it could

succeed. How, for example, can you conceive of a smoothly working board whose membership includes the heads of two successful
opera companies whose operations have become more alike every
year? Operatic managers are, by the nature of their work and responsibilities, inclined to be very uptight people, but the specter of
Rudolf Bing glaring across the Plaza at Julius Rudel, general director of New York City Opera, and Rudel glaring back, is one that
could not help but foredoom any kind of smooth operation. Bing
has made all sorts of pronouncements about welcoming the friendly
rivalry; Rudel has come to Bing's rescue any number of times by
releasing key singers to help the older company out of holes. But
the fact remains that the two companies have locked horns quite
inextricably, and probably in perpetuity. When critics proclaimed
Rudel's 1968 production of *Manon* quite possibly the best thing
that had ever happened to opera in New York, Bing had no re-
course but to withdraw his own *Manon* (which the critics had
clobbered) from his 1968–69 plans. No saint can remain patient
with that kind of problem at his doorstep.

The in-fighting among Lincoln Center's constituents goes on on
other levels besides the artistic, of course. All of them are actively
engaged in fund raising, and stand like so many suitors at the door-
steps of the city's moneyed. There, too, stands their landlord, Lincoln Center itself, looking for support for its own activities, which
run all the way from groundskeeping to its own vast, active and
valuable educational programs which bring culture to schoolchil-
dren on a year-round basis. The fight for the dollar, more than any
other single factor, establishes the untenableness of the entire Lincoln Center concept.

Thus, the analogy often made of Lincoln Center as a kind of
"cultural supermarket" is not quite accurate. Wheaties and Super-
K do, after all, coexist on supermarket shelves without going "pop"
at each other. The components of the Lincoln Center board have at
each other in ways that resemble the action on a hockey rink far
more than a supermarket, and the directions of the interaction are
devious and diverse. Balanchine has, as of now, effectively suppressed the possibility at the center of much of significance in the
way of opposing views of the dance. Bing readily admits to "having
been consulted" on the repertories of the two foreign opera com-

panies that have played at the Met during the summer Lincoln Center festivals, whose subsequent box-office failure could therefore be taken as proclamation that Bing's way was the only way.

The Lincoln Center situation is further clouded by emanations from the top. The choice of Schuman as president—a respected teacher and a composer who had earned the Establishment seal of approval—suggested from the beginning that Lincoln Center was in something more than the business of building and renting auditoriums and keeping cigar butts out of the fountains. One read of Lincoln Center in the handouts, not as a piece of real estate but as a "concept." What that was to mean came out loud and clear in 1964 when Elia Kazan and Robert Whitehead walked out of the leadership of the Lincoln Center Repertory Company while it was still operating in temporary quarters near Washington Square, when it turned out that Lincoln Center itself was to make itself felt in artistic policies concerning the company. One of the items aired at that time revealed that Schuman had dreamed up an all-star (i.e., non-repertory) production of Shaw's *Caesar and Cleopatra* (of all things!) to inaugurate the Repertory Company's new theater. Landlord indeed!

Since it is currently the home of the Repertory Company, the Philharmonic, two opera companies and the New York City Ballet, Lincoln Center has succeeded in making itself very needed. But it now seems likely that its function as a cultural power is both unneeded and doomed. At very least, its inner seethings have frightened away a lot of money.

The performing arts do not operate in the city, therefore, from the base of an efficient power structure. This is a mixed blessing. On the one hand, it rules out the possibility of a single, or at least narrow, point of view dominating the prestigious center of the city's activities, as is the case in Los Angeles. On the other, it makes the matter of financing a great deal more dangerous and diffuse. When New York had its Vanderbilts and Astors to pick up the tab for a large percentage of the city's cultural activities, life in the arts was somewhat more secure. In any case, there was money to be had, as there is money to be had today for those who gain entree in the West to Mrs. Chandler and the structure she controls.

Today the base in New York is broader, and therefore more

difficult to approach. The theater draws its support from a large network of backers, offering old money and new and in all sizes from heavy bankrolls to widows' mites. The patrons' lists for the Philharmonic, the Met, the City Opera and Ballet reach into the thousands, and the names they contain represent a diversity of ethnic and religious backgrounds and professions. Added up, they imply a great deal of money and yet, as everybody knows, the city's cultural life hovers constantly on the verge of bankruptcy.

A sold-out house at a concert or opera in one of the city's major halls does not represent enough ticket revenue to pay the costs of the evening's entertainment. A straight dramatic show on Broadway must run an average of six months at capacity before it can begin to realize a profit on its initial costs; a musical can take as long as a year. There isn't very much entertainment you can bring into Manhattan these nights, at least between 42nd and 65th Streets, at less than a six-figure initial cost; the last time the public was treated to a recitation of these figures was three or four years ago, when a concoction named *Kelly* sank on opening night with a $650,000 rock hung around its neck. Ticket prices have risen since then, and so have costs; the lines diverge more widely day by day.

Despite individual glimmers here and there, the sad fact remains that the darker side of the aforementioned mixed blessing is still in a position to put the brighter side into eclipse. New York, the performing-arts capital of the nation (some say the world) operates on a frayed shoestring. Despite the clarion calls that have gone out in the past few years to arouse the forces of private and public capital to an awareness of their responsibilities toward the arts, the response has been, to use the kindest word, spotty. One can easily hanker once again for the old days of true cultural autocracy.

In a sense, the very size of the city's cultural life creates a paradox. The outward appearance of a well-supported and prosperous theatrical life (meaning, of course, that big Broadway musicals and comedies by Neil Simon do turn-away business) has sent foundation money off to other cities; thus, worthwhile but non-mass-oriented ventures in the city, whose outlines are hard to see behind the glare from the *Fiddler on the Roof* box office, must close ranks or perish. Even with healthy assistance from the city, Joseph Papp's summertime Shakespeare Festival and wintertime Public

Theater are currently in bad trouble, as in the APA-Phoenix program, with all its faults the closest thing the city possesses to a genuine theatrical repertory. And there is a further paradox here, in that the very things that are suffering in the theater are the fare that could most readily attract the younger audience from which will grow the source of future patronage. The Broadway theater functions at its most profitable on middle-aged and elderly money, thereby choking off its own future.

Ford and Rockefeller Foundation money has gone into Establishment music and dance, spottily and sporadically, but hardly at all into the theater. So has a certain amount of business money: Eastern Airlines has pungled up half a million for the Met's new stagings of Wagner's *Ring,* and American Export Isbrandtsen Lines underwrote the Met's *Aïda* (obviously before the Suez Canal was closed to shipping). Ford has underwritten a series of contemporary operas produced by the City Opera and the Met (along with one each in Chicago and San Francisco), most of them second-rate works, to be sure, but valuable in at least creating the possibilities for a new operatic repertory, and has also placed $7.5 million into the hands of existing or developing dance companies. Rockefeller money has also gone into dance groups, into an extensive program to enable symphony orchestras (none in New York as yet) to undertake post-season exploration of new music and—aiming at the soft underbelly of the problem—programs for the training and feeding of critics in various arts fields.

There are the beginnings in all these activities of an eventual new power structure, assuming power in its classic definition as the paying of money to make things happen, that might in time form the capitalistic counterpart of the traditional European system of patronage, or its current European counterpart in the support given the arts in Europe by official governmental agencies. Unfortunately, they are at the moment only beginnings, and there have been major mistakes made. Both Ford and, to a lesser extent, Rockefeller have done their asking around for advice within a fairly narrow range of interest and this has resulted in, for example, Ford's dance money going almost entirely to groups out to perpetuate the Balanchine image. Like the situation that still obtains with the inevitable but scary full-scale entry of government into arts support, the question of corporate support for the arts must be reckoned in its birth pangs.

The closest counterpart now active in New York's performing-arts scene to the classic European patron is Mrs. Rebekah Harkness Kean of the dance world, a former dancer herself who has consistently, and with a wisdom that stops just this side of disinterest, fostered the growth of her chosen art. Currently she is known as the patroness of the company that bears her name, a new junior offshoot of that company, and a short free season of diversified dance events every September in Central Park's Delacorte Theatre. Along with this, she has in the past kept going such developing figures as Alvin Ailey and Robert Joffrey, and she has also exercised her classic patroness' prerogative in cutting her protégés unceremoniously adrift when their activities do not suit her future plans.

Harkness is unique in the performing arts in New York today, but her methods do resemble the operations of the world of the visual arts.

It is in this world that the outlines of the old feudality can best be traced. Bing and Rudel may divide the operatic world between them, but in painting, it is still the patron, not the curator, who pulls the strings. Their number is small—perhaps thirty to fifty throughout the country—but their buying activities in art constitute the signals to museum directors. When men like industrialist Joseph Hirschorn or taxi magnate Robert Scull spread their cloak of benevolence around a painter or group, the art market reacts as alertly as Wall Street might react to H. L. Hunt's cornering Comsat.

Scull made Pop Art. He bought Warhol, and then the Museum of Modern Art bought Warhol. Now he turns around and sells some gems from his Pop Art collection, and the signs are rightly taken to mean, not a panic nor the end of an era, but the establishment of a stable Pop Art market.

Scull and his group listen. They listen to the power substructure, the key gallery owners like Castelli and Ekstrom, who can themselves double the value of a painting or a painter by displaying them. The power structure in the arts is today a reasonably healthy one (injured individuals notwithstanding) because its lines of communication are plugged into the ferment. Castelli found Rauschenberg, not in the Yellow Pages but down where Things Were Happening.

This could easily be why the man who will put a Rauschenberg or a Pollock over his fireplace will buy records of the Beethoven symphonies (by Leonard Bernstein, to be sure) and take his friends to see *Promises, Promises*. And why the Harkness Ballet offers the widest range of styles, including the experimental, of any major dance company today.

Do the critics belong in the power structure?

No, not in the traditional sense, in which we have been defining power as the money that makes things happen. No also in the sense that an arts-oriented New York person could countenance the kind of ruckus Claudia Cassidy was once able to raise in Chicago (which was, in any case, a phenomenon not likely to be duplicated in a country which makes any pretense about moving toward cultural maturity).

Yet, within the realm of the most thoroughly commercialized of New York's live (i.e., not filmed) arts worlds, the theater, the critic of the city's one major newspaper is the most immediately accessible scapegoat for every failure. Let Clive Barnes write unkindly of a new play (for reasons having to do with what he had for dinner, the writer and producer will tell you) and the play will close within a week.

It may or may not be a coincidence that this phenomenon is confined to that branch of the arts with the least discernible power structure. Absence of a power structure may also imply absence of the means of communication to an audience. Lincoln Center, with its imperfect but omnipresent structure, *does* communicate by its very existence, and thus its Repertory Company operates on a near-capacity subscription business despite the fact that its press has been almost uniformly bad. The midtown theaters, each its own business with its own backers and hangups, do not individually communicate, and have abdicated this power to the critical press, which then serves it on a make-or-break basis.

But even that basis is hardly clear-cut. A bad *Times* review will, nine times out of ten, wreck a play, but this can be offset by the presence of certain star names; no critic liked Richard Burton's

Hamlet much, for example, nor, aside from Dustin Hoffman, the recent *Jimmy Shine*. And a good *Times* review, but one which implies that the play is written for a thinking audience, can damage the goods almost as seriously as a bad one. All that can really be said, therefore, is that the theater, of all arts, is potentially the one most reactive to criticism.

In other areas, criticism exists for the most part as a private correspondence between critic and thing criticized, which manages marginally to give off enough glow to alert a public to the fact that there is *something* going on. At its best it can serve to remind the public that the arts do contain an essestial challenge to the thinking process; at its worst, it can supply ad writers and the producers of brochures with a few shiny phrases.

But we are hardly ready to confuse words with power—no more ready in the area of culture power than in politics and labor. Culture power is money; its structure exists ideally to get that money spent and, as a marginal purpose, to get a little of it back.

10. Short-Wave Power, or: Hello, I'm in the Car

Ralph Schoenstein

"Are you bored in traffic jams? Then join the status-seeking hams who produce a show that blends industry, infidelity, obscenity and domesticity in a turnpike *Peyton Place*."

As darkness descends on the city, a black limousine with a high aerial and a low license speeds north to its rendezvous. In the back seat, a grim man reaches over his shoulder, grabs a telephone, and says "Hello, mobile! Hello, mobile! This is YK-46701, White Plains registry . . ."

Who is this urgent voice in the night? A detective on his way to seize some bananas? A fire chief on his way to a strike meeting? Let's stay tuned.

"This is the mobile operator, sir."

"Get me 914-732-5698 . . . Hello, Florence, I'm in the car. What are we having?"

"Veal."

"Veal? God, we just had it *Monday!"*

"Look, Joey, don't bother getting off the thruway. Just go straight to hell."

"Hey, baby, I'm sorry—I really am. It's just been one of those days. We missed a big order from National that . . ."

"Oh, sweetie, *I'm* sorry; I shouldn't go bitchy when you're calling from traffic. Honey, I'll switch to steak."

"Baby, veal sounds *great*."

"It won't be as yummy as *you.*"

"Hello, mobile . . ."

"Are you through, sir?"

"Goddamit, *no!* Florie baby, I'm wild for you."

"Oh, *hurry,* Joey!"

"I'm just passing Gimbels."

"Love you, love you, *love* you!"

"Hello, mobile . . ."

"Will you stay the hell off the *line!* Sweetie, why don't you parmigian it?"

"You got it, lover."

"Abba-dabba-*do!*"

"Oh, honey, the *hell* with National; just keep comin' to baby."

"You're loud and clear, baby. Old Batmobile's already at Castro Convertible."

"Come to Catwoman, lover. Just keep a-comin'."

For the next ten minutes, the girl with the cheesy veal and the bedroom zeal is a cooing control tower for a hungry voice heading north. Meanwhile, in another part of the busy air, another weary traveler is tuned to a succulent beacon.

"Hi, doll, I'm in the car."

"What's *keepin'* ya?"

"I need a goddam *helicopter* on this mother of a road! Just keep your pants on; I'll be there soon."

"How long we got?"

"She expects me by midnight. I'm at a meeting in town."

"How'd it go today?"

"Don't ask. You know the Paradise Homes deal? Well, the interest is due and we don't have it. The bank could end up owning everything we've put up."

"Oh, *that* wouldn't be nice."

"Mobile, Mr. Zeckendorf wants . . ."

"Dammit, I'm still *talking!*"

"Sir, this channel is busy."

"Honey, who's Mr. Zeckendorf?"

She would have known not only Mr. Zeckendorf but also Sam Newhouse and Zeppi Plumbing had she not been new to the latest chic pastime: broadcasting and bugging on the biggest party line in the world. It's the telephone company's mobile communication service, where seldom is heard a clean private word. Are you bored in traffic jams? Then join the status-seeking hams who produce a show that blends industry, infidelity, obscenity and domesticity in a turnpike *Peyton Place*. Home television may be a vast wasteland, but car telephoning is one great oasis of juicy dates.

There are only nineteen channels in this go-go version of the old party line, for the FCC gives the telephone company just a small part of the low frequency range: there has to be room for policemen, firemen and small boys with walkie-talkies. All private car phoning is on only three frequency band widths and the mobile big mouth must always be within twenty-five miles of a transmitter, which locally are found in Manhattan, White Plains, Newark and Hempstead. You can call from car to office, car to concubine, or car to car, as great a distance as you want; and the nice thing is you needn't have anything to say, for it's such bargain one-upmanship that even the elegant indigent can still afford to call a few creditors and say, "Hello, I'm in the car." The basic charge for the phone is $25 a month, but then you get 120 message units for just $7 more. Since six message units make up the average three-minute call, you can cheaply impress twenty friends with a lyrical portrait of the Verrazano Bridge.

Automobile phoning is quite different from phoning ship to shore. Not only is there the obvious lack of water, but shipboard calls are actually less salty; the sea seems to act as a conversational cleanser. However, once on shore, the party liners lose their finesse and wax creatively obscene. Inspired by the urgencies of business and sex, many rolling highwaymen sound as though they're giving dramatic readings of subway walls.

Of course, the man who phones from a car *does* have an obligation to his listeners: he's a disc jockey without music; he's unique entertainment when the helicopters above are using commercial bands to explain why you're going three miles an hour. The thousand telephonic ears in the tri-state area are really just one long bugged back fence. Some of the eavesdropping is unintentional because so many men are fighting for just nineteen lines. (At commuting times, even the men with several lines must often wait for one to be freed from executive gossip.) But there's also *intentional* eavesdropping, for 152 on your prestige dial is a cross between the

Kiplinger Letter and *Confidential,* a clearinghouse of goodies for hip wheeler-dealers and old-fashioned voyeurs. Zeckendorf reportedly lost a big deal because he put the whole thing on his radio show.

So stay tuned in: ah, ah, ah, ah—don't touch that dial! Return with us now to the swinging sound of Billy Z. and the Back Seaters, to the only Americans who are polluting the air in two different ways at once. Listen . . . it's prime morning time and we've picked up the Westmoreland of the Belt Parkway.

"Grace, what's in the mail?"

"It can all wait, sir."

"If Barton comes in, put him in the conference room! I'm just passing LaGuardia. Now give me George."

"Yes, sir . . ."

"Morning, C.C."

"George, any problems?"

"Well, they're talking strike at the jelly plant."

"Just don't let 'em run scared. Now put John on . . ."

"Good morning, C.C."

"Johnny, I'm in the car."

"Gotcha."

"What's the story on that credit rating?"

"You mean KG Products. They're broke. We could grab it for a song."

"Good. Put the lawyers right on it. And give me Phil."

"Right."

"Morning, C.C.

"Phil, do you know the definition of a Polish wedding?"

An eavesdropping shark would be foiled here, for John, using his head, gave just initials to all the fans in limousine radioland. Had he used KG's name, Roy Cohn and twenty plumbers would have known of a company ripe for plucking; but the bugging opportunist now knows only that KG may be grabbed by a firm involved with jelly. And what does C.C. make that uses jelly? Vaseline? Marmalade? TNT? All we know for sure is the definition of a Polish wedding. We'd better not wait for the Italian jokes to follow; let's look for talk more decodable. Let's move up a band to . . .

"Hi, honey, it's *me!* Sending one-two-three! Sending one-two-

three! I'm in Ted's *car*—no *kidding*—and I thought you'd get a bang outa hearing from a car. This is James Bond to Control. Am following garbage truck on Bruckner Boulevard. You're my pootchie, one-two-three."

A splendid example of the medium as the message. Even saying he was in a car was superfluous, for in most of these calls, the static could be produced only by road transmission or by the call being relayed through Radio Beirut. But the hissing heightens the drama, for not everyone is using his phone to play or impress. Somewhere out there, Sam Newhouse is snatching newspapers, and gallant Zeckendorf is stalling creditors and Mike Zeppi is speeding toward a sewer in distress and . . .

"Hello, Max, I'm in the car. Did you check that new issue?"

This may be hot. Let's avoid tunnels and see if Max scrambles.

"I sure did, Lou. The stock is way underpriced at sixteen and they're getting a defense contract. We'd better grab all we can."

"Okay, when the market opens . . ."

And suddenly, from the Van Wyck to the Garden State, the boys are trying to break the code. What new stock is coming out at sixteen to fight the Viet Cong? *Wait* a minute, where's the *voice?* Where's *Lou?* Is he being jammed by the SEC? Preempted by Barnes? No, Lou is merely passing through a bad transmission zone. There's a big dead one on Third Avenue at 59th Street, so never tell her that you love her while you're buzzing Bloomingdale's.

Actually, you don't have to transmit at *all,* for great prestige befalls the man who is merely *seen* using a car phone. Many men would rather have a Volkswagen with a phone than a naked Cadillac. It is not impressive just to roll around in a limousine; any bum can *rent* one of those. But to be seen cradling a receiver while stuck on the Major Deegan—well, that's style to be topped only by seeing stag films with Prince Philip.

There is so much glory in having a car phone that when the telephone company recently had to disconnect one for non-payment, its owner pleaded to be allowed to keep the aerial. It was a piteous scene, but the man need not have been ashamed, for the trend in car phoning is toward having no batteries. Recently *The New York Times* ran an ad that said:

PHONY AUTO TELEPHONE
only $2.98

Here's the greatest way to gain instant status. Install
your own auto telephone along with attention-getting
aerial. No wiring, no FCC license, no bill every month.

Needless to say, legitimate back-seat broadcasters are appalled
by this Woolworth crowd, by these charlatans who would replace a
real toy with a fake toy. The true sedan jockey feels that a man who
would use just the shell of a car phone is a man who would go to a
motel with a mannequin. It is not only honor that should compel a
man to have something inside his shell, it's the desire to hear the
kind of broadcasting that Fred Friendly wouldn't understand, the
kind that best captures the struggles and dreams of the American
man as he sings a new version of "The Song of the Open Road":

"Look, you can go take a flying . . . This is Dick Tracy . . .
Gotta have credit . . . The goddamn boiler's smoking, Charlie
. . . *Meatballs?* . . . This is the Traffic Commissioner: why
isn't anything moving in Queens? . . . I'm just past Secaucus and I
love you . . . Daddy's talking from a *car* . . . Overpriced at
twenty; don't touch it . . . A valve on the heater . . . So take a
second mortgage . . . Liver? . . . I'm sorry, sweetie, I've got a
lousy commissioner's meeting . . . *Please,* Al, just another thirty
days . . . You gotta tell me *now* that she puked? . . . I'm in the
car . . . in the car . . . in the car . . ."

11. Honk Power, or: You and Your Big Mouth

Tom Wolfe

"... the honks ... every day sound the secret honk of New York wealth and position; the nasal knighthood ... The Social Baritone voice cannot be achieved without some ten or fifteen years of smoking cigarettes and drinking whiskey or gin ..."

PART I

A Test

The subject should read the following passage out loud. He should not study it first but simply begin reading out loud:

> I always looked forward to going to Loew's and having a frankfurter after the movie. But it was winter and in this case the electricity in the advertising sign over the entire length of the counter was short-circuited and splashing these sparks, and I had to linger for the longest time asking myself the question: "Is this twenty-five-cent treat, this frankfurter, worth the chance of frying my hands on this manic counter?" I remember that for the moment I did nothing.

If the subject was raised in New York, he has just revealed certain intimate facts about his family background, his current class and status and his social ambitions. For example, if he pronounced

"always" as if it were "owies"; or "forward" as if it rhymed with
"lowered"; or "frankfurter" as if it were spelled "frankfooter"; or
"electricity" as if it were "electrizziddy"; or "for the moment" at
"footer moment"—then he is in all probability permanently fixed
in a "New York accent," despite all attempts at education or culti-
vation, past or future . . . never to cross over into the magical
world of the honks! Ahhh . . . so many millions, oblivious to that
sheerly dividing line.

"Dja do da chem-yet?"

Dja do da chem-yet?

—this being the voice of a freshman on the campus of CCNY
at 139th Street and Convent Avenue the other day asking the
question "Have you done the chemistry assignment yet?" The
irony of it is that here is a boy who will probably *do da chem* and
God knows how many other assignments extremely well and score
about a 3.5 academic average over four years and then go to law
school at NYU and get his LL.B—and then for some reason he
can't quite figure out, he never does land the great glistening job
he was thinking of at Sullivan & Cromwell or Cravath, Swain &
Moore. Instead, he ends up in . . . *the neighborhood,* on the
south side of Northern Boulevard in Bayside, Queens, in an office
he shares with a real estate man, an old friend of his from here in
Bayside—which some of the local wiseacres call Brayside, because
of all the "Brooklyn" and "Bronx" accents you hear here in Queens
now—

Whaddya mean it's his voice? He's upgraded the *da* with "the"
by now, hasn't he? And hasn't he replaced the r's he's been dropping all these years—well, a few of them, anyway: "This is the first
house we evuh owned. We have a gahden an my wife is the
gahd*neh* . . ."

. . . here in Brayside . . .

The same day, in the little exotic knickknack boutique on the
ground floor of Henri Bendel, on 57th Street just west of Fifth: a
nice New York girl home from St. Timothy's, St. Tim's, the boarding school in Maryland. She and a girl friend of hers are walking
around town *checking boys,* among other things. It's true! They
can tell just by looking at him whether a boy goes to an Eastern
prep school or not. Not only that, they can tell *which prep school,*
usually, St. Paul's or Hotchkiss or Groton or Exeter or Andover, or

whatever; just by checking his hair and his clothes. And *certainly* if they can get just one sentence out of him—

—like this gorgeous boy here, a tall milk-fed stud in a Brooks yellow shirt and tasseled loafers fumbling over a Cameroons egret-skin hassock with his tweedy-thatchy Prince Charles hanging over his brow and— He's Exeter, or possibly Andover. That is obvious immediately from the tie. His tie is tied properly at the throat, but the ends are slung over his left shoulder, after the fashion. And their eyes meet, and then his eyes shift to her shoes, naturally, and then he looks into her eyes again, into her soul, as it were, and says, "Those are real Guccis, aren't they?"

Bliss! It's all there! Past, present, future! Certified! The Guccis, of course, being her loafers, bought at Gucci's, 699 Fifth Avenue, with the authentic Gucci gold chain across the tongue and not any of the countless imitations of the Gucci loafer. A shorthand! A very metonymy! For the whole Eastern boarding school thing, but more than that—the *honk!* He has it, the Eastern boy's boarding school *honk,* lifting every vowel—*Those are real Guccis, aren't they?*—up over the roof of his palate and sticking them into his nose and honking them out without moving his lower jaw. And there in one sentence he has said it all, announced that he belongs in the world of the New York *honks,* of the honks who rule and possess all and who every day sound the secret honk of New York wealth and position; the nasal knighthood of the Bobby Kennedys, the Robert Dowlings, Huntington Hartfords, Nelson Rockefellers, Thomas Hovings, Averell Harrimans—for in New York the world is sheerly but secretly divided into the *honks* and the *wonks**—*Dja do da chem yet?*—and this fumbling milk-fed Exeter stud will carry a C-

---

* "Honk" is a term of Eastern prep school derivation, connoting both the nasal quality of the upper class voice and its presumably authoritative sound, commanding obedience, like the horn of a large 1936 Packard. It is not to be confused with "honkie," the current Negro slang word for white man, which is apparently a variation on a still older slang word, "hunky," originally a term of opprobrium for Hungarian immigrants to the U.S. "Wonk" is an Eastern prep school term referring to all those who do not have the "honk" voice, i.e., all who are non-aristocratic. There is some conjecture that the term is derived in the natural Anglophile bias of Eastern social life from the English adjective "wonky," meaning unsteady, shaky, feeble, awry, off. In current use, however, "wonk" is a vague, all-inclusive term, closely akin to the terms "wog" and "wop," which are sometimes used at Eastern prep schools to refer to all the rest of humanity.

plus straight to Wall Street or mid-Manhattan, for he is *one of us,* you understand—

Very ironic—the way New Yorkers at every class level delighted for years in *My Fair Lady* on stage and screen. *My Fair Lady,* of course, was the musical version of Shaw's play, *Pygmalion,* about a linguistics professor, Henry Higgins, turning a Cockney flower seller into a lady of Society by upgrading her accent. That silly, stuffy English class system!—whereupon we all settled back and just enjoyed the Cinderella love story. It was just as well. It is probably a good thing that no Henry Higgins has come along to wake up New York to the phonetic truth about class and status in this city . . .

I have just been talking to a man who could do it if he chose to, however. Professor Marshall D. Berger of CCNY. Berger is one of the country's leading geographical linguists, one of those extraordinary people, like Henry Lee Smith of the old radio days, who can listen to a man for thirty seconds and tell what part of what state he was raised in. Berger is a big man, tall, husky, casual. He is forty-seven years old and has lived in New York since he was thirteen and his family moved from Buffalo to Liberty Avenue in the East New York section of Brooklyn, where the kids all thought it was odd to the point of *weird* that he said things like *core*-respondence instead of *cah*-respondence and referred to the well-known game of *go'f* as *gawlf.* He wrote an honors thesis at CCNY in 1941 on "The Sources of New York Speech," and then a doctoral dissertation at Columbia on "American-English Pronunciations of Russian-born Immigrants." And so for the past twenty-seven years he has been doomed by his own brilliance to listen, day in and day out, to New Yorkers unconsciously confessing their ancestry, their status, their social yearnings, every time they open their struggling lips.

"This is a very sensitive area you're asking me about," he tells me. "The first thing you'll notice is that people in New York always invent euphemisms when they get on the subject of speech. They don't want to talk about ethnic background or class. In fact, people, it seems to me, are much more candid about their sex life than their status. Class—there's the truly taboo subject. So they invent euphemisms. They talk about a 'Brooklyn' accent or a 'Bronx' accent, when what they're really talking about are working-class and lower-middle-class accents found all over the city. Years ago, when Brooklyn was still a big farm, they talked about the 'Bowery' accent."

Berger's own voice sounds to me like Radio Announcer Rugged, if you know that sound. In any case—

"Even the newspaper, at this late date, observe the taboo. I remember the *Post*'s biographical sketch of a local college president. 'His speech betrays his Bronx origins,' they wrote. They were talking about 'lower class' and I suppose the readers get the point, but everyone observes the taboo.

"The same goes for 'New York accent.' Nothing pleases most New Yorkers more than to be told that they've 'lost their New York accent.' This is ironic, on the face of it, since New York is one of the great cosmopolitan centers of the world. But what they're thinking about, of course, is class. 'I've lost my lower-class accent,' they're thinking. Incidentally, people who tell you 'I've lost this or that accent' or 'I really don't have any accent any more' are almost invariably fooling themselves. What they've done in most cases is change a couple of obvious vowels or consonants—they may have changed their pronunciation of "example" from *ex-EHM-ple,* which is lower class or lower middle class, to *ex-AM-ple,* or something of the sort—but they've seldom changed their basic pattern. Even broadcasters."

The glorious New York accent!

In 'is town deh's nuh-uhn doin at da foist of da week, so I was lookin at a likka avatisement an I bought a bah-uhl an relaxed.

All this glorious dropping of *r*'s and *g*'s and *d*'s and muffing of the voiceless linguadental fricative (turning the *th* sound into *d*) and reducing vowels until they almost disappear—the usual explanation has been the waves of immigrants to New York in the 1890s and early 1900s. New York, of course, had had waves of immigrants before. But they were chiefly northern Europeans, Irish, German, Dutch, English, and they were middle as well as lower class. The new immigrants were chiefly from eastern and southern Europe, and they were lower class: Italians, Ukrainians, Poles, Russians, Greeks, Eastern European Jews, speaking Italian, Greek, Yiddish, Russian and other Slavic tongues. Part of the "New York" accent that developed was a blend of the new speech patterns with English words.

For example, of the new tongues only Greek had the *th* sound. The result was millions of New Yorkers saying *wid* for "with" and *dis* for "this." Or: in Yiddish a *t* in the middle of a word, like "winter," was pronounced much more emphatically than it is in English. To this day the New Yorker who says win-*ta* or fundamen-*t*al is usually someone from a home where Yiddish was spoken. Likewise the heavily accented *g,* as in *sin-ga* for "singer" and *Lon Gy-land* for "Long Island." Other innovations were in rhythm. Some of the most flamboyant came from southern Italian and Sicilian lower-class speech, with the old . . . *So I says to my brudd'n'law, "Awriiide, so whaddya wan me to do, I says to him, whaddya whaddya or sump'm?"*

These were all foreign flavors coming into New York English, but many of the elements of the "New York" accent had been here for years before the 1890 wave of immigrants; notably, such things as *dis* for "this" and *foist* for "first." Berger's theory hits on a far more subtle point. Namely, street masculinity. Here were millions of working-class people massed into lower Manhattan, and their sons fell into the street life. On the street the big thing was physical competition, even if it was only stickball or, today, rock'em games of basketball on a concrete slab shooting for a basket with a metal backboard and a rim with no net on it . . . In any case, the emphasis was always on the large muscles.

For a start, the street thing led to rapid speech in which words are swallowed whole, *r*'s are dropped, vowels are reduced to the vanishing point and even some hard consonants disappear. A three-syllable word like "memory" gets reduced to one and a half or less: *m'm'r.* "Bottle" becomes *bah-uhl,* "little" becomes *lih-uhl.* A pronunciation like *lih-uhl* is what is known as a glottal stop, in which the double *t* is replaced by what is in fact a miniature cough. It is common in New York City, although in England, among the lower classes, the glottal stop sometimes replaces *p*'s and *k*'s as well as *t*'s. Street masculinity has also led New Yorkers to carry their tongues low in their mouths like dockworkers' forearms. The result is some heavy handling of many consonants. *T*'s and *d*'s get dropped or mushed around. Most people's speech patterns are set between the ages of five and fifteen, and they are not likely to revamp them in any thorough way after that without something on the order of dramatic training. Often not even that will do it. A boy growing up on the street may unconsciously scorn the kind of delicate muscle play an upper-class boy learns in articulating words. The fancy work with the tip of the tongue in pronouncing "portraiture," for example, may strike him as effete, even epicene. It seems to me that when it comes to prep school *honks* like Averell Harriman or Thomas Hoving—well, it doesn't matter how many worlds they have conquered or how old they are. As soon as they open their mouths, a bell goes off in the brains of most local-bred New York males: *sissy*. Here are a coupla kids who woulda got *mashed* in the street life. Mayor Lindsay (St. Paul's) suffers slightly from this disability.

Women generally try much harder than men in New York to escape from the rockbottom working-class accents, but they are often unaware of where the true . . . *honk-wonk* divide lies. They tug and pull on their accents, but often only get them into a form that the upper orders can laugh at in musical comedies. There is the musical comedy working girl, for example, who is always saying, Oh, Mr. Steiiiiiin, I had such a foiiiiin toiiiiime—pronouncing the *i* as if she has wrapped it around a Clorox bottle. In real life she is not a lower-class girl at all, but lower middle class.

The lower-middle-class girl who says *toiiiiime* may also be aware, instinctively, that the muscle-bound tongue accounts for much of the lower-class sound. So she begins using her tongue in a vigorous way in pronouncing all sorts of things—only she overdoes it. She shoves her words all over the place but still doesn't hit them cleanly. This is the common phenomenon of the beautiful girl— "but she ruined it as soon as she opened her mouth." Here she is with her Twiggy eyes, Eve Nelson curly look, a wool jersey mini from Plymouth's, patent leather pseudo-Guccis from A. S. Beck— and a huge rosy lingual blob roiling around between her orthodontic teeth.

The *oi* sound in *toiiiiime,* by the way, is not to be confused with the so-called "Brooklyn" *oi* sound comedians always used to mimic: *"Da oily boid gets da woim," "She read da New Yoik Woild," "She lives on Toity-toid Street."* These are all examples of dropping *r*'s and substituting *oi* for the *er* sound. Today you are only likely to hear it from older working-class people, such as some of the old cab drivers. This is one lower-class sound that dates back well before 1890 and is not even a peculiarly New York pronunciation. The same sound—it is actually closer to *ui* than *oi,* more like *fuist* than *foist*—can be heard today in two Southern port cities, Charleston, South Carolina, and New Orleans, among both upper- and lower-class people. A century ago upper-class New Yorkers used the same pronunciation, only with a slightly flutier intonation. Sort of the way Berger's old party pronounced "Twenty-*thuid* Street." About half a century ago upper-class New Yorkers began changing their pronunciation of "first" from a flutey *fuist* to a Boston or English *fuhst.*

This is all *r*-dropping, as I say, and it is one of the most subtle and vital matters in phonetic social climbing in New York. This is where middle-class strivers get caught out—as usual, I suppose. The New Yorker who has risen above *wid* and ex*ehm*ple and even *toiiime* and aspires to true *bourgeois* status will next start to re-place all the *r*'s he or his family has been dropping all his life.

"The fi*r*st pahty I went to was in my senya yea*rr*"—and so forth—not realizing that in the upper orders he envies everybody is busy dropping *r*'s like mad, in the ancient English mode.

Many New Yorkers have taken conscious pains to upgrade their accents socially and confidently believe that they now have the neutral accent of "a radio announcer." Three pronunciations almost invariably give them away: *owies* for "always" (lower-class *l*-dropping); *fo'ud* for "forward" (dropping the *r* and the *w*); frank*foot*er for "frankfurter" and *footer moment* for "for the mo-ment" (lower-class *r*-dropping).

"The fact is," Berger tells me, "that a person who tries to change one or two elements in his speech pattern may end up in worse shape than he thought he was in to begin with. His original pattern may not be prestigious, but it may be very good in terms of its internal arrangements, and he may succeed only in upsetting the equilibrium. Frankly, I like to hear people like Vito Battista and Jimmy Breslin talk. They have working-class accents and they don't care who knows it. They're very confident, that's the main thing. 'Dis is da way I tawk an dis is da way I'm *gonna* tawk, an you betta lissen.' A person's speech pattern is bound up with so many things, his personality, his role, his ambitions, that you can't deal with it in isolation or simply in terms of some 'ideal.' "

Yes . . . but! . . . suppose your ideal is to get your daugh-ter's picture on the first page of the Wedlock Section of the Sunday

Times, and not in one of those scrimey little one-paragraphers at the bottom of the page, either—you know those little one-paragraphers, the ones hog-to-jowl up against the Arnold Constable ad with a little headlinette over the paragraph saying,

Horlek-Klotkin.

Suppose you're after the pole position, up at the top of the page, with a big three-column picture all downy silk with back lighting rising up behind her head like a choir of angels are back there singing and glowing, and a true headline proclaiming,

Satterthwaite-Klotkin
Betrothal Announced.

This and other matters in the world of the *honk,* such as the Spotted Bostonian and the Locust Valley Lockjaw, and the Dahling, I would like to discuss in the next installment. But I can offer one hint now. One option is to do what Mrs. Bouvier did with her daughter Jacqueline. Namely, pack her off to a country boarding school, from whence she can return to New York bearing what the press chooses to call a "little girl voice" but which is known in the secret *honk* world as the "Southern 45-degree Upturn," in which your daughter turns her mouth up 45 degrees at either end, then her eyeballs, and says,

Ah you rilly an ahkitect?
Ah you rilly a docta?
Ah you rilly a Senata?

And travel *fuhst* class forever after.

PART II

Another Test

The subject should read the following sentence out loud. He should not study it first but should, rather, simply start reading: "Mary is having a merry Christmas in Florida but she is sorry her vacation is ending soon."

The subject, if he is American and white, has just revealed what part of the country he was raised in. For example, if he pronounced "merry" as if it rhymed with "cherry" and "sorry" as if it were spelled *sahrry* and "Florida" as *flahrida,* he was raised in New York City or Hudson County, New Jersey (Hoboken). If he pronounced "merry" as if it were spelled *mairy* and "sorry" as *suwrry* and "Florida" as *Flawrida,* he is from—Pittsburgh. This is an example of "lexical incidence." Pretty deadly business, this lexical incidence. One has only to think of all the aspiring matrons who have come to New York seeking the upper reaches of the social order . . . confident that they have mastered all the tones of the languid New York Social Female accent . . . only to have Pittsburgh or Chicago . . . Midwest! the Balkans of America . . . reeking from their lexical incidence . . . see the fatback Bulgar toads parade about in Bergdorf clothes . . .

The broad *a* has very little social cachet in New York. Quite the opposite, in fact. The broad *a* is part of a pattern known as Upper-Class Schrafft's. They're wonderful women, these old babes of the Upper-Class Schrafft's world. As near as I can make out, they are the wives or widows of men like . . . a chief accountant for an "occasional furniture" wholesaler—Harry Valtin and Kidney-Kurve Koffee-Table King!—or the like, and they were born in South Akron but they have lived in New York thirty years and one thing you have to keep reminding people of in New York is . . . well, your quality . . . And they start about 11 A.M. preparing their faces with EstroDreme Hormonal liquid makeup for Mature Moderns and by 12:30 they're into their three-piece peach wool suits from Best & Co. with fur trim around the collar and the cuffs and a hat with an enormous puffed-up crown of cream-colored velvet sitting up on top of their apricot hair like a wedge of lasagna. By 1 P.M. they are sunk down in a chair and amid the wall-to-wall and the plate glass in the board room of a midtown brokerage house. They take notes when the Automatex quotation comes jiggling and simpering across the Big Board, by way of keeping up appearances. Despite which they are known to the hired help as Board Room Bums. But by 3 P.M. they can—Rapture!—begin to assemble at Schrafft's at 58th Street and Madison Avenue over cheeseburgers or milk shakes, but mainly sundaes with towers of ice cream and nuts and sauces and fudge such as the outside world has never dreamed of, crinkling the liquid base around their eyes in a thousand thoughtful ways and saying to one another:

Ackshew-ly, I think Automatex is *rahther pahst* its peak—all the while eying the great alp of ice cream, the perfect steamy circle of cheeseburger, for the secret art of the midafternoon in Schrafft's, the *pacing* and the Final Shape.

Oh, *ab-slootly,* those computer sort-of-things cahn't possibly lahst—the *pacing,* as I say, and the *final shape.* For it is not enough merely to *consume* the sundae, like an animal. No, one must pace it along with the others at the table so that they don't have some left to look forward to after one has finished one's own. And more important, one's last bite—that Final Shape—must be, in fact, a very replica, a miniature, of the original sundae. They're all sitting in there at Schrafft's at 3 P.M., a great sea of glorious old girls, nursing their sundaes and cheeseburgers down to the perfect Final Shape, as in some Taoist paradigm of macrocosm and microcosm. But wait a minute—one old babe at the table has just ordered a chopped steak:

No, I *cahn't* have to*mah*toes or egg *plahnt.* And the waitress, who has taken all this in, is saying:

Well, do you want french fried po*tah*toes? Or Julienne po*tah*toes? Or mashed po*tah*toes? Or boiled po*tah*toes? Or baked po*tah*toes? Or po*tah*toes au gratin? Or new po*tah*toes? Or po*tah*to chips? Or shoestring po*tah*toes? Or po*tah*to salad? Or hash-brown po*tah*toes?

Po*tah*toes? Is this *mockery*—or is the poor dear attempting to add grace notes to her voice? But it couldn't possibly be mockery, not here. The waitresses here are the most understanding in all of New York, even to the point of knowing, tacitly, about the Final Shape. So that when one's cheeseburger is two-thirds eaten and it is obvious that one has already consumed so much of the cheese that there will not be enough left for the Final Shape, one has only to ask her for more cheese and she will take one's cheeseburger, two-thirds eaten, back and have a slab of cheese *broiled onto* the remains—bliss!

Meanwhile, the true social heavies among New York's old babes will have gathered about 1 P.M. for the Status Lunch, and the accents will be quite different. The Status Lunch is a peculiarly New

York institution in this country, although the same thing goes on in a less manic way in Paris and London. The Status Lunch is where women who have reached the upper social orders gather during the week, so that they may . . . well, simply celebrate their status. They may be at the top through family background or marriage or other good fortune. In any case they are mostly in their late thirties or in their forties or early fifties, starving themselves to near perfection in order to retain . . . *the look,* with just a few piano wires showing in their necks and forearms and the backs of their hands, from where the body packing is deteriorating. Or maybe they have begun to let themselves go into that glorious creamy Camembert look in which the flesh on the shoulders and upper back and the backs of their arms looks like it could be shaped with a butter knife. They are Pucci'd and Gucci'd up to their temporal fossas, Pucci in the dress, Gucci in the shoes and handbags—the Pucci-Gucci girls!—yes. They start pulling into Status Lunch restaurants in the East and West 50s, such as La Grenouille, Lutece, Orsini's, about 1 P.M. and make a great point of calling the maître d' by his first name, which at La Grenouille is Paul, then peer into that ocher golden-mirrored gloom to case the important tables, which are along the walls in the front room, by way of weighing the social weight of today's gathering, as it were. Then they suck in their cheeks—near perfection!—and begin the entrance, looking straight ahead, as if they couldn't be more oblivious of who else is there, but waiting, hopefully, for the *voice*—

Dah-ling dah-ling dah-ling.

There it is!—the *dah-ling* voice, a languid weak baritone, not a man's voice, you understand, but a woman's, *The New York Social Baritone,* like that of a forty-eight-year-old male dwarf who just woke up after smoking three packs of Camels the day before, and then the social kisses, right out in the middle of the restaurant, with everybody locking heads, wincing slightly from the concentration on not actually pressing the lips, which would smudge the lipstick, or maybe even the powder covering the electrolysis lines above the lips, with the Social Baritone *dah-ling* voices beginning to bray softly in each other's ears, like an ensemble of cellos—*we are all here!* This voice cannot be achieved without some ten or fifteen years of smoking cigarettes and drinking whiskey or gin, which literally smoke-cures and pickles the vocal cords and changes them from soprano to the golden richness of baritone. It takes, on the average, at least 13,000 cigarettes over a ten-year period. In pronunciation, the *dah-ling* voice seeks to set itself off from both the urgency (what's going to hit the fan next?) of the lower-class female voice and the usual efficiency (must pronounce everything *correctly*) of the middle-class female voice with a languor and a nasal *honk,* connoting ease, leisure, insouciance. Two techniques are the most vital: dropping *r*'s, as in *dahling,* and pronouncing most accented vowels with a sigh thrown in, particularly the *a*'s and *o*'s, as in—

Dahling, I *caaaaan't.* I just did the *Mehhhht* and you know, the sets were *stunnnnnning,* Myron le Poove I think he is, but it was the most *booooooring*-sawt-of-thing—with the vowels coming out of the nose in gasps as if she is going to run out of gas at any moment.

And *yet!* She has worked on this voice for ten years, producing her deep rich pre-cancerous vocal cords, but it gives off the deadly odor: *parvenu.* The *dahling* voice, heard so often at Status Lunches and country weekends and dinner parties where two wine glasses are used, is almost invariably that of the striver who has come upon the upper-class *honk* voice too late in life. She has picked up a number of key principles: the nasality, the languor, the oiliness, the *r*-dropping. But she does not understand the underlying principle, which is historical. Her attention is fixed upon New York, and as a result her voice takes on a New York theatrical manner, a staginess, in the Tallulah Bankhead mode, which is show-business upper class, not *honk* upper class. The certified *honk* upper-class woman in New York has her attention fixed, phonetically although unconsciously, on Boston and the Richmond-Charleston social axis of the South.

The secret here, as among New York male *honks,* is the boarding school. The outstanding girls' boarding schools are oriented, socially, toward the nineteenth-century upper-class traditions of Boston and the South, which, until after World War I, had far more social clout than the upper-class world of New York. Miss Hall's, Miss Porter's, Westover and Dana Hall are all girls' boarding schools where an old Boston upper-class tradition dominates, just as places like Foxcroft, Madeira, Chatham Hall, Garrison Forest and St. Catherine's are still schools where the Richmond-Charleston tradition dominates. New York girls bring back the Boston or Southern sound in a somewhat crude form, but nevertheless it is not a New York sound. It is neither a street sound nor a theatrical sound nor an English sound. Its components are nasality, languor, oiliness, *r*-dropping—but with shorter, clearer, more open vowels than the *dahling* voice. If the girl has gone to a truly social Southern school, she will tend to have a soft, childish voice. If she has gone to a "Boston" school, the speech will be much brisker and yet still languid and oily, as if lubricated ball bearings were pouring out of both nostrils.

In the nineteenth century, the New York upper classes were much more directly influenced by Boston and the South. Boston overshadowed New York in many phases of business, finance and law and was unquestionably New York's social superior in the area of Culture and the Arts. The New York upper classes had close ties with the Southern upper classes because of the shipping trade, Southern planters came to New York continually for financing, and packet boats loaded with cotton came to New York on the way to England. About 1940, linguists at CCNY made recordings of the voices of old New Yorkers, people in their seventies and eighties, most of them upper middle class, in order to get an idea of what speech patterns were like in New York in the nineteenth century. They tended to speak in a medley of Boston and Southern accents. One old party reminisced about an old structure on 23rd Street as "the old *struk-cha* on *Twenty-thuid* Street," with *struk-cha* a combination of the clipped Boston accent of *struk* and the Boston *r*-dropping of *cha*; and *Twenty-thuid* a case of Southern-style upper class *r*-dropping, substituting a diphthong vowel sound, *ui*, for the standard *er* sound in "third." Socially, New York was considered an exciting but crude town, and New York's upper classes felt the sense of inferiority and preferred to sound like they came from some better spot. Even today some *honks* still use the Southern upper-class pronunciation of *thuid* for "third," although most have shifted over the past half-century to a more Bostonian *thuhd*. They still drop the *r* in any case.

Boys as well as girls, of course, learn the *honk* voice in prep school, and the same principle applies: the voice should suggest a languor that will separate one from the lower orders. The lower jaw is moved much less than in ordinary speech and the words are lifted up over the palate and secreted through the nose rather than merely blurted out of the mouth. The rigidity of the jaw may resemble an affliction to a person who has never watched someone speak this way before. In fact, the E.S.A. (Eastern Socially Attractive) accent that is often heard on the north shore of Long Island in communities such as Huntington and Oyster Bay is known as Locust Valley Lockjaw. The same voice is known in Riverdale as Spotted Bostonian. Socially ambitious people in Riverdale often try to keep their voices up by spending their summers in the select vacation communities of the Boston upper orders on the Maine shore.

Honk voices may fall anywhere in a range from Boston-Honk to New York-Honk. Leaning toward the Boston-Honk would be Averell Harriman (Groton), the late Christian Herter (St. Paul's), the late John F. Kennedy (Choate) and the late Robert F. Kennedy (Milton Academy). The worst liabilities of the *honk* voice to a politician, quite aside from the class overtones, are the monotony and the delicacy and weakness brought about by this sort of voice's emphasis on languor and refinement. Robert Kennedy, like his late brother, had great difficulty in a conventional oratory from a rostrum. His voice was trained in delicacy rather than strength and tended to turn shrill at the very moment when the heavy chord should be hit. He always sounded like a seventeen-year-old valedictorian with the goslings. In the case of Harriman and Herter, it was the nerve-gas monotony of the *honk* voice that caused them trouble as much as anything else.

The perfect New York *honk* voice is Huntington Hartford's (St. Paul's). Other notable New York *honks* are Nelson Rockefeller and Robert Dowling, the real estate and investment tycoon. Both Rockefeller and Dowling have the nasality of the *honk* voice but not nearly the delicacy of the same voice as practiced by Mayor Lindsay (St. Paul's). The explanation, most likely, is that both Rockefeller and Dowling went to prep school in the city, Rockefeller at the Lincoln School and Dowling at Cutler. Rockefeller has gradually coarsened his voice for his public appearances. It is a kind of *honk* with a knish jammed in it, although he uses much more a conventional soft *honk* in private conversation. One of the ironies of the 1962 race for governor was that Rockefeller's upper-class voice with a knish in it was so much more effective among the lower-class masses in New York than that of his upper-middle-class opponent, Robert Morgenthau. As a result of his time at Deerfield Academy, Morgenthau's voice had taken on a kind of *honk* subtlety and delicacy that made him, not Rockefeller, sound like the Fauntleroy in the plot.

Lindsay has come down off the *honk* accent somewhat by inserting r's where they would ordinarily be dropped, making his speech sound almost middle class at points. He also refers to St. Paul's as his "high school" from time to time, as if it were nothing more than a kind of Horace Mann or DeWitt Clinton unaccountably set out in Concord, New Hampshire. This is a laugh and a half to all old "Paulies," who are generally fond of St. Paul's reputation as the most snobbish school in America.

Even Amy Vanderbilt has been roughing up her female *honk* accent by adding middle-class r's, perhaps in an unconscious rub-off from the various bourgeois commercial interests with which she is involved. In general, the public spotlight tends to make *honks* nervous about their voices, whether they are politicians or performers or merely celebrities. Very few have the self-assurance to just keep pouring it on, the way Roosevelt did: *I hate wooouugggggg-gghawwwwwwwwwwwggggggghhhhhhhh*—meaning "war."

Boys today at St. Paul's, Groton, Middlesex, Hotchkiss, Deerfield, St. Mark's, St. George's, Exeter, Andover and the rest of them are strangely goosey about it themselves. They are apparently hung up on the masculinity thing, as they might put it, rather preferring to have both the social certification of the languid, delicate *honk* voice and the ruggedness and virility of various street voices. The upshot has been that they have kept the *honk* voice but picked up the spade-dope argot of Greenwich Village, the Lower East Side and other lower-middle-class bohemias, studding the most improbable conversations with the inarticulate litany of "like-I-mean-you-know-man" intoned in a kind of Bugs Bunny-Bobby Kennedy *honk* spew of lubricated B-B's:

Laiike, nyew nyeoow, man, *Ai* mean, *Fisha's* Island is a groove and a gas com*paaaiiihed* to *Deeah* Island and, like, now, *Ai* mean, Wildwood, *Nyew Juhsey,* is *prackly* a *mind-blowagggh* . . .

And the whole *honk* world sinks, *wonking,* into a vast gummy Welt-smeared nostalgia for the mud.

12. Club Power (for Members Only)

Jane Edmunds

"It's all a part of a gentleman's heritage: many a young blue blood was given a life membership to the Racquet Club on his twenty-first birthday."

Back in 1927, when a dollar was a dollar and gentlemen dressed for dinner, a *New York Times* reporter wrote in an article about the Union Club: "When one tires of the feminine idea of comfort, one strolls over to one's club and plunges deep in masculine good living." In 1969, gentlemen are still strolling, cabbing, and running to the safety and privacy of the many private clubs that continue to thrive.

The clubs, naturally, don't have the power or prestige they used to have. Ours is a much more free-form society. But in the history of New York, socially, civically, and politically, the clubs have had a lot of clout. The Union League Club, for example, was instrumental in dissolving the Tweed Ring, electing Benjamin Harrison, creating the Metropolitan Museum of Art, bringing over the Statue of Liberty, founding the Metropolitan Opera, putting up the statue of Lincoln in Union Square, and constructing Grant's Tomb. The Union, the oldest social club in New York, firmly established who the "400" really were, and, by its physical moves, marked the residential boundaries of the city. As the same *Times* reporter said on June 26, 1927, "All New York last week noted that great change in the life of the city indicated by the decision of The Union Club to move from 5th to Park. . . . Every new home it has found in the last century meant that society had migrated to a center before the march of trade."

But that was then. What are the clubs all about today? Hottest on everyone's mind, of course, is that big bad word of our time: discrimination. Social critic Cleveland Amory foretells doom. He says in *Who Killed Society?* that New York's club life is definitely on the way out because the younger generation will not accept the Anti-Semitism inbred in the older members. What he forgets is that when the old guard is carried out in their red leather chairs, the disenchanted will inherit the clubs. It's purely a matter of patience, which no one is very long on these days. E. Digby Baltzell, in *The Protestant Establishment,* writes with even more gloom from Philadelphia: "A crisis in moral authority has developed in modern America largely because of the WASP establishment's unwillingness, or inability, to share and improve its upper-class traditions by continuously absorbing talented and distinguished members of minority groups into its privileged ranks." The clubs, he says, are the prime example of this "caste" system because "membership in such men's clubs as the Links is a major requirement for eventual assimilation into the establishment." Words of truth for such ingrown cities as Philadelphia, Boston, or Pittsburgh, where the men's clubs are membered with the heads of corporations, state and local government biggies, real estate controllers, etc. Right across the board, the Power Elite in cities *other than New York,* can divide up the spoils over lunch.

This is not as true in New York. But there is still distressing validity to Baltzell's theory. The Power Elite with WASP credentials meet at their clubs to sniff out the big money action over martinis, while the non-WASPs meet in their private dining rooms downtown and sniff out the same action they're drinking over uptown! Exclusion from the WASP clubs is chiefly a *social* slap in the face, but that's more than enough in a status-ridden city.

The clubs are WASP time-bombs, and if their up-tight admissions policies don't ease up before the clock runs out, they will be in deep trouble. Witness the dying social clubs and fraternities at our universities. In the last two years at Princeton, for example, the percentage of sophomores joining the eating clubs has dropped from 91% to 50%. Says the president of Cap and Gown and the Interclub Council, the students are "no longer very interested in the gentlemanly pursuits and pleasures of Fitzgerald's day." So speaks the generation that the Knickerbocker and the Racquet will be depending on ten years hence. And tick tock goes the time-bomb.

Actually, the New York clubs are not powerful or important enough to be taken so seriously. Not all of them are Anti-Semitic. The River Club, the Cosmopolitan Club, the Century Association, and the Harvard Club have been happily electing whomever they *like* for years. These clubs are purely social institutions with the emphasis on the Social Register rather than *Who's Who*. Big business and blue blood are the common denominators, and though briefcases and papers are forbidden in the dining room at *all* the clubs, many is the merger that's been verbally kicked off over the Blue Points.

But who joins which club and why? An easy answer for the younger members.

They join for the facilities, the squash courts, the swimming pools, the convenience, and for personal leverage. "Many's the time older members have sat on the applications of young guys in their companies," a member of the Links said. "They don't want the young guys seeing where they spend their afternoons!" The question of which club and why is an even easier answer for the older members. It's a question that's never even raised. They just naturally joined the same clubs as their grandfathers and fathers. It's all a part of a gentleman's heritage; many a young blue blood was given a life membership to the Racquet Club on his twenty-first birthday.

And then, of course, the club life is not a bad way to live. Broken by all the petty irritations of New York, a member can shuffle unshaven, unpressed and thoroughly undesirable into the Racquet, and while his clothes are being steamed and pressed and his shoes boned, he can be steamed, shaved, trimmed and made once more a presentable gentleman. Theater tickets, dinner reservations, travel plans—all can be arranged by the club. If he's giving a party, the club sends up a bartender or two. After a good weekend in the field, his pheasant and duck are hung and plucked and then stored in his freezer. Upon leaving the Racquet Club, now as shiny as a polished apple, he can step into the club limousine, kept purring outside, and be driven anywhere on Park Avenue for $1.25. Just Park Avenue. But where else would he be going anyway?

The clubs are a great part of the Social Game. Ward McAllister the 19th-century society arbiter who invented the term "the 400," isn't around any longer to pinpoint who's in and who's out. Instead, social sleuths thumb through the Social Register like the Yellow Pages, counting the number and quality of club abbreviations after each name (few men are members of just one club) to find out who the social heavies really are. Like money, it's not important to those who have it, but it can hang up the ones who don't. The clubs are all part of the Label Game, the natural continuation of "Where did you go to school?" and "Who *was* she?" The ones with the best answers and the most exclusive labels have the easiest time getting to wherever they're going. *Fortune* magazine once said, "At the Metropolitan or the Union League or the University . . . you might do a $10,000 deal, but you'd use the Knickerbocker or the Union or the Racquet for $100,000, and then for $1 million you'd have to move on to the Brook or the Links." The initials to look for in the Social Register are: B, C, Cly, Cs, K, L, Ln, Ny, R, Ri, Ul, Un — the full social spectrum of the Top Twelve on the Club Parade.

Un. *The Union Club,* 101 East 69th Street. 1,500 members. Historically, the Union Club, founded in 1836, has to come first because "the mother of clubs" gave birth to many others in the Top Twelve. To forestall the irate letters from the remaining clubs, the rest will be listed alphabetically.

The Union Club spawned the Metropolitan Club when J. Pierpont Morgan, outraged because the Union had blackballed a business associate of his, called up Stanford White and set him to building the Met. The Knickerbocker (like the Lunch Club downtown) was formed from those on the impatient line making up the ten-year waiting list for the big mother.

The Union League Club was born in a political storm during the Civil War. It seems the Union not only retained its Confederate members, but one of the top officers of the Rebs. In a fury, rabid supporters of Abe Lincoln stormed off and founded the Union League. And then there's the Brook story. Two stories in fact. Number one: A member of the Union, Thomas B. Clarke, was trying to have a late dinner there. "The waiters by these signs," he said, "are telling us it's time to leave. One of these days we shall have a club which shall provide its members with continual service." And number two: Two devilish members of the Union were expelled for attempting to poach an egg on an older member's forehead. They subsequently formed the Brook where, presumably, poach-ins were countenanced.

Unruffled, the Union Club droned on according to the 1927 *Times,* "with names that represent great families rather than great individuals . . . assemblages of men who *are* rather than of men who *do.* Their members represent a social tradition, a way of living." So who can blame the Union for not dropping its Southern members. After all, they were Gentlemen, weren't they? And from the Best of Families?

The Union Club today is known to the younger club generation as "everyone's Grandfather's club." On the skids after World War II, the Union was forced to open junior memberships and to solicit new members, which kept the club alive, but with a slight dilution of blood lines. Now they have a waiting list, squash courts, a gym, and a men's locker room with black marble showers. The food is excellent and the chef sends out dinners to members in the neighborhood who can't make it over to the club. Members can bring their wives along for dinner and weekend lunches. There is Book Night, and Art Night, bridge, backgammon, 25¢ billiard games and Cowboy Pool (black tie) tournaments against the Racquet Club. But the Union Club is not where it's happening.

B. *The Brook,* 111 East 54th Street. 700 members. In 1904, one year after his abortive dinner at the Union, Thomas Clarke and a group of his friends stood in front of a brownstone on 35th Street. They took the keys to the front door, tied them to balloons, and sent them, along with all the dinners they were too late to eat, sailing over the rooftops. The motto of the Brook, then and now, is "For men may come and men may go, but I go on forever," and forever it went, offering twenty-four hour service to its pampered members. Said the *Times* in 1927, "The Brook is composed of gentlemen who are not averse to sitting up late, and has a membership that brings both young and old together in companionship."

Today, the Brook has amassed an invaluable collection of art (a Gilbert Stuart "George Washington" for starters), along with George VII silver and pewter. At no other club is a member so well taken care of. A young member who spent several weeks there said, "You could live in it for life with just two shirts. My shoes were boned, the change I'd left in my pockets was stacked on the bureau, and every night my evening clothes were laid out whether I

was going to the RKO 86th Street or the Pierre." The same atmosphere prevailed in the bar and the dining room, where the waiters
all knew the members by name and just toted up how much each
member had drunk and eaten and sent it to him once a month.
Then came a new waiter who knew only one member. The member's bar bill came at the end of the month: $2,600. Now the members sign chits. Sadly, the twenty-four-hour service has gone the
way of all great traditions in the jet age. But one tradition still
stands. Any member who says, "Take the orders," is standing the
whole bar to a round.

What makes the Brook the arena for the million-dollar deal?
Million-dollar members, like David Bruce, our last Ambassador to
London; Charles Engelhard, the Diamond King; William S. Renchard, chairman of Chemical Bank; Walter Hoving, chairman of
Tiffany's, and David Ogilvy, the advertising baron, to name just a
few. Then the men in the public domain, like Angier Biddle Duke,
Kenneth Keating, Claiborne Pell, Admiral Arthur Radford, and
General Matthew Ridgway. "I walked into the Brook for lunch,"
another young member said, "just after the 1960 West Virginia
primary. And here was this guy sitting in the corner and he was
running for the Presidency and no one was talking to him. He was
reading a book, for God's sake! So I sat beside him at lunch and
you can't talk about politics or business because it's a social club.
Everyone was saying, 'How nice to see you back in New York,' and
'How's your father?' and during lunch we chatted about sailing.
Sailing!" In *Who's Who,* the only club John F. Kennedy listed after
his name was the Brook.

C. *The Century Association,* 7 West 43rd Street. 2,000 members. The Century is something else. Unlike some of the other social
clubs whose members are homogenized and whose backgrounds
are Xeroxes of one another, Centurions are as diverse as men can
be. The membership is made up of "Authors, Artists, and Amateurs of letters and the fine arts," the category "Amateur" expanding to "gentlemen of any occupation, provided their breadth of
interest and qualities of mind and imagination make them sympathetic, stimulating, and congenial companions in a society of authors and artists." The rumor that the Century takes only two men
from any profession is wrong. There are many lawyers, stockbrokers and bankers on the rolls, but never a lawyer who is just a law-

yer. Though he may be known in one camp as an authority on anti-
trust, he's a Centurion because he's also an authority on, say,
Mayan culture. A Park Avenue doctor who coddles little old ladies
is a Centurion because he also happens to be a concert pianist.

Merged with the Sketch Club in 1847, and then absorbing the
Column, a literary society whose original silver lamp (1825) still
burns at all Century meetings, it is "a talking club"; it has no athletic facilities except a pool table. And talk they do, at the long
table, over lunch and dinner. No member is ever introduced to another, nor is a member's occupation ever asked about. Since every
Centurion is a person of renown, the answers to both questions are
expected to be general knowledge. Even drinking has a discreet air
to it. The Century Martini (Century Manhattan, etc.) is served in a
silver mug which is actually *two* drinks "to satisfy both the preprandial appetite and the preprandial conscience," explained Russell Lynes at the 1968 dinner for new members.

Becoming a Centurion is not easy. The Stim Committee (Committee for the Stimulation of Membership) meets every month to
decide who they want to share the long table with. (They meet *sub-
rosa*—literally. A rose is hung from the chandelier to alert and
divert the other members.) If a candidate makes it through Stim,
then a member is found to propose him, at least ten letters from
members must be written for him, and then, and only then, does
the Membership Committee submit his name to the full membership for possible election. Who's made it through? Such a mixed
bag as Whitney North Seymour, Louis Auchincloss, George Plimp-
ton, and Grayson Kirk. And you might have a drink with Eli Whitney Debevoise, C. P. Snow, Ogden Nash, Paul Nitze, or Arthur Lee
Kinsolving, Jr. Or you sit down to dinner with Dean Rusk, Ved
Mehta, S. J. Perelman, John V. Lindsay or Nelson A. Rockefeller.

There are art exhibits at the Century, musicales, and speakers.
There are Fortnightly Dinners held every six weeks, the American
Garlic Society cooks up a feast of fumes once a year, there's a
group that meets to read Chaucer, and, until recently, a Monday
Evening Dinner Club that met on Thursdays.

Cly. *The Colony Club,* 564 Park Avenue. 2,500 members. One
of the two ladies' clubs in New York where the porters look like
they're having St. Vitus's Dance pegging the members in and out at
lunchtime, the Colony is housed in a beautiful red brick Georgian

building on the corner of 62nd Street. The ladies sensibly shoe it in and out for lunch, a swim, a game of cards, a new hairdo, tea, dancing classes for the senior members, and the Philharmonic bus which leaves every Friday at 1:25.

The Colony Club is the *crème de la crème* socially and services, among other New York ladies, four Roosevelts, three Pierreponts, Mrs. William Woodward, Mrs. Thomas Lamont, Mrs. Peter Paine, Mrs. Casimir de Rham and Mrs. Fifield Workum. During World War II, gilt chairs were set up in the ballroom, where the members, dressed in waving plumes and high lace collars, were instructed in simple home repairs by the club's head engineer. On the rostrum built for this course was a toilet. Then they ran a first aid course, and applied to the Red Cross for an instructor, but with one condition: the instructor had to be a Colony Club member. Time was, then, that rooms could be rented on a long-term basis, and several ladies lived in the club. One grande dame was expelled after she was discovered washing her underwear in the swimming pool.

Nothing that interesting goes on any more. The hair is Park Avenue traditional, the hems a respectable inch below the knee, the heads have hats, the hands have gloves, the pocketbooks have "old" money in them, and the monograms in the minks are "old family." But it's a nice place to have lunch or tea or dinner or a swim and to order theater tickets. And "it's nice to have 'Cly' after your name in the Social Register," says a non-member, slyly.

Cs. *The Cosmopolitan Club,* 122 East 66th Street. 2,000 members. The Colony Club is *who* you are. The Cosmopolitan Club is *what* you are. The Cos, the other ladies' club in New York, is far less social than her stepsister, since each member has supposedly "done" something or is in the process of "doing." Doing what? Anything, from being a red-hot flower arranger to a doctor specializing in cancer research. Obviously, not all the 2,000 members are two-stepping around town doing good works, so there is the large contingent of the tweed suit, tweed hat and tweed pocketbook-to-match type that seems to crop up in any group of women larger than ten.

The Cosmopolitan Club is very active, and there are committees on finance, house, decorating, flower arranging, planting, reciprocal clubs, art, drama, music, library, public interests, and the United Nations. They have speakers, put on theatricals and musical evenings. As one member puts it: "We are fed from within." And "fed" from such members, as Katharine Cornell, Cornelia Otis Skinner, Mrs. Oscar Hammerstein II, Mrs. Richard Rodgers, Mrs. Eero Saarinen, all four Rockefeller wives (Mrs. Mary C.), the headmistresses of Spence, Hewitts, and Chapin, and Dr. Margaret Mead. Many of the husbands of Cosmopolitan members belong to the Century, which, though different in the sex of its members, is the same in spirit.

The Cosmopolitan was founded by a bunch of nannies who wanted a place to get together on their days off. Their employers took it over in 1911, and the nannies went back to the Mother Goose Playground. Like the Colony Club, the Cosmopolitan is the scene for many of the coming-out parties and wedding receptions of New York's own, and in the June crush the rice thrown at yesterday's reception crunches under foot as you head in for today's.

K. *The Knickerbocker Club,* 807 Fifth Avenue. 650 members. "The Knick," another of the purely social men's eating clubs, is nestled in a lovely town house on the corner of 62nd Street and Fifth, right across the street from Governor Rockefeller and what used to be President Nixon's New York pad. (Rumor has it that the Knickerbocker invited Nixon to join some years back, and he turned them down. Rockefeller was not so farsighted and was obliged to resign after a "no minority group" fracas in 1968.)

The Harmonie Club, 4 East 60th Street. The Social Register doesn't see fit to list the oldest and most prestigious Jewish club in America. Formed in 1852, Harmonie is the fourth oldest club in New York and is as publicity shy as it is venerable.

Writing about the late 19th century, Stephen Birmingham in *Our Crowd* calls Harmonie "the select German-Jewish counterpart of men's clubs of the era" with the emphasis firmly on "German." For forty-one years, German was the only language spoken in the club, a portrait of the Kaiser hung in the front hall, and the club itself was called "Harmonie Gesellschaft." Such mega-buck New Yorkers as the families Lehman, Loeb, Warburg and Seligman headed the membership list, though at that point in time, they were also accepted as members in the two most exclusive clubs, the Union and the Knickerbocker.

It wasn't until the 20's that the vast migration of Russian and

Eastern European Jews precipitated the beginnings of WASP discrimination and the formation of a caste system within the Jewish establishment itself. Jesse Seligman, a vice president of the Union League Club and one of its founding members, was stunned when his son, Theodore, was blackballed. The membership committee explained to the elder Seligman that it was "not a personal matter in any way, either as to father or son. The objection is purely racial." When Jesse Seligman then tendered his resignation, the membership was equally as stunned and refused to accept it. Nonetheless, he never set foot in the club again. At about the same time, with golf becoming a big snob sport, the emphasis shifted from Harmonie to the Century Country Club in White Plains. Here the Jews discriminated against their own by accepting only German Jews, and even further, only those on Wall Street. There were no "Orientals" and only a few "token Gimbels" from the world of trade.

In 1969, both the Century Country Club and Harmonie are still going strong. Harmonie is still known for its excellent food, has three squash courts, a sauna, and a swimming pool. Again a purely social club, Harmonie takes no political stands outside of monthly forums with speakers on international affairs. A most progressive club, Harmonie was the first men's club in New York to invite ladies to join the members at dinner, and later, to permit ladies to use the squash courts before noon and on Sunday mornings. But as to the number of members, or the dues, or the little tid-bits that give a club its flavor, Harmonie isn't talking.

The Knickerbocker ran into the same financial difficulties the Union Club did after World War II. The deficit at the Knickerbocker was being picked up by William Woodward until he was accidentally shot and killed by his wife. An unknown angel picked up the tab the next year, but the situation was desperate enough for a merger with the Union Club to be considered. At the meeting called to vote on the proposition, an older Knickerbocker member stood and delivered an impassioned speech; in conclusion, he pointed to the Knickerbocker flag, which is light blue, red, and dark blue, and said, "Remember, gentlemen, forever let the blue remain on top!" Unable to face the fact that the merger might let in blood less than blue, the members voted down the merger. It was the club's finest hour. Rockefeller refurbished some of the rooms, a new membership drive was launched, and the Knickerbocker remains independent to this day.

The membership is, in the words of one of its younger members, "old New York cum International." Hugh Auchincloss is a member, as are the three other Rockefeller brothers, C. Douglas Dillon, and Arthur Houghton. The International group kicks off with Prince Amyn M. Aga Khan, Count Alessandro de Guiccioli Asarta, Lord Camoys, Count Charles-Louis de Brissac Cosse, and H. E. Francisco Cancino Cuevas. Not surprisingly, The Knickerbocker has reciprocal visitors' privileges with Brooks's in London, the Jockey Club and the Nouveau Cercle in Paris, Circolo della Caccia in Rome and the Kildare Street Club in Dublin.

L. *The Leash,* 41 East 63rd Street. 125 members. Time was when gentlemen slipped out after dinner at home ostensibly to take their dogs for a walk. Walk they did, directly to the saloons on Third Avenue, where the dogs were leashed up outside and the masters got tanked up inside. When the saloons were closed during Prohibition, the Leash Club opened.

The original members were and still are, big dog people, like Basil Stetson (Norwich terriers and Irish wolfhounds) and Sam Boykin, Jr. (Boykin spaniels, natch). The Leash sponsors the Westminster Dog Show, and many of the officers of the Leash are also officers of the Westminster Kennel Club.

The Leash is lunch only, when the members swap hunting stories. Beyond dog shows, the Leash also runs quail, pheasant and turkey shoots for its members. Salmon fishing on the Restigouche in New Brunswick is also a big club project. In the bar of the clubhouse each member has a locker shaped like a kennel, with his own kennel mark on it. And when the clubhouse is closed on holidays or weekends, each member has his own key to let himself in. All he need do is sign for whatever he eats or drinks. A very snappy little club, the Leash.

Ln. *The Links,* 36 East 62nd Street. 900 members. The other arena for the million-dollar deal. As the senior partner of one of the biggest investment banking firms says to his young partner, "Now it's time for you to join a club—either the Brook or the Links." In *The Protestant Establishment,* E. Digby Baltzell writes that the Links is "the New York rendezvous of the national corporate establishment." But to one of the few non-business members, the Links is a pretty scary scene. "The last time I was in the bar," he said, "Nixon was in one group, Juan Trippe was heading up another group, and Tom Watson was in a third group. It made me so nervous I haven't been back!"

The Links was founded in 1916 as a golf club, and the constitution still pledges itself to "the game of golf as embodied in its ancient and honorable traditions . . . as it is played in Scotland and as adopted by the Royal and Ancient Golf Club of St. Andrews." But golf handicaps are no longer a big thing here. In the membership list, the "C's" alone list George Champion, ex-chairman of Chase Manhattan; Roy Chapin, ex-president of American Motors; Howard L. Clark, president of American Express; Lucius Clay, senior partner at Lehman Brothers; Lammot du Pont Copeland, chairman of du Pont, and Gardner Cowles of Cowles Publishing. You can bet they're not talking about golf.

The big action is at lunch for the moguls who work in midtown, and over drinks and dinner for the downtown boys. The food is reputed to be superb. "The Racquet is like Nathan's compared to the Links," a younger member says. There's a reading room hung with portraits of former Links presidents; the gaming room all set up for pool, backgammon, and cards; and two dining rooms, one for winter, one for summer. The Links keeps a suite of rooms at the Carlton House for members and guests, but women are taboo at the club. An older member is reputed to have said, "I'd rather see the end of the world than a woman here." Whereas other clubs will cash members' checks for fifty or maybe a hundred dollars, the blank checks at the Links *start* at a hundred.

The power-heavy structure at the Links sometimes has its drawbacks, though. As a partner at Lehman Brothers puts it, "My clients who are great snobs I'll take to the Links. But if I'm having a particularly sensitive evening I'd take him to the River instead. Too many people to run into at the Links."

Ny. *The New York Yacht Club,* 37 West 44th Street. 2,100 members. Obviously, a club of a different color. Here it doesn't matter what your mother's maiden name was or how much capital you're sitting on but the degree of salt water in your veins. Commodores of yacht clubs from Maine to Florida meet here in the winter to talk it all over. Not all the members are boat owners, but only boat-owning members are allowed to vote.

The New York Yacht Club no longer has any boating facilities, but time was when it had operating yacht clubs all over New York harbor and on Staten Island. Now they have stations as far upstream as Mystic and Newport so their members can moor and grab a hot shower on the mainland. The clubhouse itself is better than any maritime museum. The model room is world famous and is filled to the scuppers with half-models, full-models, and models of the twelve-meters. Any member can mount a half-model of his own boat on the wall—and that costs about half of what his *boat* cost. The dining room looks like the inside of an East Indian merchantman, with overhead beams, pegged bulkheads, dark stained wood, and teak tables, and the club has the most extensive nautical library in the country. The most prized possession, the America's Cup, held for years by the club's successful entries in that most famous international racing competition, sits proudly in a room all by itself, just off the bar.

The club's finest hour is the New York Yacht Club Cruise in the early summer. The smell of the salt air lures even the most conscientious Wall Street tars, and off they go for a week-long series of races. The commodore of the New York Yacht Club, flying the club flag, is always first to leave for the starting line, and the member boats, lined up like baby ducks behind him, finally get down to what they've been paying their dues for all winter.

R. *The Racquet & Tennis Club,* 370 Park Avenue. 2,238 members. The Racquet Club is a world unto itself. First and foremost, it is the singular club for sportsmen. Such venerable "old" New York and sports names as Vanderbilt, Whitney, Van Alen, Gerry, Guest, Hitchcock and Phipps dot the membership lists. For many of these families, the Racquet is their only New York club. Not only yesteryear's names, but such current sports figures as Gene Scott (Davis Cup tennis team), Steve Vehslage, (national squash champion), and the Bostwick boys (court tennis and racquets), are seen flashing through the club in their whites. Of course, the facilities are superb. Between the squash courts (singles and doubles), the racquets courts, the two *court tennis* courts (out of seven in the country), the gym, the Turkish baths, and the swimming pool, more blue bloods work up a sweat here than anywhere in New York.

But the action at the Racquet Club is not all racket and ball. After the Stock Exchange closes, members arrive by cab, subway, and limousine to begin what one younger member describes as "the biggest game in New York." Playing backgammon at the Racquet is not for kids. The game kicks off at twenty-five cents a point, so the average game pot is $200. Average, mind you. Then they get the five-way chouette going, with one man playing the field, and that runs at least $800. All debts are paid on the spot; one member keeps $2,500 in the safe for the day the dice run against him. But the really big game is a kind of three-handed bridge game played on specially designed tables at a penny minimum, but at five cents a point normally, $200 is small change at the end of one of these rubbers. (One shrewd member moved to New Jersey to better his tax picture.) With all this trust-fund gambling going on, it's not surprising that bookies regularly drop off Christmas presents to client-members at the front desk.

And then there are the parties—the wild, howling bachelor dinners suggesting that F. Scott Fitzgerald is alive and well at the Racquet. The governors have made it very plain that private rooms are rented with the full knowledge that he who rents it is responsible for the damage. And with good reason. After one party, the large marble statue in the front hall ended up on the main runway at Kennedy Airport. A waiter was left, bound and gagged, in the closet overnight. In the aftermath, fourteen members and their immediate relatives had to leave the club, in temporary disgrace. At another party, $1,000 worth of china and glass was reportedly smashed, not to mention $800 worth of Chippendale chair.

Not all occasions are so rowdy. On New Year's Day the older members gather, some done up in morning coats, and traditionally sip champagne out of the Sherman Day Cup. And more ladies get their hair done for the Annual Ladies' Day than for any other social event in New York.

Ri. *The River Club,* 447 East 52nd Street. 1,000 members. Another world unto itself, the River Club has two unique things going for it: (1) It is New York's only country club, and (2) it is New

York's only family club. These two plums make it positively the most difficult club to get into, with a bona fide five-year waiting list.

Sitting prettily right on the East River, the River Club is the scene of endless coming-out parties, wedding receptions and private parties. And it's not surprising for a hatted, white-gloved wedding guest to share the revolving door with a hair-netted, Top-Sidered member wielding a tennis racket. The River Club has two indoor tennis courts, East and West, which a member has to book at least a week in advance for prime time. The East Court, with windows on the river, freezes the marrow in the serving arm of the most agile player in the winter, while the windowless West Court is suitable for egg poaching in the summer. Nothing discourages the tennis-playing members, however, and the tournaments have been won by such society aces as Mr. and Mrs. Stanley Rumbough, Jr., Mrs. Ogden White, William du Pont and Alice Marble, Francis X. Shields, and Billy Talbert.

Women can be members in their own right at the River Club, and the vice-president has always been female. After a set or two, the attendant in the ladies' locker room faithfully gathers up the wretched tennis dresses and wraps them in brown paper for the trip home. Children are welcome, and both the tennis courts and swimming pool are available to them in non-adult hours. "It's like East Hampton versus Southampton," said one of the members. "The River Club is quiet—sort of square."

Square though it may be, the club's tennis courts, squash courts, badminton court and swimming pool are rarely empty. There are also very attractive bedrooms and suites, and many of the out-of-town members use the club instead of a hotel. Back in 1930, when it was founded, members used to sail up the river and moor their yachts at the River Club dock. Now the members cab it or arrive in private cars bearing their grand old New York family initials on the license plates.

Ul. *The Union League Club,* 38 East 37th Street. 1,800 members. After its tumultuous and idealistic beginning, the Union League Club has settled down into being a national businessmen's club without the mega-buck power boys who fill the Links. The ULC is constantly getting confused with the Union; many a wedding reception set on 69th Street finds half the guests showing up on 37th Street. But the similarity ends there. There is only a smattering of the social at the Union League Club. As one member puts it, "We don't take any sons or grandsons who live off somebody else's sweat."

Still politically minded (the ULC once passed a law requiring every member to be Republican, then softened it to include "specific men of similar political thinking"), the Union League has portraits of almost every Republican President. Only U.S. citizens are allowed to be members and all must agree [1] to give "absolute and unqualified loyalty to the government of the United States . . . [2] to discountenance and rebuke by moral and social influences, all disloyalty to the Federal Government . . . [3] to pledge . . . collectively and individually to resist to the uttermost every attempt against the territorial integrity of the nation . . . [and 4] to resist and expose corruption and promote reform . . . and to elevate the ideal of American citizenship."

There are three squash courts, a complete gym, sauna, steam room and masseur to knead away Republican tensions, and the ladies are invited. But the Union League Club is no longer where it's at.

Where are the University and the Metropolitan? Well, the University has 3,500 members and is about as cozy as an automobile convention. And the Metropolitan, though a Stanford White original, is not the "Millionaire's Club" it used to be. It has gone the way of very old men, with smatterings of oil- and admen. Besides, according to the really hot pistols on Wall Street, $10,000 deals are now made on street corners.

Then there are the smaller, specialized clubs that the Social Register doesn't recognize, but where the members have much more fun. Like the Anglers' Club, where the members sit around after dinner tying flies. And the Regency and Whist Club, where the members, male and female, gamble away their afternoons over the bridge tables. There's an anti-club club, the Coffee House (1915), which draws literary and professional people to lunch and dinner with the promise of "no officers, no liveries, no tips, no set speeches, no candidates for membership, no charge accounts, no RULES." Then there is Harmonie, the most exclusive and established Jewish club (1852) in New York, where, for the first forty years, only German was spoken. And lately there's been Daphne's, a membership club complete with party girls and the most sought-after club in town, which temporarily closed down but is reopening soon.

So there you have the Top Twelve. The dues run from a low of $180 at the Century to a high of $600 at the Racquet. The lowest initiation fee, $150, is at the Century, and the highest, $500, is at the Racquet. But the money doesn't count. The label does. As long as The Establishment survives, so also will the B, C, R, L, etc. Without these clubs, the last definition of "gentleman" would be lost, along with the last vestiges of pampered luxuries. As Max Beerbohm said, ". . . there is the notepaper, and there are the newspapers, and the cigars at wholesale prices, and the not-to-be-tipped waiters, and other blessings of mankind."

13. The Power to Exclude

Nicholas Pileggi

". . . between one-third and one-half of the East Side's luxury co-ops bar Jews completely or maintain quotas."

There has recently been much attention directed at black anti-Semitism in New York, but an older, lily-white variety still exists among the city's business, political and judicial leaders and continues to go unchallenged by its victims. It exists as a well-known though unspoken conspiracy that separates gentiles and Jews and not only stratifies the city's private schools, charities and cotillions, but also determines where New York's wealthiest, most powerful and most distinguished citizens can live. Restricted housing as practiced against Jews is limited almost exclusively to the city's most luxurious East Side cooperatives, and many of these buildings insist upon such total religious separatism that two very distinct and almost equally powerful establishments have come to live side by side in a state of chilly tolerance. These multi-family buildings, owned by their tenants, have boards of directors who give or withhold approval to prospective owners. Anti-Semitism among members of these boards has long existed and continues to exist although many of the residents of the restricted buildings are among New York's white Anglo-Saxon Protestant establishment and hold high public office, sit on the boards of innumerable philanthropic organizations and frequently act as the stewards, overseers and trustees of the city's moral and ethical life. In fact, religious discrimination against Jews is so rigidly observed in some gentile buildings that an elevator operator at 2 East 70th Street, a cooperative, recently felt free to make an anti-Semitic remark to first-time visitors to the building as he transported them to the apartment of their host. Presumably such employees feel secure in the knowledge that no one even visiting the cooperative is going to be Jewish.

Rather than fight this ethnic quarantine, the city's wealthy, powerful and influential Jews, the traditional victims of this upper-class conspiracy, have simply retired to equally expensive, and equally elegant, East Side cooperative apartments adjoining the gentiles'.

Real estate agents who specialize in luxury co-ops of the economically privileged claim that they can pinpoint building after building along Fifth Avenue and Park Avenue that is either off-limits to Jewish tenants or dominated by them. The buildings may have anywhere from ten to sixty-seven tenant owners, and while many cost hundreds of thousands of dollars, some small apartments can be had for as little as $80,000. While the cost and size of these apartments can be extraordinary (the *Times* real estate section advertised a furnished four-and-a-half-room Fifth Avenue cooperative for $550,000; and when a twenty-four-year-old heiress was married recently it was reported that she "lives in a 29-room cooperative at 120 East End Avenue"), the standard luxury apartment of fourteen rooms costs between $250,000 and $450,000 and has maintenance charges of between $950 and $4,000 a month.

The real estate agents who deal in the restricted cooperative of this type, many of whom are employed by Jewish realtors, have an extensive vocabulary of euphemisms with which to protect all of the participants in this gentlemen's conspiracy from moral embarrassment. Phrases like "It's a quiet building" or "It's a very conservative building" or "I don't think your client will be happy here" are just a few of those used among salesmen to make it perfectly clear that the building in question is not open to Jewish tenants. In such cases these real estate agents, despite the possible loss of tens of thousands of dollars in commissions attached to huge sales, do not even suggest that their Jewish clients attempt to pass the muster of certain Wasp boards.

A list of the city's restricted cooperatives, compiled by just one leading real estate firm, cites ten buildings strung out along Fifth Avenue from 62nd Street to 95th Street, sixteen on Park Avenue between East 65th Street and East 95th Street, eight on East End Avenue, Beekman Place, Mitchell Place, Sutton Place South and Lexington Avenue, and thirty more scattered over East 66th, 67th,

69th, 70th, 72nd, 73rd, 74th, 77th, 79th and 86th Streets. East 72nd Street and East 79th Street between Fifth and Third Avenues are noted as particularly "tough" blocks for Jews.

Essentially, these are the buildings that serve as the New York homes of men who run many of the nation's industries, investment banking firms, brokerages and insurance companies. They are the quiet and discreet residences of the wealthiest and most powerful men in America. Expense is not spared in services and appointments. Elderly white doormen in starched collars leap to the curb whenever a car so much as slows down outside. Well-rubbed furniture and fresh-cut flowers are characteristic. Wood-paneled elevators run by white-gloved operators open onto the foyers of apartments built to a nineteenth-century scale. Servants' quarters large enough to accommodate a middle-class family of four are not unusual (some of the older cooperatives still specify in their leases that the maids' rooms are "to be used by female whites" only).

"It used to be worse," the president of one of the city's largest real estate companies said recently. "Ten years ago there were well over a hundred and fifty of Manhattan's best buildings where a Jewish tenant could not get in. Today I would put that number at about fifty. Most of the buildings that have changed, however, haven't really changed. They've simply acquired a respectable token Jew. It helps. You get a Lehman, a Loeb or a Schiff and you're safe. For instance, the governing board of one Fifth Avenue co-op just rejected an English stockbroker who happened to be Jewish. They felt secure in rejecting him because just a few years ago they had let in a Lehman. If anyone pointed a finger at them they just pointed to their 'house' Lehman. They gave him the ground floor doctor's-office apartment, too. Imagine that! A Lehman on the ground floor.

"Best of all from their point of view"—the realtor winked—"the Lehman they let in doesn't even have Lehman for a last name. He changed it.

"This is what I'm talking about," he continued, pointing to a page in the Manhattan Address Telephone Directory which was lying open on his desk. The book, which lists telephone subscribers by their addresses rather than by their names, is widely used by direct-mailing firms who want to pinpoint residents of high-rent buildings. As he ran his finger down the tenant listings of one building in the East 70s, he read off the names: "Auchincloss, Babcock, Blodgett, Chambers, Chandler, Corbin, Gill, Grimes, Ireland, McCormick, Morey, Peck, Pickhardt, Ripley . . ."

At the bottom of the list his finger rapped a tattoo on the page. "And Dr. Ira S. Wender, Dentist."

He then turned a page, focused his finger on another building and continued reading:

"Campbell, Chaplin, deMuralt, Grover, Kirkland, Loomis, Metcalf, Randolph, Singer . . . Singer!" He arched his brows. "Doctor Singer, em dee.

"Here's another on Park Avenue. This one has a list of names that sound like Groton headmasters. But notice right next door. The very next house—doesn't have a gentile name listed. They're right next to each other. Ninety-nine per cent Jewish and ninety-nine per cent Wasp with a few rich Catholics thrown in. There they are," he continued, waving his hand toward the directory, "the city's leaders, and there's hardly one of them that doesn't sit on some brotherhood forum somewhere."

The wife of a corporation head sat in a small study of her Fifth Avenue apartment recently and told of how a prospective buyer for her apartment failed to get the approval of the cooperative's acceptance board.

"Cooperatives don't disapprove of anyone, you know," she said. "It is simply a matter of *withholding* approval from prospective owners. That's enough to keep someone out. And they don't have to say why they withheld their approval."

The industrialist's wife had agreed to sell her twelve-room cooperative apartment overlooking Central Park to a gentleman for $300,000.

"When we decided to sell, the real estate agent referred to our building as 'a very nice building,' but I hadn't a clue what she really meant.

"There hadn't been an opening in the building in nine years, and that is quite typical of these older, larger places. My husband and I came across our prospective buyer through business. A wonderful gentleman. A charming man. An extremely substantial investment banker.

"Tea was arranged with the building's board. All they needed were a few letters of reference and some indication that he was very rich. He came with letters from two government officials, the president of a major American corporation, that kind of thing. At tea the board was very cordial, so cordial that, although we never heard a thing, we assumed the gentleman had been approved.

"I found out that our gentleman had been turned down a few weeks later when the real estate woman called and asked if another couple could have an appointment to see the apartment. I told her the apartment had already been taken. In fact, in the meantime, the gentleman had given us a check for half the total price. Well, the woman just let it drop that she had heard that our gentleman had been turned down. 'Yours is a very difficult building,' she said.

"I immediately called one of the four members of the board and he told me, 'I'm sorry, but the gentleman failed to get approval of the rest of the board.' I asked why and he said, 'They just felt they could not vote for him.' "

The four members of the co-op's board, as described by the executive's wife, are an ecentric widow, an octogenarian multimillionaire manufacturer, a broker and a young, Ivy League Wall Street lawyer.

"I was hopping mad about it, so I called our gentleman, and at first he said he was willing to fight the damn thing. I even went to the Human Rights people and was assured there would be no publicity. Meanwhile, the gentleman discussed the problem with several friends and they all advised him not to get involved in the messy thing. Some of his friends told him it would look like a grandstand play for publicity. In a few days he decided to take their advice.

"I remember he wound up having to tell real estate people not to show him apartments in buildings in which he would not be welcome. When we put our apartment back on the market one salesman thanked me for calling and said he'd be 'very careful' to whom he would show our apartment. I didn't know whether I was going paranoid or something. They'd never say things directly. There was always lots of beating about bushes. Some agents would even suggest that I be cautious about certain other agents because 'they'll show the apartment to people who couldn't possibly get in.' We put the apartment back on the market on a Thursday and by the next Wednesday we had three offers similar to that of the original gentleman. We had to go through the whole awful tea business again, and I couldn't really take it, but the rental woman said 'there'll be no problem this time.' The couple who took the apartment were terribly rich, in the social register, all of it.

"Nothing has really ever been said, you know," the woman continued. "At first I didn't really know whether this had happened or whether I was reading things into a situation that weren't really there. After that second tea I found out for sure. It was raining and I was waiting for a taxi to take me downtown when the young lawyer who is a member of the co-op board joined me at the door. We decided to share a taxi since they were scarce, and on the way down Fifth Avenue he said, 'Ah! Now *that's* the kind of man we want,' referring to my new buyer. 'He's just a wonderful man. You know we have to keep away from those Seventh Avenue types.' I was so shocked I couldn't say a thing. Seventh Avenue, for godsake, the first gentleman they rejected wasn't even American, he was French."

All cooperatives, according to real estate agents, are by their very nature restricted against one thing or another. Even those cooperatives that do not discriminate against anyone because of race or religion often discriminate against prospective tenant-owners on the basis of their professions. For instance, psychiatrists, diplomats and politicians often find it very difficult to gain admittance in the city's older, more prestigious buildings. Psychiatrists are frequently rejected because tenants envision psychiatric patients wandering the halls of the building. Diplomats are usually rejected because they cannot be held legally accountable for their debts under their diplomatic immunity. Successful politicians and famous personalities are usually rejected because they draw attention to the building, clutter the lobby with newsmen and are required to entertain so often that they dominate the use of elevators and parking spaces.

Harold Braverman of the Anti-Defamation League of B'nai B'rith said that studies conducted by his office show that between one-third and one-half of the East Side's luxury co-ops bar Jews completely or maintain quotas.

"These hard-core buildings," Braverman said, "are mostly limited to the older cooperatives, those built prior to World War II. It's these old line co-ops that are generally the bad ones. The new co-ops are more open in their admittance policies. In 1958 we first studied these prestige co-ops between 42nd Street and 96th Street and Fifth Avenue and the East River, and we found that in at least one-third of the buildings examined there were no Jewish tenants. Five years later, we checked the same buildings and the situation was unchanged. There is still no discernible change."

As part of the ADL's 1958 study, a sampling of thirty-three co-operatives with 1,556 tenants was taken and it was found that thirteen of the buildings excluded Jews. In 1963 the same buildings were rechecked and the same thirteen buildings were still without Jewish tenants. Studies by the ADL also showed that where cooperatives have had one or two token Jewish tenants, that ratio remains constant. Using the same thirty-three buildings the study also found that seven of the thirty-three buildings had between one and three Jewish tenants and that by 1963 the same seven buildings each still had exactly the same number of Jewish tenants.

"It is still very obvious to us that Jewish quotas exist in these cooperative buildings," Braverman continued, "and that these quotas are maintained."

On March 30, 1961, the city's Commission on Human Rights found that the board of governors at 1001 Park Avenue had discriminated against Mr. Alfred R. Bachrach, president of Temple Emanu-El, on the basis of religion. The Park Avenue cooperative denied the ruling and pointed to the fact that it already had one Jewish tenant-owner in the building.

An aide to the commission explained: "The point, of course, is not whether or not a building has accepted a Jewish tenant. The point is that the building not discriminate against another man purely on the basis of his religion, race or color. It is apparently very difficult for lots of people to make that not-so-fine distinction. At the time of the Bachrach case, however, we didn't really have the power the commission has today, and there was no punitive action that could be taken. We pursued the Bachrach case until 1964, since it was the only one of its kind we ever had. Finally a state supreme court judge ruled that we didn't have jurisdiction in the matter.

"Anti-Semitism on that level is doubly difficult to deal with because there is the unmistakable tacit agreement by the power structure of the Jewish community not to say anything. Whether it's natural prejudice, discrimination or just old-fashioned social clannishness, I don't know. What I do know is that the Racquet and Tennis Club is filled with Wasps, the New York Athletic Club is filled with Catholics and the City Athletic Club is filled with Jews. Bachrach made an issue of the situation because he was outraged that it could exist in New York. Most of the other men who have been discriminated against are too busy. 'I don't want to live anywhere I'm not wanted,' they say.

"But as long as the most powerful men and women in the Jewish community refuse to press charges against these practices there is really nothing that we can do about it. What you find on this level is that rather than fight the Wasp establishment, the city's Jewish establishment simply indulges in a similar form of ethnic clannishness. It has created a kind of Park Avenue ghetto.

"A man wants to move into a particular Park Avenue building, and the word gets back that the building's a little 'tight,' and so instead of batting his head against the wall he picks the building next door. It's as nice. It has wooden elevators. It's got Irish doormen. The only difference is that it's filled with people just like himself."

14. Women and Power

Gloria Steinem

"To make this acquisition of the ruling group's privilege and power more or less permanent, all women have to do is marry it. The method is simple, socially approved and sometimes even happy."

Toward the end of Gore Vidal's gossipy, underrated novel, *Washington, D.C.,* a fictional girl named Elizabeth Watress meets President Truman at a Democratic Convention. She is tall, beautiful and well bred. (In fact, her whispery voice, a divorced father who "played polo and drank heavily," a public manner "simulating fear and delight in equal proportions," and her eventual marriage to a handsome young Presidential hopeful, have led a lot of people to think she is based on Jacqueline Bouvier.) So it surprises Clay Overbury, her eventual husband, when she gazes after little homespun Harry Truman with whom she has just shaken hands, and exclaims, " 'He looks so . . . sexy!' "

" 'Sexy? Good God, you *are* crazy. That's the President.' "

" 'And that's what I meant,' said Elizabeth evenly, and Clay laughed. Not many girls were so honest."

If Harry Truman had pursued this advantage (he didn't; even Gore Vidal doesn't go that far), he certainly would have known that it wasn't his beautiful soul and/or body that attracted her. Men wise in the ways of power understand its sexual uses as well. But there are a lot of men, and a surprising number of women, who believe the sexual segregationist argument that women aren't interested in power at all, that something in their genes makes them prefer to be ordered about. While this is true of individual women —and some individual men: think of all those who seek out domineering wives or job hierarchies to take orders from—it turns out to be no more fundamentally true than all the other past myths:

that women enjoyed sex less than men, for instance, or that Negroes were dependent creatures who didn't want power either.

A century ago when Henry Adams wrote *Democracy*, still the only truthful novel about American politics, he understood that women wanted power, and had quite good instincts for using it. But objective truth and social truth are two different things. As a shy pretty Barnard girl explained, surprised to find herself braving police cordons outside a Columbia building, "I guess I'm just finding out that women are people."

New York is probably one of the better places to discover it. Girls come here, after all, for somewhat the same reason that Negroes and homosexuals do: to escape the roles dictated by their background and Conventional Wisdom, and discover what they can do on their own. Frequently, it turns out that they, too, want to see tangible and intangible proofs that they make a difference in the world, that they are unique and valuable people. Power may be a dirty word, especially among New-Left-through-Hippies who fear that it must be manipulative and bad. (Though they have no double standard. Power is bad for anyone, male or female, and "manipulative" is the worst word in the New Left lexicon.) But vitality and a desire to change things are its ingredients, and the under-thirty generation has those in better supply than anyone else. They may not call it "power," but they are certainly seeking to take control away from the Establishment.

Nobody seems to be denying the biological differences, not the Barnard girl, nor those few women in New York who already wield some power. ("You lose interest in everything else for a month or so before childbirth, and several months after," explained a former State Department official, now a political science professor. "Nature takes care of that. But the women I see who continue that single-mindedness year after year because they think they ought to—they end up being a burden to the child.") It's just that the difference is less all-pervasive than it was in the underpopulated day when women had to have a lot of children (and spend all their time running a complicated household) if a few were to survive.

Now motherhood, like sex, dominates a woman's life only by its absence: nothing else may go very well without it, but once that basic need is being fulfilled, there's still a lot of life and interest with no place to go.

But the fact is, even in New York, that the great majority of women don't have the training or opportunity or courage to get and use power on their own. Probably they've been brought up to believe that such ambitions weren't feminine. (And if any group is told its limitations long enough, pretty soon they turn out to be true.) Those who hold jobs of any influence—unless they're totally concerned with makeup, clothes, cooking, and the like, and have no men in the hierarchy under them—are eventually gossiped about as pushy and masculine even now. ("What can I do?" said an unmarried representative of a fashion house who is often thought to be a lesbian. "I can't sleep with every man who thinks that just to disprove it.") It's the same kind of emotional blackmail that used to keep men out of the arts, and push them into various forms of social violence—hunting, street fights, sports and wars— whether they liked it or not.

To accuse someone of not being a "real man" or "real woman" is a potent social weapon in preserving the status quo. During each war, women discover that they can do "masculine" jobs and wield power without losing their femininity, and after each war, they are sent back home (though there are always some who won't go: wars have changed women's status more than any suffrage movement) by men who return with standards unchanged.

Even those who keep their jobs are often apologetic about it, insisting that they just work so the family can have a few more luxuries: an easy way to avoid disapproval that might come from admitting they liked the independence, and even the power. In the women's-rights movement, one of the few instances of taking this emotional blackmail head on came from a distinguished Negro freedwoman named Sojourner Truth. "Nobody ever helps me into carriages or over puddles, or gives me the best place," she said, letting a male critic have it between the eyes, "and ain't I a woman? I have plowed and planted and gathered into barns—and ain't I a woman? I have borne thirteen children, and seen most of 'em sold into slavery, and . . . I cried out with my mother's grief—and ain't I a woman?"

That was more than a hundred years ago, and now, women are defensive about commanding office staffs, much less plowing.

In fact, they don't like to admit the barrier between men's jobs (those with power) and women's jobs (those without). It's sort of embarrassing, and may lead to such dread accusations as being a feminist. (An associate producer of a television talk show, who has now seen five not-very-well-qualified men promoted to be her producers, one by one, while her capabilities are ignored, complained to a station executive. "He thought I was getting 'women's rightsy,'" she said sorrowfully. "Couldn't he at least say *human* rightsy?") But in New York, where hierarchies are probably more modern and flexible than the rest of the country, the barrier still exists. It seems impossible to find a profit-making organization of any size that doesn't discourage women, subtly or not so subtly, from aspiring to positions of any power.

In banks, female "senior tellers" and male "vice-presidents" often do exactly the same job, but salaries and promotional possibilities are as different as the titles. At Time, Inc., men write, edit and get promoted; women research . . . and then research some more. Television has women with "associate" and "assistant" in their titles, but almost none (outside public service and kiddie programs) are allowed to be full-fledged writers, producers, and directors. *The New York Times* employs more women than Negroes ("Only because," said one disgruntled newswoman, "we have a Women's Page and no Negro Page"), but they are nowhere to be seen in Editorial Board lunches or the decision-making process. Women are illustrators but rarely art directors. J. Walter Thompson and other big advertising agencies don't encourage women account executives, "because the client might not like it," the advertising successes of Mary Wells and June Trahey notwithstanding.

Politics is probably the worst of all. Even Robert Kennedy couldn't help Ronnie Eldridge, an eminently capable young politician who was then a district leader, into the job of New York county leader once occupied by Carmine de Sapio. Kennedy thought she could handle it well, but the Reform Democrats hesitated, largely because they didn't want a woman.

Sometimes women do well outside an organization, or by starting their own business, but in general, they just aren't considered eligible for power. Caroline Bird, who has done the best book on this barrier, *Born Female: The High Cost of Keeping Women Down,* comes to the conclusion that powerful women—like Mary Wells or Judge Constance Baker Motley or even Geraldine Stutz of

Bendel's or Mildred Custin of Bonwit's, though fashion merchandising is traditionally a field more open to women—have gained their positions because of loopholes and idiosyncrasies in the system, not because of any liberated attitude in the system itself.

In 1944 when he wrote *The American Dilemma,* Gunnar Myrdal added a parallel between women and Negroes. Both groups, he noted, had been slowed down by the same crippling stereotypes: smaller brains, childlike nature, limited ambition, limited skills, roles as sex-objects-only, and so forth. Neither group liked the comparison very much, but now that Negroes are throwing off these stereotypes so insidious that they themselves had sometimes believed them, women are beginning to think twice about the similarities, in kind if not degree.

Of course, the big difference is mobility: even in work, women have more leeway, and socially, their mobility is almost limitless. Spongelike, they acquire the status (even, temporarily, some of the power) of the man they're with; so much so that it's part of every girl's experience to be treated as two entirely different people just because she's changed escorts.

To make this acquisition of the ruling group's privilege and power more or less permanent, all woman have to do is marry it. The method is simple, socially approved and sometimes even happy. Women have been doing it for years. Of course, this practice makes for June-January matches: figuring out a man's power potential when he's still in his twenties isn't easy, and an important older man usually expects a wife to be young and to look good; that's her part of the bargain. (New York is full of this sort of marriage, from the short bald men and tall blond wives in the Stage Delicatessen to distinguished lawyers and Vassar graduates on Sutton Place. Washington would be even fuller, if only politicians could get divorced.) Marrying for power is slightly more involved than marrying for money and doesn't get boring nearly as fast. The wife must have had some dim appreciation of her husband's work, after all, in order to figure out how powerful he was in the first place. They may even be working together, though never on an equal basis. (Secretaries marry executives, students marry professors, researchers marry television producers; it's a giant step, an Instant Promotion.) Only Helen Gurley Brown has grasped and openly written about the idea that office proximity is to the making of "good" marriages what social connections and dowries used to be.

The bargain, if both parties are clear about it, may work out well. The man gets the pleasure of a new and admiring audience for his power displays, and the wife has the exhilarating experience of being on the Inside; a place she would never be allowed by herself. Moreover, she herself becomes a power symbol: youth and beauty well displayed. Sexually and even financially, her husband may view her that way. The sales people at David Webb, the jewelers who have a genteel air of having seen everything, nod solemnly at arguments like (one woman to another hesitating over $18,000 earrings) "It's a wife's *duty* to be a showcase for her husband's power and success."

Unfortunately, the man—believing the convention that women aren't interested in power—may assume she loves him for himself. There isn't much excuse for this, considering that he has probably used power calculatingly in order to attract her. (It's a standard part of the New York mating game for men to have girls pick them up at the office, whereupon they push every button and issue orders to every employee in sight. Lunch in executive dining rooms, police escorts on the way to the theater, celebrities produced for all occasions, a personal wine cellar at one or several restaurants: all this heavy artillery may be brought out for the wooing.) But it still comes as an unpleasant surprise to many men when they produce three Broadway flops in a row and their wives' affection cools; or when "the other man" turns out to be someone older, less attractive, but more powerful; or when they retire to long-anticipated lives of comfort and leisure, and their wives want a divorce.

They are even surprised, if not quite so unpleasantly, when their wives try to exert power through them. The simplest form is the marital "we" (as in *"We* just bought a big British company" or "Bernstein is doing *our* symphony" or "We knew *we* should have rewritten the second act"), even though the wife has had nothing to do with it. This taking of unearned credit is as ridiculous (especially when spoken by the twenty-two-year-old wife of some hardworking man) as it is popular.

Finally, there is the wife who tries to make her husband's power her own, who wants to select the companies he buys, or the scripts he produces, or the political strategy he campaigns with. She is much more admirable (at least she's trying to earn some of the credit she's taking), but if ability doesn't go along with desire to influence, she may be the most destructive in the end. There are always stories in New York of talented husbands who haven't got this or that job because they come as a package with interfering wives. The name of one movie producer gets groans from directors. His wife insists on showing up to interfere at all production meetings.

The wife looking for power and the husband who has it are dependent on a lot of outside circumstances at best. But the difference between public and private conclusions about women and power comes out in odd ways.

In Washington, for instance, it was a much-discussed fact that many of the men around President Kennedy got divorced when the administration ended. Most men assumed that the husbands had wanted out all along, but refrained from leaving because the publicity would be bad. Many of their wives, who worry about what their lives would be like should *their* husbands leave, assumed the same. But several of the hostesses and one woman high up in the State Department—some of the few in Washington with identities not dependent on marriage—wondered if the wives hadn't had something to do with it. "Why stay?" as one hostess said. "The Kennedy court was obviously their high point. Better get out and find some other interesting man fast, because it's going to be straight downhill."

Few wives, even if they have made power marriages, are that clear-eyed about it. Going along with the women-aren't-interested-in-power theory, they may assume that they couldn't possibly be, and therefore the attraction they feel must be something else. Power translates into sex, and admiration into love. But power and sex are only the same in anticipation, so the wife—who still feels her own power urge satisfied through her husband—may find herself having an affair with a more ordinary man, without any thought of leaving her husband. That's the lady married to a bigwig who goes out with her garage attendant on the side.

If she loves him, or is convinced that she does, she often finds herself jealous of the work whose results attracted her in the first place. Political wives who rarely see their husbands except on national holidays and campaign planes; business wives who get tired of having all birthday and Christmas gifts selected by secretaries; every wife of a powerful man who finds she can get anything except his attention: life and fiction are full of them.

"Never marry an important man," said a girl who observed all this from her vantage point as secretary in the White House. "Go out with them or have affairs with them, but find some other kind of husband."

According to Alice Roosevelt Longworth, even Eleanor Roosevelt didn't always enjoy her position. On hearing of her husband's first election to the Presidency, she is supposed to have run from the room in tears, and said, "Now, I've lost my identity." One New York woman complains that people she has had dinner with don't recognize her the next day in the street without her husband's famous face. A woman who marries a powerful man gets an instant identity all right, but it's his.

Still, acquiring power through men remains the only sure-fire acceptable way. Margaret Mead notes that this society approves women's power only if it's been inherited in some sense, and that widows of admired men are therefore the only women leaders to be widely accepted. Inheriting a seat in Congress is liked, but winning it is not. The activism of Eleanor Roosevelt won more affection and less resentment after the death of F.D.R.

Even Jacqueline Kennedy, regarded as ornamental but frivolous before her husband's death, got all kinds of serious suggestions that she become Ambassador to France, or even Johnson's Vice President, immediately after. But as she was quoted in a New York newspaper profile, "There are two kinds of women: those who want power in the world, and those who want power in bed," the clear implication being that she was the latter. And, almost equally clear, that she disapproved of the former.

Some women solve the problem of being limited to one husband's identity by having several. One New York widow is said to have married once for money, once for power, and once for social standing, so that she emerged, if not as herself, at least as the author of an anthology. She fell somewhere between Mrs. Kennedy's categories, but then so do most women. Sexual power may be enough by itself. (As in the case of girls who enjoy conquering powerful men, and thereby making them pathetic and human. "It's hard to explain," said one television actress, who was having an affair with a much-feared Texas business executive, "but seeing him pad around in shorts to bring me breakfast, or knowing he's switching the schedules of millions of dollars and hundreds of lives just so he can get to New York and see me—that gives me some feeling of accomplishment.") Or it may be a direct path to worldly power, as in the case of many girls who marry for it, or get jobs and favors as the result of affairs. But it's rare that the excitement and rewards are totally detached from the outside world.

"Sex," said an English historian, "is woman's only path to power." As women's options increase, that's not much more true than, "The way to a man's heart is through his stomach." But it is likely that, as long as power is seen by some women as a peculiarly male attribute which only men can confer, they will go right on confusing sex with power.

It's no accident that politicians have to devote less time and trouble to the seduction of women than anyone, possibly including male movie stars. And it's no accident that political conventions, not to mention White House workers of almost any rank, are surrounded by dozens of otherwise well-bred girls who are strangely willing. As Arthur Koestler wrote, quoting a European woman who was interested only in important men, "It's like going to bed with history."

The power-through-men theory can produce very constructive marriages and good partnerships. One of the best examples is Clementine Churchill, who simply made a decision when she married young Winston, not yet a leader of any kind: she would devote herself to him totally, to the exclusion of any separate life of her own, and chances of the couple's success in the world would depend totally on his tastes and decisions. Mrs. Leland Hayward, an adopted New Yorker who was married to Sir Winston's son, the late Randolph Churchill, believes that this investment of time and loyalty had a lot to do with Churchill's later power and success.

"Clemmie never did many of the things that other wives enjoyed —dinner parties, going out with her own friends, anything—unless it happened to be part of her husband's life, too. His friends were hers, his enemies were her enemies. I think that unquestioning support did a lot for him, especially during the middle years when his career seemed to be over. I wonder about a man like Duff Cooper

[a diplomat and a wartime cabinet officer]. He was very intelligent, very talented. His wife was a good wife, but she wasn't interested in politics, and so tended to have her own dinner parties and
activities. Would he have been more of a force had his wife been
like Clemmie? I don't know; it seems possible."

But, as Mrs. Hayward also observed, this kind of devotion
doesn't always get rewarded these days. "Too many first wives,"
she said, "find themselves exchanged for younger ones when the
lean years are over." Certainly, the number of divorces right out of
medical school, with men no longer interested in the girls who
worked to help put them through, has become a kind of joke
around colleges. Very few women find themselves married to a
man of potential power, much less greatness, whether they can recognize it or not. But this kind of partnership is still possible, and
may contribute to the rise of a powerful man.

Whether out of love and devotion or cynicism and necessity, the
truth is that most women will have to exercise their much-denied
but very much alive instincts for power through men for a while
yet, at least until the generation now in college starts taking over
the control centers. Young girls are refusing to be emotionally
blackmailed into domesticity in the same way that boys no longer
fall for the real-men-go-out-and-fight tradition, but the change will
take a long time.

Because women *don't* have power in this country or this city
except as consumers. (Which is exactly parallel to a voter's power
to run Washington. There is a choice between candidates, or
among brand names, but very little influence on what's presented
for that choice.) Or as a nuisance. (Large numbers can occasionally make enough noise so that men act just so the noise will stop.)
The myth of economic Momism that grew up in the '50s—based
on women's new consumer power, and the rise of Madison Avenue
—is, when it comes to real power and control, just that: a myth.
Women make, have, and inherit a great deal less money, and what
they do have (even the greatly exaggerated number of rich widows) is usually controlled by men. They do very poorly at getting
into the knowledge elite. (Nine per cent of professors are women;
6 per cent of doctors, much less than in so-called underdeveloped
countries; 3 per cent of all lawyers; and 1 per cent of engineers.
Professional schools habitually discourage women, and so do most

of the teachers and career advisers they meet along the way.) Of the income elite, only 5 per cent of all people receiving $10,000 a year or more are women, and that includes the famous rich widows.

Of the prestige elite as taken from *Who's Who in America,* they are 6 per cent. Of the business power elite (executives of corporations and the like), they are 4 per cent. And when it comes to elected officials, judges, and so forth, the percentage is almost nil.

Perhaps if women had more encouragement, more opportunity to gain power on their own, there would be less of the bitterness and hypocrisy that comes from using men for subversive ends. If society stopped telling girls that men can and should hand them their total identity on a silver platter, wives wouldn't be so resentful when it didn't happen. And ambitious women could relax, and look for pleasure instead of power in bed.

Men ought to encourage the idea. It might take a load off all of us.

15. Fast Money Power

Chris Welles

"Slow Money men make up most of the business Establishment . . . The Fast Money men are decidedly *nouveau,* often non-WASP, inelegantly energetic, unpossessing of the social graces and unwilling to abide by the rules if they don't feel like it."

Saul P. Steinberg is a Fast Money man.

A new kind of morality has developed in the business world, which is having a large effect on the structure of American capitalism. Its precepts are:

> Slow Money is immoral, and therefore bad.
> Fast Money is moral, and therefore good.

Most businesses are conducted with Slow Money, with only very occasional amounts of Fast Money. A shoe company takes in Slow Money in sales, spends Slow Money for expenses and perhaps for the building of some new shoe factories or even a sock factory. Over the years its reserves of Slow Money accumulate handsomely. It never loses sight of the fact that basically it is in the business of shoes and related products, comfortably and profitably occupying its small niche in the overall economic scheme.

Fast Money is the currency of the conglomerate and takeover movement. In the world of Fast Money, a dollar is never merely one dollar. It is five dollars or more. Money is hypoed, ballooned. Its velocity and vibration rate are multiplied. Its strength and energy are intensified. Even a small amount of Fast Money has a great deal of power, power especially to acquire stagnant pools of Slow Money which can then be transformed into Fast Money. The progression upward can be geometric, not merely arithmetic.

In American business, there has always been a certain amount of Fast Money around. Occasionally whole eras have been dominated by Fast Money, such as the age of the great trusts and cartels in the late nineteenth century. The present era is different for three reasons. First the techniques of making money fast are far more sophisticated, which means that the economic power per dollar is greater than ever before. Second, Fast Money users see no limitations on the kinds of businesses from which Fast Money can be generated and in which Fast Money can be used. They are in the *money* business. Profits are profits, and a man with ingenuity can make money fast no matter the source. Finally, and most important, never before has the distinction between Fast Money and Slow Money been a moral one. Devotees of Fast Money feel that users of Slow Money are encumbrances, sea anchors on economic progress. In refusing to budge their money from its stifling lassitude, its state of *underutilization,* the Slow Money men thereby *relinquish their right to it*. It is not only the moral prerogative but indeed the duty of a Fast Money man to swoop down on a pile of Slow Money, discharge its stodgy guardians and transform it into glorious, healthy, moral activity.

The result has been a vicious and bloody civil war. Slow Money men make up most of the business Establishment. They run the old, traditional well-heeled large corporations that dominate most of the major industries. The Fast Money men are decidedly *nouveau,* often non-Wasp, unseemly ambitious, inelegantly energetic, unpossessing of the social graces and unwilling to abide by the rules if they don't feel like it. In short, they are a *threat*. The current fervor in Washington against mergers and conglomerates may be in part an effort to maintain competition in accordance with the law, etc. But to a substantial degree it is directed toward maintenance of the status quo, toward protection of the Slow Money Establishment from the Fast Money upstarts.

"People want to know: Is it for real? They just can't believe it. But it's all *true.* Okay? Here we are, a *billion-dollar company* doing some of the *most important work in the world* headed by somebody who is only *twenty-nine years old*. Isn't that what the essence of America is all about?"

Fast Money man Saul P. Steinberg, who is only twenty-nine

years old and who looks something like an overgrown, aging former eleven-year-old world chess champion, was looming up over an immense, cluttered desk, his arms waving. His words caromed off overstuffed couches and chairs, polished bookcases and plush, drawn drapes. Steinberg is chairman of Leasco Data Processing Equipment Corporation of Great Neck, Long Island, which a scant three years ago was a mere $7 million company engaged in the relatively prosaic business of leasing computers.

"We do a lot more now," Steinberg thundered, moving rapidly back and forth across the room. "We don't only tell a company what computer they need. Okay? We design the system, the program, run the whole show. We produce the sales models, the inventory projections, everything. They don't even have to get involved. Okay? That's because we bring the *brainware and the hardware together*."

And that's not all. As Leasco's latest annual report puts it, today's problems "are big. They span continents. They involve the very fiber of government, industry and civilization." Fortunately, "at Leasco the power of specialization in software has been synergized into advanced group applications of diverse skills, to penetrate the bedrock of problems." A few pages away, a dazzling color photomontage shows the holes of a computer punch card exploding like fireworks over a night skyline of New York City.

Steinberg suddenly reached down on his desk and snatched a piece of paper. "Look at this," he cried. "A study for the Philippines on the reporting of election results. A systems analysis of military hospitals. A new fuse setback mechanism. A narcotics rehabilitation study. A statewide traffic record reporting system. Here's a secret one from the Government I can't even tell you about. You know, we're actually developing whole towns in several countries where there was nothing but *swamp*. In Iran, using the systems approach, we're turning the desert into productive land. Our Louis Berger division looks at itself as nation builders. Isn't that pretty good? They go into the economics of the area, the communications, the military problems, everything. And we've got techniques to solve the poverty problem, too. We can bring our brainware to bear on the ghetto *block by block!*"

A secretary rushed in with a glass of water and a pill. "My *vitamin!*" he announced. "I was wondering why I was running down."

He went on, "I used to be a selfish little kid, but I've developed a real social conscience."

Saul Steinberg started in business in 1961 with a $25,000 present from his father, who ran a small Brooklyn rubber plant named Ideal Rubber Products. Saul had grown up in Brooklyn and had obtained the idea of going into computer leasing at the Wharton School of Finance and Commerce at the University of Pennsylvania after his instructor had asked him to write his senior thesis on "The Decline and Fall of IBM."

"My instructor was sure IBM was some kind of fandangle," Steinberg recalls, "and he wanted me to go out and prove it. I was the kind of student who was prepared to believe anything was bad, so I accepted the assignment. But after I had gotten into it and done a lot of research, I discovered that it was the instructor who was really the fandangle. IBM, on the other hand, was an incredible, fantastic, brilliantly conceived company with a very rosy future. But when I told him this, he wouldn't believe me. He wouldn't even look at my research. So I ended up having to write on another subject which I don't even remember."

Steinberg's research convinced him there was a lot of money to be made in computers. IBM was charging a 50 per cent premium on rentals which gave the lessee the privilege of returning the machine before the end of the lease. Steinberg reasoned that he might be able to sign up clients for uncancelable, long-term leases at reduced rates. Computer leasing would also step up the power-per-dollar of his available cash. For one thing, he figured he could borrow all the money he needed to buy the computers because the loans could be secured by the leases. And he would be able to take advantage of all sorts of tax benefits, mainly depreciation on his equipment. Shortly after he had set up shop in 200 square feet of dismal cement floor space in a loft in one of Brooklyn's slum sections, he had assets of $100,000 and was $2 million worth of computers in debt.

Already, therefore, $25,000 in Slow Money had been "leveraged" into $2 million worth of profitable financial activity. The more computers he leased, the more his assets grew: $2.4 million in 1963, $4 million in 1964, $7.8 million in 1965. In 1965, Leasco went public which brought in $750,000. The stock—Leasco retained a good percentage of the shares—zoomed upward. Steinberg sold more stock. He sold warrants and convertible debentures and other notes. Assets grew to $21 million in 1966 and $74 million in 1967.

A pause for a word of explanation. The chief method of increasing the power of one's dollar, of making it truly Fast, is to borrow. (Only to oldtimers is it a mark of honor to be debt-free.) The business world is much different from the personal world in this regard. A private individual will almost never be able to borrow more money than he is worth—if he defaults, where will the money come from to pay back the debt? Most likely he will be able to get only a fraction of his total assets. An aggressive, growing corporation, though, can borrow much more, far in excess of its total sales and assets. Banks will loan it money, investors will buy its bonds if they feel the corporation is adroit enough to put all this new money profitably to work and earn enough to pay the interest.

Another method is to sell more stock, as long as enough buyers think the company can earn enough additional profit so that earnings per share on the larger number of shares will only briefly be lower than earnings per share on the original number outstanding. Many corporations, moreover, perform a large number of completely legal accounting manipulations to create more earnings and increase the power of their dollars. (These tactics are continually roundly blasted by more conservative financial observers.)

There is a final method, though, that brings in a lot more money much faster. That is to take control of a good-sized pool of Slow Money which may then be turned into Fast Money, and that is just what Saul Steinberg did last year. Insurance companies, awash with the slowest of Slow Money, have been a favorite target of Fast Money men. Steinberg's choice was the conservative, Philadelphia-based Reliance Insurance Company, whose assets of $700 million were three times Leasco's and whose revenues of $330 million were six times Leasco's. Reliance not only was free of debt, but it had $100 million worth of "surplus surplus"—cash and negotiable securities above the reserves it is required by law to maintain against its outstanding policies. The money was just quietly gathering mildew.

Reliance, and its chairman, W. Addison Roberts, was something less than thrilled with the idea of joining forces with Steinberg. He vigorously resisted the takeover with lawsuits and other devices. "It was pretty tough for them to take," says one participant. "Here they were, an old-line Philadelphia company being attacked by a young Jewish firm from Long Island." But Steinberg's offer of between $80 and $90 worth of Leasco convertible preferred stock and warrants for each share of Reliance, which had recently been selling in the 30s, was so attractive to Reliance shareholders that eventually management had no other choice but to cooperate. (Steinberg, in his business dealings, is really very personable and ingratiating, and much less overbearing than he would appear.) In the end, the Reliance shareholders in effect exchanged their shares in Reliance under the old management for a lot more shares in essentially the same company (plus the much smaller Leasco) run by Saul Steinberg.

It should be mentioned here that Steinberg and other Fast Money men have received considerable assistance in their takeovers from Wall Street's powerful investment banking houses, which, unlike the large commercial banks, contain large numbers of Jews and other non-Wasps. The firm of Cogan, Berlind, Weill & Levitt, which keeps a close surveillance on the insurance field, received nearly $800,000 in fees and commissions for helping Steinberg subdue Reliance. Cogan, Berlind received some interesting Fast Money side benefits, too. Before Steinberg began his takeover bid, the firm had acquired over a million shares of Reliance. A Cogan, Berlind official estimates his concern quadrupled its money, a profit, in other words, of over $75 million.

Steinberg was willing to issue all this new stock (worth about $400 million) for Reliance at such a premium over the company's former market price because he was certain that by turning some of Reliance's Slow Money into Fast Money he could produce a big jump in earnings. He has already set about improving the investment record of the vast portfolio of securities—$300 million in common stock alone—in which Reliance had its premium money invested. He has established an incentive system for the managers of the money and "to provide proper stimulus to our in-house investment people" he has given chunks of the money to the managers of a couple of go-go mutual funds. He expects the yield to move up from the former 3.7 per cent toward 10 per cent.

Steinberg meanwhile has plenty of plans for the surplus surplus. He is interested in acquiring more "software" companies—Leasco already owns a number of them and is, in fact, the world's largest independent computer services organization. He intends to offer a broad range of "information services," especially in the financial field. "Information is money," Steinberg says, "and information is more money if you can *massage* it." (He is an eager student of McLuhan.) Further along are such delights as mammoth "data banks" and huge time-sharing networks connected by communications satellites (Steinberg already has an application in) and stocked with Leasco's own "proprietary software."

Enthused by his success with Reliance, Steinberg a few months ago began eying one of the deepest pools of Slow Money around: The Chemical Bank, the nation's sixth largest commercial bank, with assets of $9 billion. "We have concluded," Steinberg announced, "that our corporate plans and purposes would be enhanced by bringing Leasco's capabilities and assets together with those of a large bank." Terming Leasco an "aggressor," Chemical chairman William S. Renchard testily replied that "we intend to resist this with all the means at our command, which might turn out to be considerable."

They did indeed. Financial executives all over Wall Street had settled back to watch what would have been virtually the ultimate imaginable confrontation of the Establishment vs. the Nouveaus, but it was clear very soon that it was no contest. Even before Steinberg had a chance to make an offer, New York bankers arose as one and made it clear that, if provoked, they could virtually put Leasco out of business—it is after all the commercial banks who make possible much of the credit on which Leasco is based, and their influence spreads throughout the financial community. Meanwhile, as a kind of warning salvo across Leasco's bow, several large institutions (mutual funds, pension funds, etc.) dropped big blocks of Leasco stock on the market, forcing the price down dozens of points. Other institutional holders of Leasco stock issued warnings. Many of Leasco's customers threatened to cancel their contracts. Finally, Leasco's two principal investment bankers—White, Weld, and Lehman Brothers—refused to back a hostile move against Chemical. Steinberg was beaten. "Hostile takeovers of money center banks," he announced meekly, "are against the best interests of the economy because of the danger of upsetting the stability and prestige of the banking system and diminishing public confidence in it."

A number of Establishment companies have been taken over, however, and the remaining ones may not escape as handily as Chemical. Currently the huge B. F. Goodrich rubber company is unleashing an incredible array of legal, political and economic strategies to resist a takeover by Nouveau Ben W. Heineman of Northwest Industries, but the outcome of the struggle is still in doubt. The giant Pan American World Airways was seriously threatened by tiny Resorts International, which owns hotels and a gambling casino in the Bahamas, until the White House intervened and caused pressure against Resorts by the Securities and Exchange Commission and the Civil Aeronautics Board. It is clear that if enough major companies pass from the Establishment into the hands of the likes of Gulf & Western's Charlie Bluhdorn (a high-spirited refugee from Austria), Ling Temco Vought's James Ling (a high school dropout) and AMK's Eli Black (a rabbi's son)—if Fast Money prevails over Slow Money—American capitalism, for better or for worse, will undergo a substantial overhaul.

As for Steinberg, he asserts he is "bloody but unbowed" by his brief tussle with Chemical. In the meantime, the Establishment can take note of the fact that if Steinberg isn't precisely one of them, he is at least learning to live like it. He will soon relocate Leasco on Park Avenue. He recently hired as Leasco's treasurer John T. Leatham, a fast-rising, young (thirty-two) lending officer at the Continental Illinois Bank, whose former chairman was David M. Kennedy, Richard Nixon's Treasury Secretary. Steinberg's stake in Leasco is around $50 million now, and he and his wife have purchased a large house over on the south shore of Long Island.

"It's a modern palatial mansion just like that of any other successful kid of twenty-nine," says Steinberg offhandedly. "You know, twenty-nine rooms, a tennis court, two saunas, six or seven servants, a couple of chauffeurs. *House and Garden* even had my bedroom on the cover. Big deal. I collect art, too. Picasso, Kandinsky, everybody. It's a much fancier place than I ever thought I'd have. I guess I was a little embarrassed when I bought it. But I've learned to live with the burden of my wealth. You gotta understand, a lot of things have happened very quickly."

16. The Power of Positive Fidelity

"Adam Smith"

"The compounding of wealth . . . suggests immortality, [a stronger itch] than the more recognizable and well-advertised summer and seven-year itches."

I have only a footnote, a kind of grace note, to contribute to this social-history business about summer in the city. It is only a footnote because it is very hard to do a story about nothing happening, as Henry James demonstrated in *The Beast in the Jungle*. My footnote concerns what the daddies do in town when the mommies are out at the beach with the kids. You think you know what the daddies are up to? Exactly, it is all part of contemporary mythology, out of *Playboy* by the *Seven Year Itch*. They are getting a flowerpot dropped on their terrace by the redhead above, they are chasing the secretary who always says they are in a meeting when you call, they are up at Daphne's Health Club. Daphne's was a brownstone on Lexington Avenue with a swimming pool, a sauna, masseurs, a game room, movies, drinks, food, and girls, all for $100—until it got busted. Daphne's, now that it is busted, is building up into a regular legend; Daphne's had the late tape from the Coast, Daphne's was so elegant you could sit discussing the utility turnarounds, have a drink, watch a blue movie, and then go home, if you were really feeling strange. "One guy," reported the *News,* as Daphne's was busted, "was even eating grapes." Grapes! Orgy time! It is too bad about Daphne's, it would have been a great summer lightning rod for all the hostile electrical energy of all the wives on the Cape and in the Hamptons and at the various other sandy spits around.

My footnote concerns one typical summer evening spent with

Arthur, a friend of mine and a hedge-fund manager by trade. Arthur and I had been on the phone with this summer stuff—"When are your bride and moppets departing?"—all that terrible emotion-disguising neo-Madison Avenue talk. So we arranged a dinner date, and Arthur said we would go get into some trouble. (One of his partners had a cousin who had these marvelous British secretaries.) Sounds like *Marty,* right? Where are the tomatoes, right? I want to have a date for New Year's Eve, right?

We met at Oscar's, hard by Lehman Brothers off Wall Street.

"Where are the girls?" I said. This is a funny, because at five o'clock on a summer afternoon there are no girls at Oscar's, at least none that I can see. Instead, there is a pride of hedge-fund managers, an exultation of brokers, and a covey of institutional salesmen.

"In a minute," Arthur said, and he introduced me to one of these young tiger partners you see these days. The young tiger partner has this Scheherazade spell on Arthur. The story he is telling Arthur is that they have a nice little hi-fi set company that has always lost just a little money. Now they are going to comb its hair, brush its teeth, put clean short pants on it and sell it to Solitron.

At Oscar's even the waiters are men.

"If we can't find any girls," I suggested, "we could go to a movie. I never did get to see *The Sound of Music.*"

"Sit down," Arthur said. "This is a college friend of mine, I never get to see him any more, it's a nice story. You might make two, three times your money if it's true."

"Of course it's true," said the tiger-partner-college-friend. "We have new management, we have a new product line, and Solitron already wants it."

For two hours and several rounds of drinks we discussed how to clean up this company, what to do with the old management, where we could get some acquisitions for it, what other lines we can introduce. After the drinks we are all salivating like hounds before the hunt, the stock is going to go from 7 to 50, and we can hardly wait to get out and carry the word to the heathen. I looked at my watch.

"It must be time to go meet some girls," I suggested. "The summer is wasting away."

"Right," said Arthur. "One of my partners has this cousin who knows these marvelous British secretaries, like I told you, but I'm starved. Let's go up to a steak house and get something to eat first."

So there we are at McCarthy's on Second Avenue, and at the next table is another sometime-friend of Arthur's who is a vice-president of United Fidelity Life. There are people at insurance companies who sell and then there are vice-presidents who manage what the salesmen sell, and Arthur's friend is one of the latter. He and Arthur trade all the stuff about old Charley and whatever happened to so and so, and then the United Fidelity Life man joins us at our table. The United Fidelity man says he and Arthur should get together more.

"Why don't you get together more?" I asked. It seems a logical question, and I am looking at my watch, because the summer is wasting away.

"You know how it is," the United Fidelity man said. "I live in New Jersey, and our office is uptown, and Arthur's wife and my wife don't hit it off. So summer is the only time we can get together, when the wives are away. Say, Arthur, what would you say the compound growth rate of your fund has been?"

"Arthur and I are going to meet some marvelous British secretaries," I suggested. "Why don't you come along?"

"Over thirty per cent the last couple of years," said Arthur, figuring on the tablecloth.

"Really?" said the United Fidelity Life man. "You know, all the insurance companies are looking for funds with a record, and yours certainly has a record. Would you consider being acquired, if the terms were sexy enough?"

"We want a couple of more years to build it," Arthur said, "but I'm just curious as to what you think it's worth."

"I'd have to talk to the Old Man," said the Fidelity Life man, "but we'd either take the whole thing aboard, and you'd all be vice-presidents, or we'd buy just the name and the assets, and you could start another fund."

"Suppose you just bought the name and the assets," Arthur said. "Just off the top of your head, no commitment."

"Just off the top of my head, no commitment, for a name and assets like yours, we might say something like three-four million in stock, maybe more. Maybe more."

"I haven't talked to any of my partners," Arthur said. "We

haven't even talked about it. But six is more what we had in mind, if we ever did talk."

"Six is not impossible," said the United Fidelity Life man, and I look at my watch again.

"I'm glad we ran into each other," Arthur said, and they made a date for another dinner.

Now Arthur and I are sitting in his mother's apartment, empty for the summer. It is 11:45 P.M. and we have bought two copies of tomorrow's *New York Times,* and the Oppenheimer type we met on Park Avenue as we were getting out of the taxi has left. The Oppenheimer type had a suitcase and had just come back from visiting some pump company newly dubbed Air Pollution Control or something like that. The stock is going to go from 7 to 50. The British secretaries spent their evening blissfully unaware of our plans. Arthur calls his wife in the Hamptons, and the conversation goes something like this:

Arthur: "Hello, sweetheart."

Wife: "What did you wake me up for?"

Arthur: "I'm sorry, honey, but I got a message to call you earlier and then you were out. How are the kids?"

Wife: "Fine, will you bring their raincoats on Friday? I forgot them."

Arthur asks, Why, is it raining? And then errands are traded which need not be detailed.

Wife: "What did you do this evening?"

Arthur: "I had a drink at Oscar's—"

Wife: "What was her name?"

Arthur ignores this, coolly: "—and then we had a steak at McCarthy's and then a beer up here and we're reading the papers."

Wife: "Somebody's there with you?"

Arthur: "Yeah, he's reading the paper."

Wife: "Is she that redhead from the office, or the blonde from the Christmas party?"

Arthur: "That's not so funny. I'll see you Friday night."

Wife: "Arthur, I asked you an honest question, I think you could give me an honest answer. The kids have been fighting all day and I have a headache and you woke me up and you've got some blonde in your own mother's apartment and you won't even talk to me, you won't even try to communicate."

Arthur: "What do you want communicated?"

Wife: "I want to know what you did tonight, and you might at least make up something I could believe."

Arthur: "I had a couple of drinks at Oscar's, a steak at McCarthy's, and a beer here, and in a minute I'm going to get mad."

Wife: "That's better, I can always tell when you're guilty. Is she still there or did you have the decency to send her out? Maybe you're going to *her* apartment."

Arthur: "I'm going to hang up before I get mad."

Wife: "Just tell me what you did tonight. You sound like you're having a ball."

Arthur: "I am having a ball. I got something looks like a sure triple, I got a bid for our outfit of six million dollars, and I saw four guys I never get to see since I've been married. *And I like them.*"

Arthur and his wife hung up.

Well, I don't really expect anybody to believe this, but there it is. One could tell the ladies at the beach that the compounding of wealth is a sexy thing and that commerce is intercourse too, but they would consider it some sort of double entendre. The compounding of wealth, after all, suggests immortality, and the itch for immortality is sometimes even stronger than the more recognizable and well-advertised summer and seven-year itches. Summer is beautiful. You can see all its fruits as the days shorten: they appear as mergers and rekindled friendships and as million-dollar bills.

I have lost the real name of that pump company, but there are still bewitching opportunities and soft summer evenings ahead.

17. Private School Power, or: Life in the Clean Machine

Julie Baumgold

"Macabre tales of ossified applications, filed and forgotten. Supersnubs. Schools that won't even let you apply. Plangent parents before the Community Elders, birth pangs barely over when they are writing checks for scholarship funds."

Remember the messy old woman from Mother Goose? She lived in a shoe. She had so many children she didn't know what to do. Especially about getting them into Riverdale. Collegiate. Maybe Dalton.

A wistful Republican malaise has settled over Mother Goose's playground at East 72nd Street. Two young mamas, more *Vogue* than *Redbook,* rock spanky navy-blue English prams. It is Wednesday, nurse's day off. The Jungle Gym is hung with scions and siblings, their Indian Walk souls taunting the skies. Pretty toy boys. Little girls who curtsy. Nothing elaborate, the bare bob of breeding. The mamas are rocking and talking in the fairytale playground. They are on private schools. Only they do not say the word "private." To them they are just plain *schools.* Assumptions of life. Spence versus Chapin. Trinity versus Collegiate. Buckley. Brearley. Maybe Dalton. But first the nurseries. Christ Church or Everett? The names flip from their tongues so easily. Those brief uncomplicated names. Nothing inspirational like Joan of Arc Junior High. Just the Trads (traditional schools) versus the Progs (progressive). And they love it. It's the most fascinating thing to come along since orthodontia talk. Really everyone's a Raving Expert. Now they are into how Bitsy's boy was rejected at St. Bernard's. They giggle over Maureen's disaster at Chapin. But the Mother Goose malaise gets to them. They shiver in their second best playground furs. Gripped in the gorgeous grimness of it all, one of them tucks a squirrel carriage cover more closely around her future Buckley boy. Or will it be Allen-Stevenson?

At age seventy, Queen Mother Moore, a leader of the black nationalist Republic of New Africa, also has private education on her mind. She wants to form an all-black school commune in the Catskills. The Manhattan Country and Downtown Community schools, too, live in the present tense of New York private education. As do the Co-ops, parent-participating cooperative schools with one-third non-white enrollments. These are private schools gone quasi-public.

But never mind about them. Almost Nobody (with an irrevocable capital) goes there. They go to the Brearley-Buckley schools, which have remained as private as liberally possible. Together these schools constitute a mere 2 per cent of the total school population. Both are alternatives to what the headmaster of Dalton labels "the nonsense called public-school education in New York." The Co-ops might seem a bit pinko to the Mother Goose mummies, but then just look what's happening in some of the presumably safe schools. Financial problems. Expansion. Co-education. Ghetto faces (when they had just gotten around to Negro doctors' children and Jews). Mandarin Chinese courses. Beads at Collegiate. Chinos, if so desired, all year round at Trinity. The atrocious appearance of the Stark's Skulkers (on view slumped against cars at Madison and 78th) or Malkan's Monsters (haunting 79th between First and Second). All this is so expensive. So hard to get into. So very worth it.

In one of the Dead End Kid episodes Huntz Hall, Leo Gorcey and the Bowery Boys en masse attack this sniveling snitch of a rich kid, a real Freddie Bartholomew type. They tear him apart by his fancy seams. Everyone in his heart of hearts says "Good." Give it to him. Maul him, the twerp. Rub his face in the essence of democracy. Until the good cop (played by greasy-haired Ronald Reagan) blumbers in and breaks it up. The private schools have been

Freddie Bartholomews (and Margaret O'Briens) in a world of Bowery Boy public schools. Country gentlemen in seething cities. Orphaned sensibilities.

They have been clean machines, oiled by unreality, with freshly waxed floors, hot nourishing lunches. Headmasters' offices crammed with luster plates and candlesticks, hard shiny-leaved plants which bloomed inexplicably here like nowhere else in the city. Wood furniture scarred with the rounded characters of the private school hand. Midmorning juice and graham crackers. Courteous preserves of Misses in tailored suits of fine English stuff, linen blouses, onyx lapel pins. With Private School Brown hair. Sourball dispositions. To love or hate, but always to fear. They broadcast waves of it. Who ever dared to fill his blue book with a manifesto on how very boring they were instead of taking his Dostoevsky test? And then, as four Dalton students recently did, turn in the manifesto in lieu of Dostoevsky.

Schools have always been big on the teaching of tenses. The stress turns out to be symbolic. They have been living in their tenses. The Imperfect Tense. The Present Tense. The magic world of the Subjunctive "Ifs." The private schools today function in the Past Perfect/Future Tense.

They are facing a reality crisis. No longer can the ark float serenely on seas of applications and drowning humanity. Now, just like their nubile-puerile students, the schools must go on an Identity Quest: the private school as *Bildungsroman*. Confrontation. Cultural shock. The nasty emphasis of real life sticking its grubby fingers in the face of the Universal Lady. Who? Just listen to the voice that answers the phone at these schools. The same clenched tones, reeking of widowed gentility fallen on hard but proud times. Parched. Remote. Restricted. It is the same voice at all the schools, the same lady. The Universal Lady. Nice but distant. Having nothing whatsoever to do with reality. A masterpiece of irrelevance. She is the lady who takes you on tour.

A mother being guided through Spence was shown the dining room. One look and she was suddenly transported back to her own embalmed days at Dana Hall where she choked down stiff meals with the Universal Lady. "My God," she said out loud, "it's just like the dining room at Dana Hall." The claustrophobia in her voice was unmistakable. The loathing and panic. But the Universal Lady with the archaic smile just murmured (they always murmur), "Yes, it is lovely. Isn't it?"

The school crisis means different things to different classes. In the Mother Goose world it means Mummy must take Jennifer Perfect school shopping ad exhaustion while Dad, a walking Fabian Bachrach portrait, must spend part of his day wooing board members for letters. Jennifer must be on her best behavior or, if she is going to Dalton, display ample "pizzaz" (Headmaster Barr defines pizzaz as "a non-possessive love of something outside oneself") as she is inspected like a piece of meat. The Perfects must all show the right degree of togetherness at the interview. They must try to refrain from gasps and jerks in their seats when Jennifer doesn't know an answer and invents a whopping lie. Then they become Strangers in Paradise and take one of those Corridor Grand Tours that rival the European Experience in thoroughness. And, oh yes, Mrs. Perfect must never again on one of those tours point to a closed door and ask ever-so-brightly "What's in there?" Or the Universal Lady will answer, "Mops and brooms," and Jennifer will be rejected and *her life will be ruined*.

In this world it's a matter of getting into the Right nursery school and then, once caught in the Clean Machine, whirlpooled on to Princeton. But even here where people float in on Generational Rights and the wings of Waspdom it's hard. For others, the big strike has led to the big strive. The schools got hundreds of calls from parents wanting to go private. After 450, New Lincoln stopped taking names. Trinity got sixty in one week and was not, when one mother called in mid-November, seeing applicants till mid-February. Ethical Culture told a first-grade mother to call back when her child was in seventh. Town School had a 100 per cent increase in 1968 over 1967. Its acceptance ratio is one out of eighteen. At Ivy League colleges it's about one to six. One school sent out Dear Parent letters when it had fifteen hundred applications for twenty places. "Applications have blossomed to frightening proportions," says Collegiate's headmaster (using the nature metaphor so popular nowadays in describing applications. They are "floods," "avalanches," "mountains").

There are *such* stories to tell. Macabre tales of ossified applications, filed and forgotten. Supersnubs. Schools that won't even let you apply. Plangent parents before the Community Elders, birth pangs barely over when they are writing checks for scholarship funds. It becomes an obsession.

Witness the pretty, very pregnant lady crying in the rain, a two-and-a-half-year-old clutched to her bulging coat. Sobbing because she can't get a taxi and is late for her appointment at Temple Emanu-El Nursery School and she is afraid this will "prejudice" her child's chances. Therein *ruining his life.* Or the mother who enrolled her two-year-old in an art class at the Met, not because she thought his crayonings showed particular promise, but because she thought it would "look good" on his Nursery applications. Or this from a father:

"Last year I tried to get my kid into Dalton. I had letters from four professional athletes (including Dick Lynch and Don Meredith), the late Senator Kennedy, Senator Javits and thirty top businessmen. Our kid is a really sensational ballplayer, but he doesn't get in. A lot of parents think they can worm their way in through the summer programs, but it's a real con job. I can smell a racket real fast. Now the kid is back at The Little Red Schoolhouse where the economic and racial breakdown is terrific. Really sensational."

Says one Chapin mother, "All the horrors are understated. It's simply agony, worse than sorority rush. I could have used a slug of Mary Poppins' tonic while I was making the rounds."

The private school by definition is based on exclusion. Or as Grace and Fred Hechinger call it in their *New York Times Guide to New York City Private Schools,* "selectivity." They have many inventive variations on the theme: X is "highly selective," Y is "very selective," Z is "one of the most highly selective schools in the city," Q is "among the very selective schools in the city." Is this code? The "very selective" schools are, mainly, second rate. The "one of the most highly selective schools in the city" are all academically good except for one which is known for girls in tweed jackets, fawn jodhpurs and $150 custom-made riding boots. Girls who, after receiving an education costing $15,800 sans extras, matriculate around the corner to the famed alma mater of Trish Nixon. What is this nonsense? Selective for what? Against what? Can't a guidebook tell the truth without equivocation? That certain schools take 8 per cent Jews and others 92 per cent? That some schools don't adore Italians or Irish Catholics? That some sell places? That some have suspended all dress and hair regulations, therein changing their physical character, while others are uniformed and astringent? No, everything juicy is to be inferred. It doesn't do to chafe the schools with vulgar fact, such as follows.

First: The private schools of New York, with few exceptions, are not As You Like It, but As *They* Like It. As The People Who Give Them Money Like It. (One outstandingly courageous exception here is Dalton, which, after extensive renovations by a prominent real-estate family, took only one of the clan's eleven applying grandchildren, though they promised the other ten places over a seven-year period. One is sweating out his seven years happily in Browning.)

Second: If a school wants three Puerto Ricans, four Negroes, one hundred and seventy-five bright whites, thirteen friendly, gregarious dumb kids, seven Orientals, fifteen incipient millionaires, three neurotic geniuses, one Swiss, one son of a Spanish grandee and one son of a bitch, all qualified, it can probably pull what it wants right now from its applications (referred to in the non-nature metaphorical collective as "an annoyance of applications").

Third: It takes a lot of bread to get one meatball in.

Fourth: After accepting alumni kids, siblings, returning students, the rich to donate, the poor to be liberal, and the clergy to be holy—the schools have no room left. The scramble in the private school is for a couple of thousand places.

Fifth: Within the clean machine there are gradations. There are specific sets of schools. The Sir Schools (so-called because the masters are addressed as "Sir"): Trinity, Collegiate, St. Bernard's, Buckley, Browning, St. David's, Allen-Stevenson. At kindergarten level Buckley's the one. At the first grade level Collegiate, Trinity, St. Bernard's, Allen-Stevenson, in descending order of difficulty. The Six Curtsying Sisters: Brearley, Spence, Chapin, Nightingale-Bamford, Lenox, Hewitt. Both the Sir Schools and the Six Sisters are academically Trad, Christian-in-character schools. Jews do well in some of these Aryan schools where they want a few white Jews on display. Then there are the Schools on the Hill (the Hill being Van Cortlandt Hill in Riverdale Heights): Riverdale, Fieldston, Horace Mann, large, excellent, co-ed or on the way, and religiously City Mix. The City Progs: Dalton, New Lincoln, Ethical Culture, Walden, Friends. The City Trads: Town, Birch Wathen.

Then the Special Schools: École and Lycée, the UN School—all international in tone, these are the Ivylet League.

Some are simply second string. They are referred to in the vernacular as less pressured, less competitive, lower keyed: Bentley, Calhoun, Rudolph Steiner, Columbia Grammar, Barnard School, Franklin.

Sixth: The schools right down to the nurseries have Reps. Reps are formed on Park benches, in doctors' waiting rooms, on the banquettes of fancy French restaurants or the leatherette seats at Indian Walk shoe store. Brearley is the best girls' school in the city, very aggressive academically and athletically. But Spence is prettier. And less competitive. Oh, how the schools must fight to get rid of their reps nowadays—reputations of exclusivity built by earnest generations.

A Spence mother calls Chapin "locked-in Wasp, with no loosening or limbering in its integration ration or scholarships." She calls Spence a "swinging place" and speaks of mixed religious backgrounds, exotic ethnic minorities (she cites a Jewish-Arab girl), and a teacher who worked for McCarthy. A Chapin mother speaks of pictures of all-white graduating classes hung in the Spence halls and says it is Chapin that is becoming less exclusive. Dalton, which might be the most popular and showbizzy school in the city, is known for its contemporary values. Buckley is known for inbreeding and snobbery so very unadulterated that it becomes at least awesome. Buckley's sources of admission seem to be firmly three-fold: alumni sons, siblings, and the Episcopal School (a nursery) right across the street. Friends Seminary is very good but inconvenient. Collegiate has a wider sort of public and is more liberal. Riverdale is a haven for urbanites and has good college connections. At Trinity not all the parents are so very rich and the boys never talk about or display money. Certain schools are known to accept only family. Others are known deliberately not to favor alumni and siblings: Brearley, Ethical Culture, Dalton, Town.

Then there is the whole You Are Whom You Graduate complex. Or, Whom You Have Now. Or, better still, Whom You Expel. Humphrey Bogart and Truman Capote were Trinity students who left under dubious circumstances. Jackie Kennedy Onassis, Gloria Vanderbilt Cooper, Oona O'Neill Chaplin and the Misses Nixon went to Chapin. Penelope Tree sprouted at Town. Dalton has the Javitses' youngest daughter as well as Walter Cronkite's child, Fritz Weaver's, the Delacortes' son and formerly the children of Sammy Davis, Jr. Ethical Culture has the progeny of Steve Lawrence-Eydie Gorme. Revson's boy is at Trinity, which also had the Ralph Bunches' son. David Susskind's son is at Allen-Stevenson. Sons of *Esquire* editor Harold Hayes, *Time*'s managing editor Henry Grunwald, Edgar Bronfman and the late President Kennedy are at Collegiate. So was the McGeorge Bundy boy; no wonder Headmaster Andrews is off on a six-month Ford Foundation grant. The Rockefeller girls have always gone to Brearley. John Kennedy, Jr., was supposedly asked to leave St. David's, but descendants of Peter Lawford, Romeo Salta, and William Randolph Hearst remain. Also at St. David's is Javier Serra III, grandson of the maker of Tabu perfume, who revealed to the world through the medium of the *Times* that John F. Kennedy, Jr., ate erasers.

You Are also Whom You Have on Your Board. Brearley: Arthur T. Hadley, Mrs. Gabriel Haug, Samuel Pierce, Jr. Collegiate: John S. Hilson, Mrs. John L. Loeb, Clarkson N. Potter, Samuel B. Payne. Hewitt: John G. Husted, and Mrs. Preston Long, Mrs. Clark Roosevelt, Mrs. John M. Schiff. Manhattan County boasts such exotica as Zero Mostel and Robert Motherwell. Chapin: Mrs. Albert H. Gordon, Mrs. Osborn Elliot, Harry W. Havemeyer, William L. Cary. Spence: Mrs. Edgar Bronfman, Mrs. Robert J. Edmondson, Mrs. Harold R. Medina, Mr. Donald Stralem. Dalton: Malcolm Delacorte, the Honorable Roy M. Goodman, Joseph S. Clarke, Jr., Mrs. Schuyler G. Chapin, Lawrence B. Buttenwieser, Albert Bowker, Mrs. Anthony B. Bonaventura. Oh, the weight of these names, the sheer oppressive clout of power!

These realities of private school life discourage absolutely no one from applying, least of all the middle class. The most ferocious desires and disappointments belong to them. It is they or their fathers who walked a mile barefoot through Midwestern or Latvian snows to get to school every morning at 5:30 A.M. who want the "best" education for their children. Set among the smartest students, if one abides by tests geared to middle-class mores such as the white IQ's and ERB's, in whose pamphlet is stated the reassuring fact that the independent school child is, in 97 per cent of tested cases, smarter than his public counterpart. This is all any self-made parent has to hear. In his day, if it wasn't walking the snows, he could go through PS 10 Manhattan at accelerated speeds and be out, say in CCNY, at fourteen or fifteen. He sees this is not going on except in the rare case of a Bronx Science or a Music and Art, and even the specialization of such schools as these is now being questioned. He sees the private schools with a rosily bigoted Old Grad mentality, peculiar to those who are not Old Grads. He sees their safety. Their toney panache. For some parents there is the social motive of advancing through one's child, hinged on the theory that if you beat up a ten-year-old Auchincloss in the Collegiate yard, he is yours for life. Well, so it costs a lot. He is ready to sacrifice. But no altars are open to the public this year.

Many of the schools feel the perplexed indignation of these parents. But middle-class desperation never seems quite as desperate. The parents are moths banging softly against the lightbulb of wisdom. The schools do not want to switch off. There is simply not much they can do. Their giant corporate forehead is wrinkled in pain. Pain for the parents, but mostly pain for themselves, so much so that one of them is translating the schools' Identity Quest into action. Carl Andrews, headmaster of Collegiate, the country's oldest private school, went off for six months to study urban day schools all over the country under the sponsorship of that organization with "a better idea."

Andrews' tone is one of regret as he says, "The schools are entering a period of self-evaluation which will take several years. I hope we can increase in public service all the time. Our existence is based on the theory of choice between public and private education. Our strength has been the public school. If the public schools are strong, we are strong. If they are not, then we have a tendency to become complacent. If the middle class is forced to leave the city we will again become bastions of privilege."

In other words, there is trouble. The bastions are full of velvet problems. Though the demand for their service is greater than the supply to the point of embarrassment, they are poor. They are essentially closed structures and, like European royalty in decadence, they may have inbred and infestered to death.

The schools are moving in four directions to bring themselves into contact with reality. The first two are changes in their life cycle. The second two are what the newborn school must face.

First is *co-education* (mating). Then *expansion* through construction and conglomeration (pregnancy leading to birth). The other two situations are *rising costs* and an academic, social and governmental *liberalization* or loosening.

Sexual segregation in education is an idea we copied from England. Certain schools abolished it under the Progressive Movement, then resored it, and now are banishing it again in favor of the old nursery-school idea of co-education. Trust a three-year-old for the proper instincts. So the schools rush in to foster nymphomaniacal desires to mate or cross-fertilize. Co-education is back on all levels up to the LUX ET VERITAS gates of Yale. Dalton graduates its first co-ed class in 1969. Calhoun is taking in boys, Hackley, girls. Choate is combining with Rosemary Hall. (Its football team is coyly known as "Rosemary's Babies.") Lenox, which did not join with Horace Mann, is reportedly still thinking co-ed. Horace Mann, of course. There's a glimmer in the staidest eye. "Trinity believes there will always be people who think the separate education of boys is a wise thing," says Headmaster Richard Garten. But in its new building Trinity is including separate facilities for girls in its summer program. Ties are kept tied with Nightingale-Bamford and Spence through chummy seminars.

Expansion is even more prevalent under the pressure from alumni, current parents, and the "sheer turmoil" (to quote Headmaster Robert Thomason of Horace Mann) of increased applications. Many of the schools have Five- and Ten-Year Growth Plans. There is a movement to the total grade-spanning school. One way to move is through merger or sub-merger. In favor of expansion by conglomeration is economic survival through a combination of resources (one Latin teacher may reach more students and therein justify his existence to the fullest) and a sharing of such "hardware" as gym and lab equipment. Against Congloms is the loss of esprit of place in the massive institution. Some schools hold out. Town School resisted the Gobbler, Horace Mann, which went on unmiffed to acquire the School for Nursery Years and is now looking frantically for a city-based primary school. It has felt out Lenox and Birch Wathen. Meanwhile Town School has planned its own Five-Year expansion to raise its student body from 225 to 340. Collegiate has just finished a new building and added twenty-five more places. Calhoun and Barnard for Boys talked merger, but that collapsed. Trinity has gone into an $8.4 million investment partnership with the city. Theirs is a pioneer program, combining private and public capital to benefit private education and public middle income housing.

The schools are truly poor little rich kids. Orphans with no State Sugar Daddy. They are tax-exempt and so non-profit that some run at a deficit. If their land has not been inherited it may still have a substantial mortgage. Most of the schools are not endowed. Brearley is a rich exception, but Horace Mann with $750,000 says, "We have virtually no endowment," and means it. Costs are rising and competition is high over teachers' salaries, which consume 50 to 80 per cent of the budgets of many schools. Still they usually pay less than public schools by a hefty two thousand. (The lowest-paying of all are reportedly the Six Sisters.) The new teachers are not the Miss Jean Brodies of this world . . . teaching for love and $1,200 a year pocket money. No, they are often Andover-Harvard bred draft dodgers. Sometimes family men. It is they, with their hair and beards and corduroy clothes who often inspire student rebellions and change. Many of the schools offer no tenure. The headmaster is the captain to an uptight ship. The first crack has already appeared. A few years ago at one of the lesser Hill Schools a new headmaster fired a teacher who had been at the school twenty-five years. A group of teachers and some UFT friends supported her. They were all fired. Nobody much liked this and the school had very little left in the way of faculty. The new teachers would never stand for something like this even when compensated by smaller and calmer classes, shorter hours, parents more awed than interfering, and no need for a state license. Should private-school teachers ever unionize, it could mean the end of private school education in the city.

In addition to teachers' salaries most of the schools must finance their expansion plans. Barr at Dalton finds the situation bleak: "The demands cannot be met. It costs about $5,000 in construction to make one additional place, and at that figure, you won't get the best real estate. For a thousand places that means five million dollars."

Where can they get the money? Government aid has been suggested for years by such as Christopher Jencks of Harvard. Without public money can the schools be expected to face public problems?

Garten of Trinity cites the fact that Pennsylvania provides its private schools with state aid and seconds this on the justification that parents in independent schools are now paying twice for education, once in tax and once in tuition. Thomason of Horace Mann thinks it unlikely that New York could afford aid and thinks it would have to be on the Federal level. Barr of Dalton says the answer is to make tuitions totally tax deductible. Another supporter of government aid to private education is President Nixon, who paid two Chapin tuitions and knows. The schools that favor aid of this sort all shudder at government intervention. Augustus Trowbridge of The Manhattan Country School, however, thinks that community service is the only justification for accepting aid, much in the manner of private museums and private hospitals. But the schools fear having to take any child the government might send their way. This might result in "standardization." Standardization, by the way, is the word that private schools hate most. Their favorite word is "independent," which is what they call themselves. Independent schools. It's so much more democratic than "private," while still retaining memories of the august right to raise one's snub nose.

The schools have found their own answer. They just raise tuitions—$100 a year, 5 per cent, whatever. There's always someone to pay. The Hewitt School catalogue has a label pasted over last year's tuitions. Upon peeling, it reveals a $100 hike at each grade level. If this keeps up they may even be able to print a new brochure.

The cost of one education in the private school system from 1947 to 1966, nursery through college, was $25,650. Today it would cost $35,375, and that is just at this year's prices. The figure includes only straight tuition and none of those fetching extras like lunch (c. $200), milk and cookies (the $45 Mallomar theme), textbooks, Christmas presents, school publications, athletic fees, tests (aptitude tests cost $18 at Spence), diplomas (Hewitt's diploma costs $7 after $15,800) and clothes. Then there is the whole $250-a-Term-to-Ride-in-the-Back-of-the-School-Bus Syndrome. In ten years the same $25,650 education might easily total $45,000 or more, plus extras. Schools argue that all costs are rising, but clearly this system will force out the middle class, leaving only the ultra rich and the ultra poor. The costs of city schools have affected boarding schools whose applications have been a little off. Trinity found a decrease in its annual prep school exodus, with only five out of forty-five boys leaving last year. Yet good old Buckley is still able to say to a parent on the phone, "Of course, you realize *all* our boys go away to school."

The costs so far cited do not take into account the whole "We depend on generosity beyond the fees charged" state of affairs. This generosity is, of course, tax deductible. The parent is bombarded with an incessant gay whirl of theater parties, teas, thrift shops, and school bazaars full of homemade brownies that taste like baked chalk and little hand-knit adorables which have the magical property of making any infant shriek upon bodily contact with them. Yes, a whole holy host of pleasures await the parent, succulent as the Calhoun School's "Sparkling Sweets Soirée." But sweetest of all are the gifts to be given out of pure good will and because one has another child whom he wants to get in. Rodman G. Pellett, headmaster of the new Birch Wathen (with a name reminiscent of the rabbits caged in the old B.W.), says "We rely on our Annual Giving from parents. Some are very very generous." Barr of Dalton says, "People in New York are better able to pay. They are reconciled to pay whatever the costs."

Certain of the schools take advantage of the demand for places. Usually the dirty work is left to the trustees. The whole soiled business of grubbing. Drubbing on the sensitive silken tissues lining the pockets of the unwary and the unwilling. Not that being a trustee on the board of a good school ever hurt anyone's business. Those approaching the trustee for a letter describing little Carter Perfect's multiple perfections are brought to a dignified grovel. They must feel immense gratitude. The trustee, intoxicated by the uprightness of his position, requires nothing in return. But he would not refuse a donation to the school scholarship fund . . . say, $2,500, $1,000 . . . whatever. Then Carter's test scores look so much prettier. Then one overlooks the fact that Carter sucks his thumb in a corner or has a hostile streak. This practice is known as selling places. It is a publicly condemned no-no. But it is a private, albeit limited, fact.

Once money talk arises, the schools begin to look like poorly run businesses. There are the mergers and acquisitions as in the Market. High finance in the funding programs. Contacts to seek and nurture. Corporate structure with the headmaster as big boss, the trustees as executives, the directors of the high and lower schools as junior execs, the admissions as personnel, the teachers as labor cogs. Substitute teachers come and go like office temporaries. An ominous symbol of this in some of the schools is the changeover from the old bulging cowhide briefcase to the trim attaché case (with sliding metallic airline luggage locks which the boys manipulate with the full expertise of Street men). Of course, there is no greater example anywhere of a seller's market than the schools. They are even equipped with tax dodges in tuitions. Serious business-like machines are used. There are computers to figure scholarship costs. Xerox machines for letters and tests, and closed circuit television. In the worksheets for the development of a Ten Year Financial Plan put out by the National Association of Independent Schools (known to all swingers as NAIS) this entry is included under Assumptions for U.S. as a Whole: "World will remain at peace. Neither major war nor widespread disarmament will occur." A flash on the ticker tape, no?

Many of the schools justify their eligibility for public support and, indeed, their very existence, on the ground that they are working models of new educational techniques. In this aim they are limited only by tradition, the archaism of the College Board tests, and parent-teacher mystification when faced by the demands of college acceptance. It is very easy to tell a Prog from a Trad school. Progs move in wondrously collegiate ways their miracles to wreak. They have independent study programs, laboratory and non-graded methods that let the student move at his own rate, and a diversified curriculum with electives. These schools, when they work, are refreshing smiles on the somber country-parson face of education. Why shouldn't the student who has struggled through incalculable hours of homework get a couple of weeks in his senior year to write a string quartet or paint a picture or apprentice himself to a doctor as Horace Mann permits? Why shouldn't he be allowed to choose among eighteen English courses or ten languages or take African History as Dalton encourages under its restored Dalton Plan? (One teacher doubts Dalton will ever be able to return to the old progressivism in its new mood of expansion, which is destructive to close student-teacher contact. Horace Mann ships its eighth-graders off to the John Doer Nature Lab, where the high-rise darlings study science in the field, sleep in open shelters, learn axman-

ship, how to prune trees and generally Fend. At one Trad school
we heard a Latin class discussing the influence of a particular Latin
writer's style on Thurber's prose and thought. Things like this
might go on at Brearley, but who knows? Brearley doesn't talk to
strangers. Chapin has A, B, C groups moving at their own speeds.
The Collegiate curriculum is under a two-year study and "There
will be major changes," says Headmaster Andrews. Schools as diverse as Buckley and New Lincoln use the Initial Teaching Alpha-
bet. Birch Wathen is moving in this direction under Pellett.

Then there are leaders like Orson Bean's Fifteenth Street School,
so Prog that the students don't even have to attend classes. The
headmaster of New Lincoln received a mandate from his board to
make his school a center of creativity. He talks of getting rid of all
grades and letting the students proceed at their own level, having
advanced seniors enrolled in college courses for credit, using students as teachers in the summer programs and full time. Since he
must assure parents that, with all this freedom the student will still
fulfill one of their last golden goals for him and get into college, he
is looking for a city college to work with on a six-year program.

Some schools may want to adventure but cannot because they
are too small and do not have the money for a widespread curriculum. And many students do better under Trad ways. Still there are
the reactionary schools who pride themselves on never having
changed methods of curriculum. They proceed along in lockstep
. . . all the kids on the same paragraph of the same page of the
same book at the same time. Is it any wonder that they turn out
with the same mind?

What of the private-school student? The one not rooting through
the streets. Bid Dink Stover goodbye.

The rhododendron leaves are rustling. A Viva Zapata musta-
chioed fifteen-year-old who still doesn't eat California grapes is
slouching along with a Russian Lit text and a radical publication
tucked under his sweatshirted arm. He meets his drugged girl
friend in the neon corridors of a giant private-school complex. She
has gotten a little dumpy since starting on the Pill. Is this the future
of the Stark's Skulkers?

The private-school student voice has always been limited to the
polite peep of Blue Books, class discussions, a censorable student
paper, a student council, and a social org to debate over the Plaza

versus the Waldorf for school dances. "Student government is a farce in most schools," says Thomason of Horace Mann. And he's right. The baby radical waits trembling on the bench outside the headmaster's office, rehearsing speeches asking for "another chance" before his parents are called. Now with drugs, the Pill, hyper-politics (even if this only means Nixon stickers on the attaché cases at Allen-Stevenson and St. David's), and revolution in the wind, some schools are afraid of eighth-grade Columbias.

This year marked the fall of the jacket, tie and hairline at Horace Mann.

"It was instigated by me, not from a confrontation and demand situation," says Headmaster Thomason proudly. In an explanatory letter to parents he referred to the move as a turning away "from standardization" (*that* word again) and "an alternative to anarchy." It was also pretty crafty, in that it left such issues as curriculum content and graduation requirements in the hands of his faculty and administration. Thomason feels that the students have not got time "to inform themselves properly" on these things and still get into college. He had a further heartwarming message to parents telling them that Horace Mann was giving seminars on the dangers of drugs.

One morning in December, the headmaster of Trinity, Richard Garten, walked into chapel and announced first that a workman had been killed in the construction of their new building site and second, that the Trinity boys, within limits, mind you, had won Trouser Power. Said Garten later that day, "Trinity will move slowly. We always move slowly."

At Collegiate the headmaster is reportedly receptive to liberal ideas but has not had the courage to follow them through. "The dress is still coat and tie. Students do not have free reign here as elsewhere but we're more tolerant today than five years ago," he says. At Chapin the sea-nymph-green jumpers always had to touch the polished floors when the girl knelt, today they have crept to one dowdy inch above the ground when kneeling. The girls now have to wear hats only in the winter. They wear Green Berets. Whenever the Chapin Green Berets misbehave in Schrafft's, the Girl Scouts of America receive the calls of complaint.

Ho hum, yes. But, in context, this is revolutionary.

Private-school children have always had a different look. For one thing: the Posture of Privilege. For the boys this means walking on the balls of their feet, pitched forward as though leaning into the current of a giant magnet aimed up at them from the sidewalk. You can pick them out of a crowd twenty years later in their velvet-collared Chesterfields. For the girls there is always the Spence Posture Award to consider. Should the book be *on* head or *in* head? For another: Private-school children always tend to dress younger. They persist longer in short pants and other Brooks Brothers Anglicisms. Those little princess coats for girls, smocked dresses. Mary Janes, anklet socks.

A strange thing has happened with the private-school uniforms. Designed for economy and democracy, they wound up with the opposite effect. One little girl, after a heady round of school shopping, came home and said, "That school must be a pill, Daddy; they don't even wear uniforms."

In schools where uniforms don't exist, signs of the times can go further. At Dalton, a group of guerrillas barely out of their Monkee phase started an atrociously misspelled underground paper with a Chinese name which, when written out on posters, strongly suggested a classic obscenity. Its editor-founder accused the headmaster of having a dirty mind when he suggested that the title might be offensive.

"Everything is up for grabs" in New Lincoln, according to Haizlip. He went to his high school students and told them that, as adults, they should have equal status with the staff and administration. He said they could dress themselves, have freedom of speech and all the other rights optimistically granted to American citizens under the Constitution.

Another liberalizing trend is apparent. Ever since the election of a Republican-Soul Wasp to the head of this city, interest in urban affairs and community concern has been given the Goodcitykeeping Seal of Approval. Until then, there had always been a well-developed strain of Christmas Basket Charity, but now good works became more important than ever. Candy Basket Night at Chapin was no longer enough. After hours during the school strike Brearley took public-school students into the cold bosom of her gymnasium. The Brearley staff taught them from the goodness of their outrageously underpaid hearts. There were similar programs at Spence and Nightingale-Bamford. Birch Wathen took a student from Brooklyn, but he lasted only two days. Trinity had a neighborhood boy sit in on English classes. But then, Trinity, located at 91st Street between Columbus and Amsterdam, has always been exposed to life right at its *bodega*-ed doorstep. The neighborhood is surrounded by a complex of public schools so big and modern-brickish that they shame the dark Trinity stone. The Trinity boys in their hacking trousers and blazers with the Episcopal cross walk through blocks of black leather and pomaded pompadours. Every year during its bazaar the stately doors open up to the neighborhood, and the West Side is invited in to buy the rejects of the East Side.

"At New Lincoln the kids define themselves in terms of externals. The old Protestant ethic can't work for them. Their studies are not the only thing," says Headmaster Haizlip. New Lincoln, located in a heavily Negro-Puerto Rican district, is in touch with the area schools with which they discuss and share problems. They are active in the Frawley Circle Re-Development area, the Real Great Society Programs, and a 110th Street version of the Street Academies. The Downtown Community School recently held a meeting on "How Best to Educate to Eliminate Racism" in which they mixed such Establishment educators as Harold Taylor and James E. Campbell with Ralph Pointer of I.S. 201 and Queen Mother Moore, both of the public school system. Now even schools like Lenox have planned courses on urban affairs. Who ever heard of the urban affair before Lindsay?

Probably not the thirty-nine members of the Guild of Independent Schools. Their function had been primarily social, limited to the coordination of calendars so that the kids could all be in Palm Beach at the same time. Recently the Guild began talking about scholarships. There was a similar swing at the meeting of the Headmistresses State Association. Recently the Independent Schools Opportunity Project was formed and each member school paid $100 toward black scholarships in a member school. A series of seminars on urban problems has been organized this year for the senior classes of Browning, Collegiate, Trinity, Chapin, Spence and Nightingale-Bamford. The programs include films and visits to the city centers of grief and this, as one member said, "may stimulate some of the students to change the course of their lives." The schools are also participating in running the impressive Harlem

Preparatory School. Riverdale has lent teachers and board members, Trinity has given advice, and some of the parochial schools have lent nuns.

It was also in this time that many of the beknighted wandered out from their White Castles and took a look around and saw that there were black faces and they were suddenly, if not good, then mandatory. So they took some of these faces in and sprinkled them with the hand of a stingy baker putting raisins in big sugar cookies. Public schools are over 50 per cent non-white and private schools are barely 3 per cent. Sometimes it seems as though the black faces are there chiefly for the day the yearbook photographer shows up.

The issue in the more understanding schools is pluralism ("a theory that reality consists of two or more independent elements," according to the Random House dictionary). In the others, and they are the majority, it is simply tokenism. Yet that word falls into the hush of headmasters' offices like "brainwashed" dropped at a Romney dinner party or "bag woman" on the island of Bimini. No, they have taken up the White School's burden, turning away a white minister's daughter for a black minister's daughter and then a black minister's daughter for a welfare child at percentages ranging from zero to thirty. Some Browning students became so discontent with the situation there that, as their senior gift to the school, they gave money earmarked toward a scholarship for a Negro student.

Once the burden is assumed, the schools really do try. They give extra help and even include some uptown addresses in the lists of their doggedly exclusive Goddard-Riverside Community subscription dances.

"They all want more Negro students, but as it is now, the concept is compensatory," says New Lincoln's Dr. Haizlip, the first Negro headmaster in the history of this group of independent schools.

"To actively integrate there must be at least thirty per cent non-white enrollment," says Augustus Trowbridge of the Manhattan Country School.

To some extent the classic school dodge of "They Never Apply" still has validity. Why would any Negro girl rush to Spence to become the first black face in the graduation photographs hung in their halls? Of course, there are always many ways of recruitment: public schools to contact, faculty friends. And after a while, direct applications ensue, as has happened at Manhattan Country and Dalton.

"The schools which say they can't find Negro applicants are putting up a smokescreen. Many Negroes do not apply because they feel they need a strong racial identity, especially early in their education," says Trowbridge.

Early is just the time that the private schools like to get the black students. "Not when they are sixteen and six foot four and have to repeat a year, though then they make wonderful additions to our basketball teams," said one Sir school, somehow forgetting to add that Negro students also have fantastic rhythm in glee club practice.

"New Lincoln is highly verbal. When the Negro kids have not been through the lower grades there's a vast difference, they tend to withdraw. My own bias is that the children need to be together. What the black student needs is a vehicle whereby he can have his own voice, like an Afro Student Union," says Dr. Haizlip.

Some students in schools without Afro concessions manage well.

The question in the French class of the Trad school was *"Votre mère, porte-t-elle des bijoux?"* *"Oui,"* the Negro boy replied smoothly. *"Ah, ça c'est charmant,"* said the teacher. *"Quel genre de bijoux?"* And the student rattled off a list. Necklaces. Bracelets. *"Une tiara?"* *"Oui."* *"Un collier de perles?"* *"Bien sur."* Ice cool.

Haizlip finds a variation in terms of militancy among the black students enrolled in independent schools. "I'm surprised some of the angrier kids don't walk out. But they feel they need some of whitey's magic so they bend and stay."

The choice is to be in with the white middle class but out with their own or out with the middle class and then they are out completely. Then the schools find them a problem.

Dalton, which has always taken the children of professional Negro families, is now involved in a unique integration program. It has adopted a four-block area in East Harlem and placed twelve children from there in their first grade this year. It supplied them with busing, a psychiatric social worker to advise the families, plus the guarantee of a fully paid twelve-year education. Next year it will take another twelve students, and so on, until these students constitute a sixth of the student body. Naturally with a program as well meant and healthy as this, there have been objections from parents because some of the children are discipline problems. Dalton already had to get rid of one teacher whose way of controlling the kids was to take away their lunch.

Harold Taylor, former president of Sarah Lawrence, *the* man to call in for scholarly after-dinner talks on education, believes that "Given the increased need on every income level for private schools there should be more cooperative schools where parents get together and form their own schools while working directly through the public schools. It is the function of the private schools to show how experimental education can work."

Such schools as Harold Taylor recommends already exist on a small scale. They are the 30 per centers (30 or more per cent of the students are non-white) and the Co-op schools. They are alternatives to the brand name private schools.

Among the 30 per centers is the Downtown Community School, 235 East 11th Street. Downtown was founded right after World War II on an "intercultural" theme, as a direct reaction to the racism of Hitler. Many schools were connected in this effort, including certain public schools. The basis of the idea was a broadened curriculum; parent participation and the interrelationship of child, parent, and teacher to one another and to the intercultural theme. A Downtown Community persisted in these methods and beliefs when they were no longer fashionable. It spent twelve years sifting through textbooks to find those most relevant to intercultural themes. When eighth-graders study American culture, the literature and history of minority groups is woven in. Downtown Community justifies the second half of its name by making its materials and curriculum available to anyone who shows interest. The Downtown Community School has recently redefined itself through struggle. It survived a crisis over control similar to that in the public school system. The conflict lay in the board, which was composed equally of faculty and parents. It had to decide whether the school was to become a refuge for middle-class parents or stick to its original founding ideas.

"The board wanted to make us just another private school. We reviewed their relation and the relation of all the parents to the school. We replaced the board by another moving in the direction of our beliefs," says Headmaster Norman Studer.

Modeled in part on the Downtown Community School, Manhat-

tan Country School was begun in 1966 by Gus Trowbridge, a former Dalton teacher. It was formed with good intentions and foundation support and is now struggling to survive. It runs at a deficit,
since tuition covers only half its needs. It gives 20 per cent full
scholarships and 30 per cent partial. It was located symbolically
and very deliberately at East 96th Street, on the borderline between
high-rise residential turf and East Harlem. Right away the difference is obvious. Its theater benefit is *The Great White Hope*. The
dolls in its classrooms are both brown and white. Headmaster-
Founder Trowbridge stated his theme in its prospectus: "Integration is beneficial to all children. Differences must be immediately
experienced to be treasured and understood, and a school which
avoids differences, directly or obliquely, places education outside
the context of living."

Trowbridge believes New York is moving inevitably toward decentralization and that the private schools must connect with this
trend. He sees in place of the giant monolithic public school system
a "series of quasi public-private schools which are sub-contracted
to carry out the work of public education."

A couple of years ago Robert Lowell walked past the teeming
yards of a New York public school. He said he wondered whether
his daughter might not be better off there than in Dalton. When he
returned home, he found his Dalton daughter on her stomach on
the floor coloring in cartoons from *The New Yorker*. Safe. Warm.
Intellectual in a sweet and quiet way. Private.

Private schools never play Show and Tell and yet their whole
existence is an exercise in that game. Sometimes they seem very
remote. Are they Kafka's castle? Parents tangled in the village bureaucratic machine or lost in the climb tend to think so.

Or could they actually be parables of life? Maybe they are life—
complete with its multiple-choice questions, tests and grades, passing and failing and learning. Social Studies. Assignments to accom-
plish. The conjugations of life. The tenses. The fractions. God as
Headmaster. National Loyalty, a version of the old school spirit.
Teachers. Rivals. The love-hates. Of course, socially divisive.
Classrooms that are rooms of fledgling class, to be peered at
through frosty glass by those trying to get in. And upperclassmen,
just that. The uniforms grow up into the uniforms of dictated fash-

ion. How far a step is it from the Chapin monster shoe to the Gucci? The lunchroom grows up to La Caravelle, where you still want to sit at the right table with the right people. The constant struggle to get in. To stay in. To fill up your workbook. To be approved of. All the inflated quibbles of existence tidied up. Once the first application for admission goes out there is no end. Perpetual programmed motion. You are caught in the Clean Machine.

18. The High Price of Power, or: How to Stay (Barely) Solvent on $80,000 a Year

Jane O'Reilly

". . . you will always spend at least 20 per cent more than you make; it's part of 'the Law': current expenditures will expand to override expanded paycheck."

An Englishman who comes to New York from time to time to revive his confidence in the future of Great Britain said last month, "Something has gone wrong here, the city has become a totem of capitalism. It seems that people have forgotten that something is supposed to happen *after* they get the money."

If they have forgotten, it is because few people in New York ever feel they have reached the point *after*. In New York most people *feel* poor, no matter what they earn. People who relate the question of poverty to their own $50,000-a-year lives, in a city where 916,-000 people are on welfare, and where the official United States Government guess at the poverty level is still around $3,500 a year, may seem lacking in compassion and imagination. A $50,000-a-year man is only mildly inconvenienced by living in a city where the cost of living has risen 29 per cent in the last ten years, a number that is statistically shocking when it is compared to the 25.1 per cent rise in the rest of the country.

The reason middle-class New Yorkers feel poor, even with Harlem staring them in the face, is that New York is also the city where the wave of the future is test marketed, the city where ways to make, and spend, money are invented, the city with uncounted resident millionaires. New York is where it's at, and part of "it" is looking up at the millionaires, not down at the welfare cases.

The "it" factor is not included in the Bureau of Labor Statistics City Worker's Family Budget for New York City, which says that, as of spring 1967, it cost $14,868 for a family of four to maintain a good standard of living (up from $5,970 seven years ago, and $900 above the national norm). The BLS budget is reasonable and thorough for, say, a policeman or fireman (the backbone of the middle class) who owns his house in Staten Island or Queens and leads a model life in which his television set plays the largest entertainment role. The budget allows 80 per cent of the total worker's budget to food, housing, transportation, clothing, personal care, medical care and other items used in family living. The rest covers allowances for gifts and contributions, basic life insurance, pensions and social security, taxes and occupational expenses.

The New York City family the BLS budget is talking about lives more expensively but essentially no differently from average families in the rest of the country. It is a family of four: an employed husband, thirty-eight, a wife not employed, and two children: boy thirteen and girl eight. "This type represents a middle stage in the typical family life cycle. The man is presumed to be an experienced worker, well advanced in his trade or profession. He has been married for fifteen years or more. The family group is well established and has average inventories of clothing, household furnishings, etc."

If this average family (we are not concerned with single people, or older couples whose children have left home, or couples without children, because the range of possibilities is much greater for them) is moved into Manhattan, where living "a decent middle-class life" means something far more than living the way most other families live, then the $14,868 is immediately too little.

The City Worker's Budget knows this is true, and speaks of "aspirational needs," and how "the prevailing judgment of the necessary will vary with the changing values of the community, with the advance of scientific knowledge of human needs, with the productive power of the community, and therefore with *what people commonly enjoy and see others enjoying.*" Because New York is the city of great aspirations, as well as being dirty, overcrowded and chaotic, it is not only impossible to live in Manhattan according to prevailing life styles on $14,868 a year, but it is possible for a man earning $80,000 a year to consider himself both middle class and broke.

Naturally, a family living decently and honorably in Queens on $10,000 would be distressed and skeptical to hear it, but proof that such a case is not only possible, but general, lies in the fact that the $80,000-a-year man can say he is broke to his poorer friends without being laughed at.

Sociologists, economists and the mayor's office will also mutter about the idea of placing a man earning $80,000 a year in the middle class. But defining a "decent middle-class life" in Manhattan is not a problem of determining an economic condition so much as it is a problem of style. If the $80,000-a-year man puts himself in the middle class, that says something about his society, and by accepting his definition we can avoid a lot of statistical arguments and come to terms immediately with that isolated hothouse breed, the New Yorker, whose first instinct is to ignore the rest of the country anyway.

LIFE STYLE I:

Basic middle-class model with a couple of options: $18,000 after taxes

"Ten years ago," says Peter, thirty-four-year-old junior executive, husband of Marion and father of two boys, eleven and seven, "we were your basic stripped-down middle-class model: Chinese restaurants on Sunday night, post-graduate decor, the whole bit. I was making about $12,000, and out of the maybe $10,000 that was left to my discretion after taxes, we paid rent (rock bottom West Side rent-controlled five-and-a-half-room apartment for $195), food (always Key Food sale specials), clothes from post-Christmas sales. Our furniture was added to every time somebody died, miscellaneous aunts and so forth. We had a car but the outdoor-parking-lot attendant destroyed it, so we saved on that and borrowed Marion's parents' car for camping vacations. I hate camping.

"Then, this year, I got a big raise, up to about $24,000 gross, or

$18,500 after taxes. And now I know one thing, you can never have enough money in New York. We talked about all the wonderful things we were going to do, and then we all went to the dentist and I took a loan—$450 for me, $250 for Marion, and $750 for one kid's braces. I figure you will always spend at least twenty per cent more than you make; it's part of 'the Law': current expenditures will expand to override expanded pay check. Of course, we did add a few options, like buying a car. That's $1,000 a year—and forty-five minutes out of Marion's life while she parks it every day. And we decided to abandon the Adventure Playground for August and rented a house in Quogue: $1,500, plus weekend train trips, ravenous guests, and an extra phone bill. But we really saved on laundry; the kids never got dirty out there.

"Still, even counting in the $50 I sent to Hotchkiss, it seemed peculiar for us to expand $6,000 in one year, so we got a computer budget analysis. Right away it says, 'Saving: $2,060.47 a year.' We don't have any savings; we operate on the fine old New York principle that the captain will live at least until the ship gets into port, and then there will always be another ship. The only people we know who save do it for fun; they spend three hours with the stock quotations instead of at the movies. We drink our savings allotment, in house brands. We used to go to Vermont and haul the booze in, but that's like going to New Jersey to save on the sales tax. Sordid.

"Medical care was listed as $81, including health insurance. Ours is higher because every time the kids go out they come back in sick, and because I have some major medical insurance policies; my brother didn't and for ten years he has been paying off a three-month stay in the hospital. Then the computer told us we could have $50.60 for recreation and $10.80 for reading. It's closer to $100 a month for each, especially with the kids. After all, you can't get out of the zoo for less than $2.

"Now it looks like it will have to be private schools next year: instant poverty or working wife, or—the final solution—move out. But I like New York. I *won't* leave the city. A man who rides a train an hour and a half to Connecticut, where is he? In Connecticut, owning his own highly taxed home. He's traded his marriage for a back yard, and he's not here. So what if you can live better, cheaper, in Topeka? Who wants to live in Topeka? I'm here, and therefore I'm making it. I'm where the action is. The last time we went to the theater was in 1965, but I can wander down Madison Avenue and look at the people who have come from Topeka to stare at me, a New Yorker."

Peter and Marion think that they could begin to save a little (savings, to them, means reaching the upper middle class) at $30,000 gross a year. Maybe, although at $32,000 they would theoretically be paying $8,660 plus 10 per cent surcharge in taxes, and at $40,000 theoretically $12,140 plus 10 per cent in taxes, plus state and local taxes. And their "aspirational level" shows no sign of remaining steady.

LIFE STYLE II:

Hand to mouth at $35,000 a year

Last week a group of women met for lunch at L'Etoile, resplendent in midtown, chunky-heeled, hatless chic. All of them had family incomes from $30,000 to $35,000 a year, and both their lunches and their chic were a gesture to midtown and a friend visiting from Cincinnati. The friend from the provinces lives in a nine-room $32,500 house, convenient to shopping centers and good public schools. On $25,000 a year, her family is solidly, comfortably middle class, with money in the bank and books on the shelves. She assumed that her elegant friends all dipped directly into the pot of gold under the Manhattan rainbow, especially since she had a vague idea of their incomes, although not a direct idea; everybody in New York admits to being poor, but never to *how* poor.

The other three women were New Yorkers, and nothing short of a mugging or a six-month garbage strike would make them consider moving out (their children are already in private schools). The lady from Cincinnati began to wonder why. She thought New York matrons discussed culture at lunch, mixed in with a little vicious gossip about the In people. Instead, her friends sounded like walking household computers. They remembered the day taxi fares jumped 29.5 per cent, the week milk jumped to twenty-nine cents a quart. They quote statistics with some feeling for what they mean:

medical costs up 125 per cent since 1946, ladies' shoes up 6 per cent this year, soda pop up two or three cents, oranges up nineteen cents a dozen. Even comic books are beginning to appear with twenty-five-cent stick-on labels pasted cunningly over the twelve-cent printed price. Clothes up 7 per cent in the last year. Apartments, ha! Don't mention apartments.

They referred to the good old days when the movies were $1.50 instead of $2.50, when the best seat in the house was $6.90, a postage stamp was four cents and a hot dog was twenty cents, not thirty cents. Restaurant meals have gone up 6.8 per cent over last year. Live-in maids were $35 to $40 a week two years ago; now there are none available at the $66 minimum. They remember the dreadful day when their husbands were no longer allowed to include them on expense-account evenings.

Their knowledge of the New York cultural scene seemed to come entirely from the Sunday *New York Times* (up to fifty cents from twenty-five cents). Really, the provincial lady said crossly, what, aside from rent, could possibly be all that much more expensive about New York? *"Children!"* the ladies shouted in unison. "Schools! Walking Around!"

Lillian lives in the Village, off Fifth Avenue. Her small income, and her husband's salary as a design consultant, plus occasional parental gifts, bring them up to $32,000 a year. But their apartment ($350 a month, a bargain) has to be big enough for her husband's visiting children, and their income has to cover alimony and child support ($750 a month). The children visit and eat a lot (food, $270 a month). Their neighbors, unlike most New York neighbors, drop in and drink a lot ($200 a month). They have a car, a baby, and although they can't afford to replace the dishwasher, Lillian has her hair done once a week ($6 plus tip, around the corner). She isn't sure how they survive, and she is afraid to find out.

Edith has a precise idea of how her family lives: hand to mouth on $35,000 a year. A few years ago, when the children were young, they lived in restrained comfort on less, and never had a bill they worried about. But then the children entered school, and because they live just outside the PS 6 district, and just inside the East Side Ethic, it had to be private school: $1,700 for the sixth grade at

Dalton (plus an ignored request for a "voluntary" contribution of $300 more); $1,300 for the fourth grade at Spence, plus $30 for milk and cookies plus a few more assessments. School bus: $375 a year. Piano lessons: $6 a lesson, plus bus fare, twice a week (the child is, unfortunately, talented). Pediatrician: $15 an office visit, $20 for a house visit, about six or eight visits during a plague-ridden New York winter. And the birthday parties: once a month at least—requiring a $3 to $5 present, a fifteen-cent card, and wrapping paper. And a toy for her own children occasionally.

Even then, Edith and her husband, a highly paid editor, could manage (their apartment is $400 a month, but too small), except their definition of a "decent" life includes a way to get out of town, and the house that was such a bargain at $35,000 in Westport is a millstone. It isn't just a question of the mortgage payments, which they like to think of as hidden savings, but the upkeep, the car to get there ($1,000 a year plus $60 a month garage), and insatiable weekend guests ($100 a weekend for food). This, of course, doesn't include the expense of summer sports lessons for the children and a couple of club dues in the country.

America's favorite ways to save are haircuts by mother and clothes by mother. Edith simply stopped cutting hair one day, the same day she stopped sponging and pressing her husband's suits. She does make her own evening dresses and all the curtains. She refinishes furniture, shops all over town, and does all the things suburban housewives do to ease the family into the comforts of affluence, if not the convenience.

They never invite people over for a drink before they all go out to dinner ($50 for four); she feeds them at home ($40 for dinner for four counting a bottle of Scotch, two bottles of wine, and special meat and desserts—no maid), but fairly often, about twice a month, because, to her, New York is the people. She has a cleaning lady ($16 a day now, plus carfare) who refuses to iron, so her husband's shirts go out to the laundry he deems suitable, a minimum of seven shirts a week, at forty cents a shirt. On Tuesday mornings she goes to the YWHA to swim ($85, plus $10 registration the first year, after an eight-month waiting list) and grudges the twenty-cent charge for a towel and use of the dryer.

She thought at $35,000 a year she would be able to go through

Bloomingdale's and just say "Charge and send." Instead, she goes to the basement (which recently rose above the Budget Standard Service of the Community Council Bureau's level for low-priced and moderate goods) and gets what she hopes is her swinging uptown matron's kit. Her husband has settled on $200 Brooks Brothers suits (one a year), and now accepts as average a $6.50 price for dinner when working late, but he thought that by now his insurance would be more, his portfolio respectable, and that they would be able to get away for a vacation in the winter. As compensation he sometimes brings home a new millstone, such as $1,500 worth of camera equipment, and his wife retaliates by buying a $400 set of china.

The third lady at lunch, Frances, is a lawyer; her husband is a physicist, and their combined income is almost $35,000 a year. Because she works she has a maid ($75 a week), and she has to keep up a respectable semi-fashionable midtown wardrobe ($750 a year). The maid stays at home with the baby while the seven-year-old goes to private school (cheap private school, $600 a year) on the bus ($250 a year). She likes to see her children in the evening, so she meets her friends at lunch or for a drink before she goes home. She goes to an analyst three times a week ($25 a visit, but he is trying to raise it to his new low of $35). Last year she took almost $600 in taxis off her income tax, as deductible transportation cost for getting to the doctor and back. At that rate, she figures she and her husband, and the rest of the family (sending the maid off with the children, etc.) spend about $2,000 on taxis. And they have a car to get away in, even if it is only to Brooklyn.

"You have to understand," Edith said, "that the minute you have a baby in New York you are sunk. It costs about $1,000 just to be born now. Baby sitters are up to $1.50 or $1.75 an hour; a new apartment with an extra room is at least $100 a month more. Then there's the school, and the mothers at the school who are always cornering us for their benefits, and we have to go because we want them at our benefits. I'd much rather have time to give money and myself to a real slum neighborhood, but I don't. But children—just moving them around town costs money. And entertaining children, aside from taking them to the park, is an enter-

tainment-recreation-culture budget in itself; one Saturday afternoon movie with a hot dog can be $10—and without bringing
along any friends."

"But what about the *New York* things?" asked the Cincinnati
lady. "The movies and theater and openings and galleries and museums, and . . ."

An evening at the movies, counting baby sitter and taxi, costs
$15 to $20—more if the couple insists on a cozy drink somewhere.
Lillian goes to the theater—that is New York to her—but only
because they bought $350 worth of subscriptions, and she has to
go. "But," she says, "even if it costs money to walk around in New
York, it is exciting to walk around. I couldn't bear to live in the
suburbs and do nothing but drive all day. Someday, I'm sure, the
children won't need a sitter, and my husband's investments (professional) will pay off, and we'll be here, to enjoy it."

LIFE STYLE III:

$60,000 a year, East Side over-reacher

For Tom and Sheila the investments, other people's, should be
paying off right now. He is a thirty-six-year-old stockbroker, and
for the last couple of years he has been making so much money
that they thought they would be completely out of the woods and
into the clover. They made a few subtle but very expensive changes
in their life style, succumbed just a little bit to the ideal New York
life as pictured in the ads and gossip columns, and now Tom isn't
laughing when he describes himself as "just an average middle-
class clod."

Their new co-op in the 80s, $75,000 purchase price and $650 a
month maintenance, is one good reason why $60,000 is barely
enough. Another is taxes. Another is the marvelous farm in upstate
New York they just picked up for $45,000 (with a twenty-five-year
mortgage, an extra car, and those usual summertime expenses). A
big reason is that, now that Tom and Sheila are no longer rent and
tuition poor, they have time to think about things like "getting the
children ahead." The Central Park skating rink and a Boy Scout

troop used to be enough, but now they are applying for membership in the New York Skating Club ($125 for one child, last year. This year it may be higher because of new facilities). The oldest marches around twice weekly with the Knickerbocker Grays ($95 a year, plus uniforms). The youngest child goes dancing every other week at Mrs. de Rham's classes. ("It's just like a rhythm class, and they really love it; it's $95 a year.") The good old days of Pin the Tail on the Donkey and $25 worth of party favors are over. Now no birthday party is worth giving unless it includes a magician, the balloon lady, or the poodle lady ($50 to $100). Children's clothes can be bought at Alexander's, but everyone else seems to be going to Brooks or Best's. At this level, people believe that no one in New York City sells children's shoes except Indian Walk. Since the private schools are mostly half-day for children in the earlier grades, Tom and Sheila's two boys go off to All-Star Day Camp every afternoon to play games in the park, which frees their mother for the fulfillment of her own aspirational needs.

Sheila feels that they have to accept more invitations to benefits these days (most of them school or mother-of-school-friend oriented), and that means something to wear. Goaded on by ads that suggest that $100 is a basic minimum to pay for a little nothing daytime dress, she thinks she is actually saving by owning only three fur coats. She reads Eugenia Sheppard, and *wants* things—to Sheila, "things" are what make New York New York. While she is acquiring things at Bendel's, her guilt level changes. She used to worry if she took a taxi when a subway would do; now she worries if she buys a $75 pair of loafers when $12 might have done.

Sessions at a gym ($4.50 to $15 each) keep Sheila fit and busy, while various apartment cleaning services keep her apartment waxed, washed and suitable for entertaining. The cleaning service is about $40 a day for a crew of men, $25 a day for a woman; and the maid who serves at parties is about $16 an evening, plus food and drink. By midwinter Sheila is so exhausted that she has begun dropping in at the doctor's for vitamin injections ($20), and she will decide that the family has to get away to someplace where it is warm for a while ($1,500 economy trip).

Tom has begun having a regular monthly nervous breakdown about the bills. "It's not as though we were living in really high style; we don't collect paintings, we don't go to Europe, my wife isn't dressed by Dior. My shoes don't come from London, my whiskey is just whiskey. But the trouble with New York is, we're not keeping up with the Joneses; we're keeping up with the Rothschilds. When we were looking for our apartment, we shopped and shopped and found this one. Sheila's best friend was also shopping and shopping, but her apartment was $125,000.

"I have taken out much more insurance, and of course I'm investing some money, so I guess you can say we are saving something. But I find that my expenditures are creeping, no, leaping, up without my really noticing why or how, and I know we can't ever go back. For example, I thought it would be good for business to belong to a club. My father always belonged to clubs, and I thought it was a normal middle-class thing to do. Now I get my exercise at the West Side Tennis Club for $250 a year and $2.50 each time I play. I joined the University Club—in my age group there's a $150 initiation fee and annual dues of $250. The Union Club, which is a little too stuffy for me, is $480 a year with a $360 initiation fee after age thirty-six. At this rate, if I really lived the way I want to, I'd need $200,000 a year. I figure it takes that to live *really* comfortably in New York."

LIFE STYLE IV:

$80,000 and comfortable but not glittering

Nobody could say that Sara and Dick aren't comfortable. He has a private income and a large earned income as a television producer. In Boston or Baltimore people with that much money retreat into genteel silence when asked to discuss their budget. Dick obviously doesn't think he is rich, just getting by, and he talks about his expenditures with a sort of fascinated horror.

"We've got four kids, a terrible mistake but we were living in the country at the time and we liked children, and we thought we could afford them if anybody could. So now they're all in school. On October first, a real black day in New York City, worse than April fifteenth, I had a due bill of $6,000 in cash, for tuition, extras and buses. We own a brownstone that isn't the world's greatest brownstone (a great one might cost $10,000 a year in taxes); in fact we think it's close to a slum dwelling. The bill, for a half-year's taxes, was $2,000. Then my wife, like a good middle-class educated woman, wanted to go back to graduate school—$1,000 due on her tuition.

"That was October first, and we were just back from a vacation in our house on the Cape, where the contractor wanted $3,000 for a modest wing we put on the house so all the kids wouldn't have to sleep in one bunk room. The boatyard wanted $1,500 for winter storage and repairs on our sailboat. We discovered that no one would set foot in our house to work as a maid unless we were paying $125 a week, plus extra help. The car broke down, and the garage rent went up to $80 a month—I remember when my apartment rent was $80 a month—and all the appliances broke at once, and someone told me I shouldn't be expected to fix my wife's *hair dryer* any more. My God, if I take it to a repair place it will cost $10 before they even look at it, and if I don't fix it my wife will start getting massaged ($17.50 an hour) and curled ($11) and facialed ($12.50 an hour) at Kenneth's and we'll go under. We may already have gone under, I went to the dentist last week; he peered inside my mouth, muttered about 'where did you have this work done?' and offered me a special package to get everything redone for life—$3,000, with handy financing plan available. It's a choice between my teeth or my kids' teeth.

"This morning I got fifteen invitations to benefits, and two requests to serve on boards. Serving on a board means donating more, and entertaining a lot of people at great expense so that they can be persuaded to see a show they don't want to see in order to please their friends instead of their consciences.

"Every week I give my pay check to my wife, unopened, like any blue-collar worker. I keep a small side bank account, and I cash about $80 a week for walking-around money at my local bank—the liquor store. If my great aunt comes into town and I have to take her to lunch, there goes $20. Taking the kids to a hockey game is $30 without a dinner. And try to persuade the kids that a hockey game is a major event. In New York a child of ten will throw a ten-dollar-a-week allowance back in your face. Not my kids; I compare what they are spending with what the average working man makes so often that they think I work in a steel plant."

"I am still as far from the glamorous kind of New York life as a steelworker. My wife's only extravagance is a $250 Yorkshire terrier that costs $25 to be groomed. My only extravagances are $10 haircuts and a membership at Raffles—but I have to be careful there; the place is full of people who suggest things like flying off for the weekend in Paris, and once you get into that scene you never escape until bankruptcy. We don't glide around in hired limousines, we don't have a staff of four silent servants to attend to our every physical need. I have a private income, but the money is going out faster than it is coming in. The only people I can think of who don't have to worry are people like the Whitneys and the Rockefellers, and I wouldn't be too sure about them . . . The only way out is to inherit money, or to have an important corporate job with stock options and complicated expense and tax procedures."

Living in a city where making $12,000 to $80,000 puts one in the middle class is obviously absurd to some people, and they move to Seattle to begin life anew, or they move to Ridgefield to get time to think about what to do next.

A family that moves to Seattle saves immediately on local taxes, automobile insurance rates, private school fees and rents. They save about $800 a year on cleaning costs. They save two or three hundred dollars in Christmas tips, a few hundred dollars on humidifiers to protect themselves and their furniture against the steam heat. If 80 per cent of the people in midtown Manhattan need a psychiatrist (as a recent analysts' study claimed), maybe they relax in Seattle and let their little troubles vanish as they enjoy such treats as washing their own windows instead of paying someone to do it. Locks, and locking themselves out, can cost a New York family $100, certainly $50, not including extra personal property insurance to replace the goods after the burglars have gotten in.

But after a few months in Seattle, the wife starts missing her friends and her friend's friends who can get it for you wholesale. They move back.

They move back and find out the cost of living has gone up

another 3 per cent. But they are home. The people in Seattle will never understand, but the people in New York will. As Peter ($18,000 a year) said: "New Yorkers are all crazy to begin with, and crazy to put up with it all. We live here because we can all be together, sharing the craziness."

19. All-the-News-That's-Fit-to-Print Power

Paul H. Weaver

"In recent years a new style of reporting, 'interpretive journalism,' has emerged and the *Times* is among its leading exponents. . . . The new 'hard' reporting has put a strain on neutrality. . . ."

Usually, *The New York Times* only reports the news. On the afternoon of February 7, 1968, it involuntarily made news by enacting a real-life drama of bureaucratic politics that ceded nothing to *The Ipcress File* for Machiavellian subtlety nor to *The Perils of Pauline* for suspense. The setting was the *Times* Building on West 43rd Street. The action began as Arthur Ochs (Punch) Sulzberger, president and publisher, was preparing to announce the reassignment of two middle-level news executives. His intention was to appoint James Greenfield, a newspaperman who had been assistant secretary of state for public affairs, as chief of the *Times'* Washington bureau. Six months earlier, Greenfield had been hired by the *Times'* top news executives in New York—executive editor Turner Catledge, managing editor E. Clifton Daniel, and assistant managing editor A. M. Rosenthal—on the understanding that he would receive a significant editorial-level assignment. At the suggestion of those executives, Sulzberger had decided to send Greenfield to Washington.

The Washington bureau, however, already had a chief in Tom Wicker, an experienced correspondent who wrote a tri-weekly political column, "In The Nation," which appeared on the editorial page, in addition to overseeing the work of twenty-seven *Times* reporters. Although he was reputed to be an indifferent administrator, Wicker was in other respects a worthy successor of James B.

Reston and Arthur Krock, who had distinguished themselves not just by their outstanding reporting but also by the jealousy with which they guarded the Washington bureau's independence from the home office in New York.

Wicker and Reston (who held the position of associate editor) were outraged by the news of Greenfield's impending appointment. It was, first of all, an insult to Wicker who had not asked to be relieved of his non-reporting duties; it was a slap at Reston as well, for he worked out of Washington and, as bureau chief, had selected Wicker to be his successor; and it was an obvious snub to the *Times'* Washington reporters whose ability and seniority were considered to put them first in line for Wicker's job. (White House reporter Max Frankel was prominently mentioned in this regard.) It therefore seemed that the principal reason for appointing Greenfield was to bring the Washington bureau under New York's control, and Wicker and Reston resisted this not only out of pride but also out of the conviction that, since the New York news executives could not be fully in touch with the Washington scene, New York control was likely to impair the quality of *Times* Washington coverage and disrupt the harmony of the bureau.

That afternoon, Wicker and Reston flew to New York to confront Punch Sulzberger with these arguments, and soon Catledge, Daniel, Rosenthal and Greenfield were called up to the publisher's office. On the third floor, reporters watched their superiors' comings and goings with fascination, and the vast newsroom came alive with speculation. Although the general shape of things was clear enough, they did not know for sure exactly what was transpiring, nor has anyone since given a definitive version of the afternoon's events. Some argue that Wicker and Reston threatened their own resignations and those of other important Washington reporters. Others insist that the discussion was conducted in more discreet terms. And nobody knows (or is telling) how many issues were involved in the settlement which finally emerged.

Whatever their methods, Wicker and Reston were successful. Sulzberger changed his mind and rescinded Greenfield's appointment. Greenfield resigned on the spot and went downstairs to clean out his desk. Catledge, Daniel and Rosenthal had been seriously embarrassed, and when the story of the Washington revolt appeared unexpectedly in next day's *Washington Post,* their embarrassment turned to public humiliation. It was, everything considered, a stunning victory for the Washington bureau. Not only had its independence been successfully defended, but the New York executives had been sufficiently chastised that they would doubtless think more than once before trying such a move again.

About two months later, the *Times* announced an important reassignment of executive duties. Although the intentions and implications of the change were by no means clear, there was a sense in which it seemed to undermine the Washington bureau's recent victory. The facts were simply that Turner Catledge was to be relieved of his responsibilities as executive editor and would assume the undefined positions of vice president and director of The New York Times Company. Catledge's successor as chief executive of the news and Sunday departments was to be James Reston.

The move appeared to imply no disparagement of Turner Catledge, who, at the age of sixty-seven, was ready to step up from his demanding job into a quieter, more elevated status from which he could still make a contribution. For over fifteen years, Catledge had played a role of extraordinary importance in the history of the *Times,* and if his energy had perhaps begun to wane just a bit, his abilities and insight remained as impressive as ever. As well as a personal friend, he had been Punch Sulzberger's closest professional adviser, and it is difficult to imagine that the publisher "promoted" him for any reason other than age.

Why Sulzberger chose Reston, on the other hand, is a more difficult question. For ten years, Clifton Daniel had been generally regarded as the heir apparent. Reston's unexpected appointment was more than a rude shock; it also meant that Daniel, who was only three years Reston's junior, could never hope to become executive editor. Had Daniel been discredited by his part in the Greenfield affair? Had his strong unpopularity with *Times* reporters affected Punch Sulzberger's estimation of him? Thus, one hypothesis attributed Reston's appointment to a conscious desire to keep Clifton Daniel out of Catledge's job, perhaps even to induce him to resign.

The more plausible explanation, however, was that Reston was simply the better man for the job. Twice a Pulitzer Prize winner, Reston was clearly one of the most talented and distinguished journalists in the country. He was energetic; he had wide contacts; he wrote well; he had a good analytic mind; and his column was unsurpassed for consistently insightful interpretation of significant current topics. Moreover, he had proved himself an able executive when, as bureau chief, he had built up the *Times'* gifted Washington staff. He had even written a book about the problems and opportunities of modern journalism, and if it was not very imaginative, it was always intelligent. Although more than competent, Daniel just did not measure up to Reston. Besides, Reston had long been an especial favorite of Punch Sulzberger's parents, who owned the vast majority of voting shares in The New York Times Company.

The meaning of Reston's appointment was equally ambiguous in terms of the Washington-New York split. By one reading, it consolidated the Washington bureau's recent victory over the home office in New York. The opposite interpretation, however, was even more plausible. With Reston backing him up in Washington, Wicker had been able to talk back to Catledge and Daniel at relatively little personal risk. But once Reston had assumed control in New York, the Washington bureau chief would not only have fewer resources with which to resist the home office, but he would also probably be less inclined to balk the man to whom he owed his job. Over time, there was a distinct possibility that Washington's independence from New York would weaken, perhaps to the point of vanishing altogether. It was therefore conceivable that Reston was appointed not because of his special qualifications or because of the disfavor into which Daniel had allegedly fallen, but rather as the only practicable way of realizing Catledge's and Daniel's aim of establishing central control in New York. In this connection, there was speculation that Wicker, who *was* overburdened and therefore less effective as an administrator than he might otherwise have been, would resign in order to give full time to his column, and that Max Frankel would succeed him. The decision would be Reston's, and it would come from New York.

However one interprets them, the recent events at the *Times* are undeniably interesting. That, no doubt, is why the Washington *Post* and many other papers carried the story. In the final analysis, however, these fascinating machinations were unimportant and therefore unworthy of public attention. They were unimportant because, in the ways that really count, Reston's leadership will not be substantially different from that which Daniel would have provided, nor would Greenfield's Washington bureau have behaved significantly differently from Wicker's. What really matters, after all, is not what goes on inside the *Times* organization but rather what comes out of it. And in terms of the scope and quality of *Times* journalism, the fuss and bother of recent months will almost certainly prove to be quite irrelevant.

More than anything else, then, it is the *news* of the Washington revolt that is really significant, for it illustrates in microcosm a fundamental dilemma which, in various forms, plagues American journalism. That dilemma arises out of the disjunction between the two principal ends which any reporter—or newspaper—pursues: to *interest* readers and (in the broadest sense of the word) to *educate* them. The story about the Greenfield affair, for example, was published because it was interesting. The fact that it was published at all, however, inevitably suggested to the reader that, in some sense, it was also important—which almost certainly it was not, except to the careers of the men immediately involved. In the process of interesting its readers, then, the Washington *Post* was imparting information—implicitly it was telling its readers it was important—which was misleading.

One reason why newspapers are prone to this kind of error (and the *Post* is guilty in this respect less often than most papers) is that their stories typically focus on some discrete event. This practice has its advantages. Editors and reporters simply do not have the time to sit down every day, think carefully and at length, and finally make a list of the really important things going on whether or not they are expressed by some happening. It is much easier just to look for happenings in predetermined places, write them up, and make an intuitive determination of their relative importance before putting the paper together. In addition to its economy, this focus on daily happenings has the virtue of heightening reader interest by increasing the value people attach to mere newness or currency. These advantages, however, can exist only by virtue of (and are "purchased" at the price of) ignoring the basic issue of interestingness versus importance. The result is that newspapers are often shortsighted and misleading.

Sophisticated newspapermen—of whom there are many more than one might guess from reading their stories—are not unaware of these problems, nor have they been totally inert in responding to them. During the past ten or fifteen years, a new style of reporting has grown to the point of dominating serious journalism, and its principal concern has been to remedy the myopia of traditional reporting. Although it was by no means among the first papers to practice the new "interpretive" journalism, *The New York Times* is today among its leading exponents. And what is really important about the goings-on of the last ten or fifteen years at the *Times* centers on the process of adoption, benefits, costs, and future of this new style of journalism—of which Turner Catledge, Clifton Daniel, James Reston, A. M. Rosenthal, Tom Wicker, and even James Greenfield are equally the partisans—as a better way to cope with the fundamental dilemma of the newspaper.

The *Times* began moving in this new journalistic direction once Turner Catledge, an able and amiable Mississippian, assumed control of the news department in 1952, but to begin with, change was modest and progress generally slow. During the '50s, the foreign staff and most members of the Washington bureau adopted the new style of reporting, but they made up only a third of the *Times'* vast corps of reporters. It was not until late in 1963 that the *Times* fully committed itself to change by appointing a Pulitzer Prize-winning foreign correspondent named A. M. Rosenthal as metropolitan editor. The consequence was that within two or three years, the *Times* was a very different newspaper.

An uninstructed observer would be unlikely to guess that Abe Rosenthal is one of the most important men on the nation's most important newspaper. His appearance is entirely unexceptional. His build is medium; his height a shade less than average; his dark hair plentiful and well groomed; his clothes, except for an occasional incongruous mod shirt, unobtrusive; and his face, partly obscured by the heavy dark rims of his glasses, is neither long nor short, neither attractive nor ugly. In conversation, he comes into somewhat sharper definition. He is articulate and intelligent. His voice, though perhaps a bit unctuous, conveys an unmistakable sense of authority. But most of all, one begins to perceive the absence of exceptional characteristics as a characteristic itself: his personality is oddly impersonal, and his presence is quite neutral. At least this is true of the outward Abe Rosenthal. On the job, however, he is intense. He has a passion and talent for finding news and telling it well, and he is as critical and demanding of himself as he is of others. If these qualities made him an extraordinarily good reporter, they also made him a difficult man to work under, for he expected much of his reporters but was rarely particularly supportive toward them.

Rosenthal brought to the metropolitan desk a style of journalism which differed radically from the one which had been entrenched at the *Times* for decades. That he had a different style at all was due to the special character of his career. Recognized as an unusually gifted reporter during his undergraduate days, when he served as the *Times'* CCNY correspondent, Rosenthal was assigned shortly after graduation to cover the United Nations. As a result, he was spared the long apprenticeship which the *Times* generally required of cub reporters and which served to perpetuate the old style of reporting. Like other regular *Times* reporters, Rosenthal received little editorial supervision, and the consequence was that he was free to develop and practice a personal journalistic style, which he did at the UN from 1946 to 1954, and thereafter in India, Poland, and Japan.

The character of Rosenthal's journalism was heavily influenced by the demands of foreign reporting. Since he had to cover all kinds of developments in a wide variety of countries, he had little opportunity to acquire and rely on the kind of detailed knowledge that a veteran city hall reporter, for example, can bring to bear on his work. Rosenthal was of necessity a generalist rather than a specialist, and he had to learn to grasp the essentials of unfamiliar situations quickly. His reporting naturally tended to reflect the interests of the average intelligent *Times* reader. Over the years, then, Rosenthal evolved a style which was geared to rendering intelligible and interesting what were to the general reader complex and obscure developments in unfamiliar places. This style featured contextual description, analysis of cause and consequence, clear and brisk writing, and the use of revealing detail (or "color"). In all these skills Rosenthal excelled.

By virtue of their training and assignments, however, most of the 110 reporters on the metropolitan staff assumed a very different approach to the job of covering the city. Implicitly they regarded news as the sum of the discrete daily happenings to be found in and around major social, political, and economic institutions. News was, therefore, to be gathered by assigning reporters to "beats." As an editor of this journalistic persuasion once explained, "News breaks through definite channels; it cannot do otherwise. Cover these channels and you catch the news—much like casting a net across a salmon stream." Once something newsworthy was encountered, the reporter's job was to witness the happening, get the facts, and write them up. It was felt that a good story highlighted the most striking facts and events, made no errors, showed no prejudice, and offered no unsubstantiated statements. Thus the *Times'* traditional journalistic style enshrined novelty as the principal news value and factual accuracy as the major reportorial value.

The metropolitan staff had been run accordingly. Since good reporting mainly required respect for facts and an instinct for the newsworthy happening, all reporters were made to serve apprenticeships, which could last as long as two years, before receiving significant stories or beats. This was not because the *Times* particularly wanted reporters to acquire a deep understanding of some subject matter: on the contrary, it was held that a capable reporter did not need any special study or substantive knowledge to write an adequate story about most things. The long apprenticeship was necessary because the *Times* felt that a record of reliable performance in getting and presenting facts was the best indicator of a reporter's ability. It also gave a reporter time to learn the territory —who was who, and what was really new. Once assigned to a beat, the reporter was regarded as a fully competent specialist, and editors did not interfere with his work, for it was feared that to do so would compromise the accuracy of his stories. Editors tended to confine themselves to making assignments, and their typical practice was to assign the best stories and beats to the most senior reporters. These might not have been the liveliest writers—in fact, they tended to be the dullest—but they had proven their ability to get the facts and to treat them with respect; and that, in those days, was all that really mattered.

Times reportage was, therefore, reliably accurate. But this approach to reporting also had its defects. Because it was so very dependent on the system of beats, coverage tended to be excessively narrow, and there were many interesting and important phenomena which the *Times* underreported or ignored altogether. Prose was long-winded, turgid, and wooden. Although *Times* stories recounted all the facts connected with a happening, they did not always succeed in rendering it fully intelligible or meaningful to the general reader. For *Times* reporters, being specialists, tended at times to focus on matters which were principally of interest to other specialists; and as dedicated respecters of facts, they often avoided making interpretive statements which could not be fully supported with facts. Finally, the *Times* was not really edited, with the result that its news columns were flawed by frequent repetition and overlapping.

As metropolitan editor, Abe Rosenthal was determined to remedy these faults by making *Times* city coverage more informative and more interesting. To this end, he began to inaugurate his own style of journalism, which he termed (more appropriately than perhaps he knew) "hard" reporting. This, he explained, "is not taking things at their surface value. You try to find the genesis of the thing, the why. What motivates the people involved? Basically, hard reporting is a style of inquiry, an approach to reporting. It has nothing to do with subject matter."

The doctrine of "hard" reporting thus changed the going definition of the good news story. No longer could it be merely a listing of facts in order of their purely descriptive importance. Now a good story had to explain the significance of a happening—that is, it had to tell what its causes were, what its effects might be, and how it would bear on the private citizen's concerns. Because the *Times* was thereby gearing its reporting to the general reader, two things followed. For one, the reader had to be persuaded to read the story in the first place; "hard" reporting therefore required a brisk, clear, colorful prose style. Second, events had to be explained in readily understandable terms without resorting to jargon. By exhortation and blue pencil, Rosenthal encouraged metropolitan staffers to follow these precepts, which were the same ones which Turner Catledge and his associates had propagated throughout the foreign and Washington staffs some years earlier.

Despite Rosenthal's statement to the contrary, "hard" reporting had a great deal to do with the subject matter of the news, and it led directly to a significant expansion of the scope of *Times* city coverage. By looking beyond the mere happening to the broad issues and trends it symbolized, "hard" reporting admitted into the news columns phenomena which had previously been excluded. It was no longer strictly necessary for a phenomenon to be expressed by a major discrete happening before it could be reported in the *Times.* Thus, diffuse, ongoing, or typical developments began to receive attention, and the *Times* began to cover such noteworthy non-happenings as neighborhood changes, life styles, and other aspects of the sociology and anthropology of New York City. News was no longer just what happened on a beat but now could be anything of "significance."

As it was put into practice, "hard" reporting required not just a redirection but also a substantial increase of the skills reporters brought to their work and the effort they put forth in the course of a day's reporting. Rosenthal became fond of remarking that the *Times* was "not a gentleman's club." Although all the changes he introduced he considered important, he placed greatest emphasis on the search for significant non-routine stories. Reporters were hired and promoted in no small part for their demonstrated ability in this regard; and, in a break with *Times* tradition, Rosenthal himself played a particularly active part in looking for and thinking up ideas for stories. As he explained it: "When I got to New York I set out to know the mayors, judges, lawyers, theatrical people, and all the other important figures in the news. I did this because it's interesting and I did it because you get stories by knowing these people. I don't see how an editor can judge what is a good story, what isn't, without knowing the people involved. My assistants and I try all the time to think of stories, and the only reason we can do it is that we know the people."

As a part of the continuing search for more and better stories, Rosenthal refocused and expanded the system of beats, especially those having to do with city politics and government. The police department reporter was directed not to focus on crime but rather on the "big issues" of law enforcement, such as mayoral control of the police, defendants' rights, civilian review, and so on. New beats were created to cover the health and hospitals departments, for example, and those public bureaucracies having responsibility for maintaining the quality of the urban environment. The political reporters were told to curtail routine coverage of club meetings and to begin to report on such other typical aspects of the political process as campaign methods, testimonial dinners, campaign

finance, and the like. All these changes were not uniformly successful, of course, but they did succeed in substantially broadening the
scope of *Times* coverage.

Rosenthal also made new demands with regard to the structure,
composition and content of news stories. Reporters were no longer
permitted simply to dig out facts and set them down. At the very
least, they were required to write short sentences, include illuminat-
ing color, and offer statements (usually attributed to a source)
which explained the "meaning" or "significance" of the phenomenon under consideration. Rosenthal and his assistants involved
themselves actively in the writing and rewriting of news stories to
their reporters' frequent displeasure. And as with a reporter's news-
finding ability, Rosenthal paid considerable attention to writing
skills in making judgments about hirings, assignments, and promo-
tions.

As it became apparent that large numbers of the metropolitan
staff did not have the skills, energy, imagination, or inclination to
practice "hard" reporting at anywhere near an acceptable level of
proficiency, the old system of seniority and specialty rapidly broke
down. Young reporters who demonstrated they were energetic and
imaginative seekers of stories, perceptive interpreters, and talented
writers no longer had to serve the traditional apprenticeship. In
fact, they did not even have to wait in line behind their seniors for
good assignments. A zealous believer in the capability of the able
generalist to grasp and explain even the obscure events of municipal budget-making within days if not hours, Rosenthal had few
scruples about disregarding the territorial claims of specialists and
specialties.

By themselves, these changes would doubtless have been quite
sufficient to create a great deal of discontent. The added factor of
Rosenthal's personality, warm toward his few friends but cold and
abrasive almost to the point of hostility toward those whom he
perceived as neither friend nor stylistic ally, threw the metropolitan staff into an uproar. If it was not fully justified, their disaffec-
tion was entirely understandable: Rosenthal had had no professional experience covering New York; he seemed to pay little heed
to the possibility that his changes could be for the worse; his rhe-
toric reflected little respect for the traditional ways and values; and
there he was, intense and assertive, telling them—*experts*—what

would make a good story, what its significance was, and even how to write it. Many staffers, particularly the more senior ones, were profoundly offended, and they told one another in private that Rosenthal was "wild," "crazy," "ignorant," and "paranoid." Even some of the young reporters who had been hired by Rosenthal disliked him and kept their distance although they fully shared his approach to reporting. It was not long before resignations began to increase. Although some of the reporters who were leaving the *Times* were excellent, Rosenthal seemed not particularly to mind the exodus, for he had decided that many on the staff were incompetent, lazy and sullen and so should be washed out. It was not very hard to find able replacements who were adept at "hard" reporting.

Thus, by virtue of the rapid turnover and his intensive supervision, Rosenthal succeeded in substantially changing the character and quality of the metropolitan staff and its work. And in mid-1966, his reform of the goals, structure and operations of the metropolitan staff largely accomplished, Rosenthal was promoted to the position of assistant managing editor, replacing Harrison Salisbury as second in command to Clifton Daniel. The new metropolitan editor, Arthur Gelb, was Rosenthal's former assistant, and he energetically continued his predecessor's politics. The traditional canons of journalistic practice at the *Times* had been fundamentally and irreversibly revised.

The introduction of "hard" reporting accomplished much of undeniable value. That turgid prose in which local events had previously been related had hindered clear understanding and wide readership. Now that metropolitan stories were written in short, vigorous sentences which used significant detail to engage readers' attention as well as to inform them, the dual aims of the newspaper —to educate and to interest—were much better served. They were also better served by the *Times'* broadened definition of news, the consequences of which were most dramatically evident on the first page of the second section, which usually offered a "feature" story making extensive use of pictures and colorful detail and dealing with some current and significant (or, at the very least, interesting) topic, which would not have been covered by the pre-Rosenthal *Times*. More important, though, was the fact that even on the most traditional local beats, reporters were casting a wider net and dealing with a far broader range of concerns. The total amount of metropolitan news may not have increased very much during Rosenthal's tenure, but the scope and amount of information which was significant to the general reader grew substantially. Finally, by explicitly offering interpretations, by relating happenings to the values and interests of the general reader, the developments which the *Times* covered at all became more intelligible and the news grew generally more meaningful.

The "good, gray *Times*" of popular epithet, exhaustive but narrow, scrupulously accurate but difficult to understand, was gray no longer. Indeed, during the '50s and '60s it had in some respects become practically rakish: foreign reporters began occasionally to file "talk-of-the-town" pieces; more and more pictures of increasing quality were published; coverage of such fields as the arts, religion, publishing and education expanded and grew more sophisticated; Russell Baker began to write his column; and, in the most radical departure of all, the women's page, under the imaginative and mordant editorial leadership of Charlotte Curtis, became chic and witty. Although it retained its neat but staid format (except for the Sunday feature sections, the design of which became positively *Herald-Tribune*-ish), the *Times* of the mid-'60s had undergone an otherwise thorough modernization which made it at once more interesting and more informative.

But if it was no longer the gray *Times,* had it really remained the good *Times?* The metropolitan coverage produced under Rosenthal gave many readers reason to doubt it. It was as if for every improvement that was made, a new journalistic defect emerged. The *Times,* for example, had always been scrupulously careful not to "boost" political candidates (or any other person or institution relying on public good will and patronage for a livelihood) in its news columns. "Hard" reporting appeared to put this traditional value under strain. Previously, the *Times* had avoided this journalistic vice by limiting its coverage only to people and institutions of established and unquestionable importance. That way, publicity was kept proportional to an individual's public eminence. But once Rosenthal had declared news to be anything of significance, editors and reporters found themselves faced with choices they had not had to make when news was only what happened on a beat. The inevitable result was that there was a better chance that factors other than "public importance" (the vaguest and most ambiguous of concepts when used as a guideline for action) would enter into these decisions. For this or some other reason, there was a better chance that politicians might receive more publicity than their political importance warranted.

An example of this problem was the fate of an idea Rosenthal had for a story on New York politics. He wanted to do an account of how a neophyte politician goes about campaigning for his party's nomination for assemblyman—an interesting, important, and typical element of the political process—and assigned one of his best young reporters to it. The candidate selected, who was running for the first time in his life, was a young lawyer who, not just accidentally, was an old college friend of the reporter's. The story occupied a prominent place on the first page of the second section, and the visibility it gave the would-be assemblyman was a great boon. He was forced by a technicality to withdraw that year, but the following year he found little difficulty in mustering the money and support necessary for a successful campaign. Without the *Times* story, in his emphatic opinion, he would very likely not have been elected so soon, if ever. To *Times*men brought up in the old tradition and to political professionals around town, it appeared that this young politician had been "boosted," and that the *Times* was editorializing in its news columns. Rosenthal's view, of course, was that the *Times* had merely offered its readers an interesting look at an important political phenomenon.

In general, "hard" reporting found it difficult to be neutral. Like most serious newspapers, the *Times* had traditionally been reluctant to present on its own authority explicit assessments of the meaning of the news or to offer such assessments in a prominent position in the story. But making such judgments was one of the defining characteristics of "hard" reporting, and under Rosenthal these began to appear "high up" in stories, sometimes in the lead paragraph or headline. The problem was that there was often room for differences of opinion about what interpretation was the proper one. And since how an event was interpreted would affect how readers would perceive it, the participants in the event often stood to gain or lose according to the interpretation adopted. "Hard" reporting therefore inevitably led the *Times* to take sides in its news columns, which is what the non-interpretive style of journalism of the earlier era had successfully avoided. A city hall reporter offered an illustration:

"For example, to take an unimportant story from 1966, Albert Pascetta was here in the press room the other day. He was the Commissioner of Markets under Wagner, and what he had to say was highly critical of Wagner, Screvane, and Beame. Only by inference did he say anything good about Mayor Lindsay. The reporter called the office and read them his lead, which was that Pascetta had read Wagner, Beame, and Screvane out of the party. The office had formed the preconceived notion that the story was in reality a statement of support for Mayor Lindsay, which the reporter didn't think it was, except by implication. The desk insisted that he had defended Lindsay and that this should be the lead."

Many *Times* reporters and local Democrats regarded such stories as evidence that the *Times* was strongly favorable to Mayor Lindsay and "slanted" the news accordingly. They noted that Rosenthal almost doubled the number of reporters covering city government and politics when Lindsay took office, and also that Rosenthal had established relationships with Lindsay and deputy mayor Robert Price which, in the case of Price at least, were personal as well as professional. To Rosenthal, who rejected the notion of biased reporting as emphatically as the most traditionalistic *Times*man, these charges were absurd. As he saw it, there was a big difference between "slanting" the news and interpreting it. And as he explained it, that difference was his own and his reporters' professionalism. He had expanded city coverage because, objectively, Lindsay was an important phemomenon to New York and to urban America generally. The allegation that his contacts with the Lindsay administration made him biased, he argued, was just the opposite of the truth. As a newsman, he needed to have close contacts with everybody. The closer they were, the more he could learn; and the more he could learn—that is, the more his judgment could be affected—the more objective and unbiased his view of the city would be. Thus, he argued that his detractors were simply misinterpreting the facts of his conduct as well as of the *Times'* coverage. And as evidence that he was not "slanting" the news, he adduced the many bitter complaints he received about *Times* coverage from Lindsay.

Beyond the problem of neutrality, "hard" reporting appeared to encourage another serious journalistic flaw. There is unfortunately no feasible way to prove this observation definitively, but from many quarters, including some *Times* reporters, came the considered judgment that *Times* city coverage was less accurate than it had previously been. To an unknown but possibly great extent, this decrease in factual accuracy may have been the temporary result of hiring and assigning a large number of young reporters with (by *Times* standards) relatively little training. But it is at least plausible that the increased incidence of mistakes of fact was a real and lasting result of "hard" reporting. Reporters, after all, have only so much time and energy. The pre-Rosenthal *Times* asked reporters to use almost all their resources to guarantee accuracy. Rosenthal, by contrast, was asking his reporters to do much more: to find interesting out-of-the-way stories, to write engagingly, to gather color, and to provide sophisticated interpretation. By valuing these things more, the "hard" reporter of necessity cherished the old values somewhat less.

20. The Ultimate Power: Seeing 'Em Jump

Tom Wolfe

"It's not even the exercise of power . . . It's a feeling . . . knowing that anywhere they go, people will move for them, give way, run errands, gather around . . . and *jump* . . ."

One of the last big objects that symbolize power in New York is the private plane, on the order of a Lear jet or a Fairchild F-27. But even *this* all those millions of picky little bastids don't understand . . . William Paley has a G-2 Grumman Gulfstream. Among the planes owned by the Rockefeller family are an F-27 Fairchild two-engine turbo-prop, a Jet Commander, and a twin-engine Beach Baron. Marion Harper had a DC-7 that cost $300,000 a year to maintain . . . yes . . . and that was precisely what all those small-minded picadors, stockholders in Harper's advertising firm, Interpublic, picked on when they decided to force him out. *The sheer morbid expense of it*—but they never understand why these things are so necessary to men of power . . .

—*the offal chomping grin*—

. . . in New York. It is not because the private plane saves vital time by allowing Mr. Wonderful to take off for anywhere at a moment's notice. Actually a private plane almost always loses time. Even three years ago private planes trying to leave in the afternoon from LaGuardia, Kennedy or Newark had to wait 45 minutes to an hour and a half for take-offs, because commercial airliners always had priority.

—but *the offal chomping grin,* friends—

And it is not because private planes save wear and tear on vitally important people or enable them to hold important conferences while en route, or go over vital data, and so forth. In fact, the cabins of most private planes are as cramped, crabbed and uncomfortable as a Sheraton hotel room, and the alleged air conferences almost never take place. Invariably the whole time is cluttered up with serving meals and fixing drinks.

But—*the offal chomping grin,* I tell you!

That's what all those picky little bastids out there have never experienced in their lives—that magical moment before take-off when the pilot and co-pilot come back into the cabin with these wonderful offal chomping grins on their faces and their little eyes open and round as friendly as a dog's, and then their lips part and these yassah-massah voices begin, welcoming Mr. Wonderful and his guests and describing today's flight plans and telling about the food and drink on board, all the while smiling their beautiful offal chomping grins—

—and it is at this point that it registers on everyone aboard, like a 50cc. injection of warm Karo syrup into the main vein . . . these are not the pilot and co-pilot with the comic strip profiles who rule your destiny on a commercial airliner even when you ride first class, the ones who give firm orders one minute and then homespun talks on flying conditions the next, like stern parents trying a change of pace . . . no; these two are . . . chauffeurs! air butlers! *servants,* in a word—marvelous!—Captain Lackey, Co-lackey, and when you say move they will *jump* . . . and that, alone, in itself, justifies the executive jet in New York and makes it necessary and proper, that beautiful offal chomping grin—but how can all those picky bastids out there be made to understand?

One of the few powerful men who has spoken frankly on the subject is Senator Abraham Ribicoff. One night about fifteen years ago he was talking to eight or ten students in the American Studies Club. The students got on the subject of what really drives people like congressmen and senators—fame? money? the exercise of power? So Ribicoff says: It's not fame, at least not in the sense of publicity. They see their names and faces in the paper so often they take it for granted. It's not money. There may be some congressmen with deals going, but most lose money while in office because of the cost of campaigning and entertaining. It's not even the exercise of power, at least not in the sense of putting a bill through or having a part in policy decisions. For most of them it is something else. It's more . . . *seeing people jump.* It's a feeling . . . knowing that anywhere they go, people will move for them, give way, run errands, gather around . . . and *jump* . . .

Jump! Power is, after all, control over other people's lives. So perhaps it is natural that the symbols of power—as opposed to mere fame or wealth—should involve people *jumping,* i.e., acting like servants or loyal vassals. This is more so even today when New York is so full of rich men and celebrities who have access to the more obvious symbols of rank: e.g., publicity, expensively decorated apartments and town houses, beach houses in the summer, country houses in the winter, big cars, big boats, art objects, Persian rugs, kids in private schools, and wives starved to near perfection in elephant-cuff pants. But as for the real thing . . . a mere celebrity, for example, may get preferential treatment in certain restaurants, but that is as far as it goes. As for really making people jump—

—it is subtle stuff to which many rich and well-known New Yorkers are even oblivious. They never really understood Robert Kennedy, for example. In other areas his appetite for luxury was average or even restrained. But he derived enormous and, no doubt, enormously useful satisfaction from the real thing: *seeing 'em jump.* In his latter years, for example, he developed the habit of changing his shirt four or five times a day. Even allowing for his highly active schedule, this habit was incomprehensible to the people around him—except that it created an exquisite form of *jumper* in his retinue: shirt bearer. Kennedy beckoned and the bearer brought him a new shirt. It was nice stuff! The most distinguished of the shirt bearers was reputed to be Manhattan lawyer and socialite William vanden Heuvel. Kennedy also enjoyed seeing aides like vanden Heuvel and others run down the street after his motorcade if they were late for the take-off. There was no cruelty about this, however. After a block or so he would order the cars to slow down to take the man aboard. It was just routine *seeing 'em jump.* Kennedy also put various members of his staff on weight loss regimens and would actually make them march up to the scale to see if they were sticking to their diets. This was regarded at the time as part of the Kennedy emphasis on physical fitness, although in fact it was another nice way to see 'em jump.

A more solid symbol for true men of power, however, is having *brain jumpers* around. Now this form of seeing 'em jump is well known in the highest circles of government as having a brain trust. In New York men of true power in private as well as political positions like to have brain trusters around, intelligent men they can summon, and see jump, at a moment's notice. Like most status symbols, this one has a sound and practical origin. Today more than ever, information, rather than goods or personnel, is the most important resource of the powerful man. This is especially true in New York, where so much power, in all sectors, flows from the financial world. One of the great symbols of power currently is having an "eyes only" report—i.e., to be seen by the head man's eyes only—waiting for you on your desk every morning, much in the manner of the morning reports distributed to top brass in the State Department, Department of Defense, CIA, ambassadors, and key officials in oil or defense-industry companies. It really doesn't matter too much that a great deal of this information, even in the case of the CIA, tends to be lifted from *The New York Times*. Because very quickly the *idea* that he is at the center of a vast early-bird warning system becomes a psychological necessity to the powerful man in New York. This explains the significance of the radio telephones in the limousines that so many powerful New York executives still insist on, despite the fact that outsiders can easily intercept messages, making the phones useless for sensitive conversation. But so what! The car phone is . . . an information totem. The very king of information totemism, by the way, is Aristotle Onassis. In those marvelous pictures Onassis likes to have taken aboard his yacht—the ones where he has his shirt off and a great tire of fat enveloping his waistband—he always has a telephone to his head and more on the desk in front of him and a Telex machine to one side and various receiving sets in the background—so many brains jumping for the Early Bird!

Many men of power in New York have informal brain trusts, experts of various sorts whom they like to convene to discuss critical problems. The *brain jumpers* they call in may very well be younger men from outside their own fields—even from journalism or show business. There's no money involved. The brain jumpers get their satisfaction from the feeling that they have somehow hooked into the power circuit. The man of power gets useful information . . . sometimes . . . and always the satisfaction of seeing well-bred brains jump in his behalf. Over the years the Rockefeller brothers have actually institutionalized this sort of operation, setting up ostensibly independent information-gathering organizations and hiring experts at heavy salaries.

As for the daily life of the powerful in New York . . . they strive not only for insulation from the public—almost every wealthy New Yorker tries for that—but for various nostalgic trappings of European feudalism, which is, of course, the most venerable form of *seeing 'em jump*. They tend to live almost exclusively in large cooperative apartments on upper Fifth Avenue ("Central Park East"), Park Avenue, East 57th Street and Sutton Place, or in their own town houses in the East 50s, 60s, 70s, 80s and low 90s. The older co-ops are really more like feudal bastions than the town houses. They have amazingly large staffs of doormen and janitors and ingenious walls of privacy. On each floor the elevators tend to open up on a small vestibule, which is the outer chamber of only one apartment. Unlike the new UN Plaza building—which is more Show Biz than Power—the older buildings have no mail boxes. The mail is sorted by the house staff and delivered to the door. The doormen tend to be aging servitors of English stock and feudal-service disposition. They never engage a tenant in conversation unless invited to do so, and indulge in no personal remarks even then. They run interference, carry bags and chase cabs with a feudal zeal despite their years. They are almost always starchily turned out in wing collar, white tie and military frock coat. Somehow in non-Power co-ops, no matter how expensive, the wing collar gives way to an ordinary turned-down collar; the doormen themselves are *ethnic,* as it is called, meaning Irish, Italian, Puerto Rican or something else non-English; and they may engage in direct conversation at any moment. At the bottom of the Power scale are the West Side co-ops, where the doormen never seem to be able to pull the full uniform together at any one time. If they have on the jacket, they have on baggy gray khakis below. If they have on both the jacket and pants of the uniform, they have on no tie, or else the jacket is dangling open. What a world . . .

Many wealthy New Yorkers travel around the city by limousine. But the most powerful tend to engage in a kind of British reverse snobbery, using old or inconspicuous cars. David Rockefeller is driven about in an old Buick; Walter Thayer, in a old green Chrysler; Averell Harriman, in an old Mercury. The late Cardinal Spellman had a private black checker. Black Cadillacs are still common, but Rolls-Royces, among the powerful, are looked down upon as vehicles for women or Show Biz jaybirds. Jaybirdism is avoided by men of power of New York at all costs. They may wear their hair on the longish side, but it will be combed straight back and there will be no sideburns. Sideburns are a very strong dividing line between the powerful and the merely celebrated. They also avoid all mod or Cardin-style clothing. English custom-made suits of hard worsted used to be a hallmark of men of power in New York. But now the jaybirds—chiefly people in communications or show business—have discovered English tailoring, and men of power currently tend to concentrate on three articles of dress; shirts, ties and shoes. The shirts are usually custom made at $25 to $40 apiece. The collars have straight points and no gap above the button. Ties are almost invariably a solid color, and usually dark blue. Prints and even stripes smack of juvenilism, collegiatism or jaybirdism. In shoes they look for the "old leather" look of English bench-made shoes. They prefer capped toes and avoid heavy soles, which smack of collegiatism.

At their offices, elevators have great symbolic significance, since elevators in large buildings are places where it is easy to be trapped with the public. Where the buildings have elevator men, they are instructed to close the door and ascend as soon as certain VIP's step in. The very top NBC executives, for example, enjoy this sort of *jumping* in the RCA Building in Rockefeller Center. A very few New York executives have the ultimate symbol, a private elevator in a large building. One of the final inducements offered to Bennett Cerf to get him to agree to move Random House out of the Powerhouse mansion at 457 Madison over to the new building going up at 205 East 50th Street, reportedly, was the promise of a private elevator. Where the elevators are automatic, the problem requires more ingenious solutions. In the Time-Life Building the starters were instructed to put Henry Luce's elevator on "go" as soon as he stepped in. The first stop in this bank of elevators was his floor, so that the system was almost private. (At 40 Wall Street one elevator serves only the seventeenth and eighteenth floors, the offices of Kuhn Loeb, which is corporate privacy at least.) The rationale for all this is that the time of top executives is exquisitely valuable. In point of fact, of course, it is to *see 'em jump.*

Men of power in New York tend to give their offices the look of an expensive home, preferably that of a medieval baron's. The look they strive for is not Knoll Associates, but French & Co. In the classic mode, the carpeting is not wall to wall but Persian. The furniture runs to antiques. This is partly because men of power tend to look upon antiques as a sound investment that increases in value with time, but chiefly it is psychological. Antiques smack of feudal power, for a start. But chiefly the general look of an expensive home suggests the idea of a man of power as a paternal ruler, an absolute monarch, whose power is not corporate but personal. In the new CBS building, a strict corporate rule controls the decor of every office but one, giving the building an absolutely uniform look of Eames-Saarinen-Florence Knoll modernity. The one exception, of course, is the suite of CBS Chairman William Paley, which is furnished . . . yup . . . completely in antiques (he also has a private garage door in the base of the building).

The office suites of the very powerful typically include one or more bedrooms, private bathrooms and a dining room. The private dining rooms are perhaps an even more potent symbol of power than private elevators. The man of power in New York does not even go out to a private club for lunch. He tends to have a rather baronial dining room with full staff of maids, butlers and the chef. Some corporations, such as Chase Manhattan on Wall Street, have even gone into competition with Manhattan's leading restaurants to obtain top chefs for their top executives. The ultimate is Lehman Brothers at 1 South William Street, whose reigning patriarch, Bobby Lehman, is one up over the entire field. Not only does he have a private dining room for the firm's important executives and guests, but also another for himself alone. The daily question at Lehman Brothers is "Is Bobby coming down or is he dining alone?"

See 'em jump . . . for one alone . . .

Index